Copyright

IN

CYBERSPACE

QUESTIONS
AND
ANSWERS
FOR
LIBRARIANS

GRETCHEN MCCORD HOFFMANN

NEAL-SCHUMAN NETGUIDE SERIES

NEAL-SCHUMAN PUBLISHERS, INC.
NEW YORK   LONDON

Published by Neal-Schuman Publishers, Inc.
100 Varick Street
New York, NY 10013

Printed and bound in the United States of America

The paper used in this publication meets the minimum requirements of American National Standard for Information Sciences— Permanence of Paper for Printed Library Materials, ANSI Z39.48- 1992.

PLEASE READ THIS:
We have done our best to give you useful and accurate information on copyright law. But please be aware that laws and precedents are constantly changing and are subject to different interpretations. The information presented here does not substitute for the advice of an attorney. You have the responsibility to check all material you read here before relying on it. Of necessity, neither Neal-Schuman nor the author make any warranties concerning the information in this book or the use to which it is put.

"This publication is designed to provide accurate and authoritative information in regard to the subject matter covered. It is sold with the understanding that the publisher is not engaged in rendering legal, accounting or other professional service. If legal advice or other expert assistance is required, the services of a competent professional person should be sought." *From a Declaration of Principles adopted jointly by a Committee of the American Bar Association and a Committee of Publishers.*

Library of Congress Cataloging-in-Publication Data
Hoffmann, Gretchen McCord.
    Copyright in cyberspace : questions and answers for librarians / Gretchen McCord Hoffmann.
        p.   cm. — (Neal-Schuman NetGuide series)
    ISBN 1–55570–410–7
    Includes bibliographical references.
    1. Copyright and electronic data processing—United States— Miscellanea. 2. Fair use (Copyright)—United States—Miscellanea. 3. Cyberspace—Miscellanea. I. Title

KF3030.1.Z9 H64 2001

                                                                00–067869

Contents

Part II: Applying Copyright to Cyberspace

Part IV: Copyright Information Sourcebox

Foreword

Only a few short years ago, if asked what was the most important skill for today's librarian to acquire, I would have responded "an in-depth understanding of electronic search and retrieval systems." While knowledge of traditional library processes continued to be very important, the challenge was applying those traditional skills to the digital environment. It seemed apparent then that the electronic world would have a huge impact on the library landscape and be the source of our most difficult problems.

And indeed, the impact has been immense.

However, I was only half right. While the digital environment was certainly the challenge, I was wrong about what aspects would be the *most* challenging. I naively thought that the technical and managerial problems would be the greatest challenge — and got degrees in information science and management to prepare myself for the future.

I now know that the biggest challenge is not the technical issues that confront us, nor is it the managerial issues — it is the *legal* ones.

Today, no librarians can do their jobs without a strong understanding of intellectual property law as it relates to the digital information environment. What used to be arcane knowledge that only interlibrary loan librarians needed to possess (and then only the CONTU guidelines), has transformed into a passionate rallying cry for library leaders, an obsession for library professional organizations, and a major concern for university leaders and library boards everywhere. There is no other issue in recent history with such potential for turning cherished library principles upside down. From open access to restriction, from privacy to invasive monitoring of research activity, from the ivory tower to the bombardment of Madison Avenue, the new electronic world is changing the environment in which we work.

Today, the question is no longer *whether* the world will change, but *how* it will change. The list of issues is long: copyright in an environment where information moves without regard for place or time; the ability to exercise fair use in electronic systems controlled by security protocols and license provisions; the increasing emphasis on intellectual *property*; the underlying shift in "ownership" of information and knowledge from many authors/publishers to a few multinational companies whose focus is financial gain, not open access. How will any librarian make sense of these complex issues? How will we prepare ourselves to represent our crucial professional values in this dynamic, and increasingly economics-dominated, environment?

The answer, as always, is to educate ourselves. Ms. Hoffmann has provided an excellent starting point in this education process. Her organization of this complex material is effective not only for cover-to-cover reading but for quick reference on specific topics. Her experience as a frontline reference librarian and heading a library instruction program, in conjunction with her legal training, has ably prepared her to provide the library profession with a resource that is not only legally accurate, but communicates effectively on these pressing issues. And, in so doing, she has found that elusive balance between presenting the legal issues precisely without sacrificing clarity for those of us with no legal training.

I highly recommend this book as a valuable resource for professionals in all stages of their careers and degrees of experience with copyright issues. By providing a critical tool for meeting the inherent educational challenge of struggling with these issues, Ms. Hoffmann has made an important contribution to our professional literature.

Marilu Goodyear
Vice Chancellor for Information Services
and Chief Information Officer
University of Kansas
Lawrence, Kansas

Preface

Copyright in Cyberspace: Questions and Answers for Librarians is designed as a basic guide for librarians who need to understand and apply copyright law to information obtained from and/or transmitted through the Internet.

Although the last copyright act—written and adopted almost thirty years ago—was intended to be flexible enough to apply to new technologies as they arose, its authors could not have begun to fathom the technological changes that have occurred in the last few years. The Internet is developing much more rapidly than the law that governs it. This results in confusion to everyone: Internet users, lawmakers, judges, lawyers, and librarians. *Copyright in Cyberspace* attempts to provide the best answers currently available to the many complex copyright questions confronting librarians. Although statutes have been passed dealing with a variety of Internet-related issues and the body of Internet case law grows daily, we still do not yet have statutes or case law in many areas concerning copyright and the Internet.

As librarians know, people tend to make numerous faulty assumptions about the Internet: if it's on the Internet, it's free; if it's on the Internet, I can do anything I want with it. These assumptions are, of course, false. Perhaps because it is a very complex area of law, copyright discussions are often over-simplified and participants make too many assumptions in their attempts to explain the law. Many people believe, for example, that it is legal to make multiple copies of anything as long as the copies are not made for a commercial purpose. This is simply not true. Many, though not all, copyright experts believe that it is allowable to make copies for one's individual use, but probably none would argue that one can make scores of copies of a work to distribute to friends and family as long as one doesn't charge for the copies.

Copyright in Cyberspace was designed to meet three goals:

1. To provide a general understanding of copyright law as it relates to the librarian's use of the Internet;
2. To provide an awareness of the issues that the Internet brings to bear on copyright law, the fact that most of these issues are undecided, and that how they are decided is of the utmost importance for the future of libraries and library users; and
3. To inspire a sense of responsibility for helping our society and its decision makers to resolve those issues.

Copyright in Cyberspace: Questions and Answers for Librarians is divided into four parts. Part I, Essential Background of Copyright Law, provides the basic information needed to understand how the Internet as a communications medium affects the application of copyright law to content. Chapter 1 describes the history and purpose of copyright law, while Chapter 2 provides an overview of various current copyright laws by discussing what can be copyrighted, how you get copyright protection, and the possible limitations of these rights. Fair use, that favorite copyright topic of librarians, is discussed in Chapter 3, followed by Internet Basics in Chapter 4. Chapter 5 examines recent copyright legislation, such as the Digital Millennium Copyright Act.

Part II, Applying Copyright to Cyberspace, applies copyright law to various aspects of using the Web and analyzes what may or may not be legal. Chapter 6 answers questions on hyperlinking and framing; Chapter 7 covers browsing; and Chapter 8 is devoted to digital images. Chapter 9 explains related but noncopyright issues—including trademarks and words used as logos and links. Chapter 10, Realizing Legal Liabilities, discusses what kind of exceptions or damages a court might assess a "good guy" like a library and the likelihood of a library being sued for infringement.

Part III, Specific Library Applications, covers copyright in libraries' day-to-day use of the Internet. Chapter 11 covers the library's liability for copyright infringements as both content provider and as an Internet service provider. Copyright considerations related to interlibrary loan and resource sharing, electronic reserves and classroom copying requirements, and library instruction and distance education are covered in Chapters 12, 13, and 14 respectively. The last chapter in Part III addresses the librarian's role in advocating for the rights of library users as copyright law evolves in this area.

Part IV, Copyright Information Sourcebox, presents a wealth

of documents that reference librarians need to properly develop and administer copyright policies and procedures. Source 1: Selected Excerpts from the Copyright Act of 1976 (17 U.S.C.101 *et seq.*) provides the significant excerpts of the copyright statute. This section also includes copyright term durations, fair use guidelines, and a model policy statement from the American Library Association. In addition, there are many "how-to" sources providing information on obtaining permission for copyrighted material, protecting your own work, and representing the needs of your library. The sourcebox concludes with helpful resources from organizations, publications, and Web pages.

The book is written in such a way that you need not read it from beginning to end if you don't wish to. If you feel grounded in the basics of how the Internet works, for example, you might skip Chapter 4. If your library is looking at using the Internet for electronic reserves, you can skip to Chapter 13. However, do keep in mind that if you have questions as you read, they are likely answered in other chapters, so you might want to refer back to earlier chapters because many of the topics are interrelated.

As an instruction librarian teaching classes on Internet research, I quickly came to realize that few people—librarians, professors, or library users (including me) — seemed to know exactly what copyright meant for their day-to-day use of information sources. This realization led to my growing interest in copyright, eventually to law school, and now to writing this reference book about this vital new frontier of librarianship. I hope *Copyright in Cyberspace: Questions and Answers for Librarians* will plant seeds in your mind and give you a solid base for searching for new ways of thinking about our new cyberworld. I trust it will help librarians gain a fresh understanding of copyright law. My goal is that you and your patrons can explore what the cyberworld offers with a renewed sense of safety and confidence about the adventure that lies ahead.

Acknowledgments

I need to thank several people for their contributions to the writing of this book:

First, the numerous librarians who contributed ideas and questions for the book and general inspiration for writing it. Second, my editors at Neal-Schuman, Michael Kelley, Charles Harmon, and Kevin Allison, who made the experience of writing a first book as painless as possible. Third, Myrtis McCord, an excellent writer who has taught me so much by patiently editing much of my work. Fourth, Professor Wayne Schiess, writing instructor at the University of Texas School of Law, for bringing out my dormant ability to write well. His encouragement to write *expressively* and *concisely* led my husband to recently exclaim: "When did you become a good writer?!" (One of the greatest compliments I've ever received, considering he is a devoted yet critical reader of my work.) Fifth, Professor R. Anthony Reese, Assistant Professor of Law at the University of Texas School of Law, whose course "Intellectual Property in Cyberspace" formed the basis for much of this book, and whose patience and assistance in answering questions (often with other questions, in the fine tradition of the legal education system), general availability, support, and encouragement were extremely valuable in completing this book. Sixth, Professor Neil Netanel, Arnold White and Durkee Centennial Professor in Law at the University of Texas School of Law for his guidance, encouragement, and support, both in class and out; and special appreciation for taking the time to review and critique the manuscript of this book. And finally, and most importantly of all, my deepest gratitude goes to Peter Briggs Hoffmann, who never flinches at any of my crazy ideas, the pursuit of which dramatically affects his life; who offers only support, admiration, and encouragement.

Part I:
Essential Background
of Copyright Law

1

History and Purpose

At each turn [during the 210-year history of American copyright law], copyright's adaptation to a new technology was a rocky one, and there were those who argued that copyright simply could not be adapted to fit the new technology. (Merges et al., 1997: 323)

There is nothing new under the sun. (Ecclesiastes 1:9)

Knowing a little about the history of copyright law helps us to appreciate its intricacies and complexity and to understand its purpose. Understanding the purpose behind the law, in turn, helps in understanding the law itself. I have found that many people who criticize the very application of copyright law to the cyberworld, who make arguments that copyright should not apply to the Internet, or who argue that "information wants to be free," often do not understand either the purpose of copyright law or what it really protects. With just a general understanding of both, you will be one step ahead of many Internet users.

The fundamental base of American copyright law always has been the attempt to find a balance between the necessity of protecting the rights of authors in order to encourage production of intellectual works, and the necessity of providing public access to works in order to maintain a democratic and educated society. Thus, copyright law attempts to balance the rights of authors with the rights of the public to have access to the author's work. It is interesting to note that the needs on each side of this scale reflect two broad values that have played vital roles throughout American history: on one side, protection of private property and the right of every member of American society, no matter his position, to own private property; and, on the other side, the fundamental right of every member of American society to better himself and his position in life through education. Maintaining such a balance, however,

Q: Isn't copyright all about protecting the rights and ownership of the author?

A: No! American copyright law has always emphasized the need to balance the rights of the author with the need for a democratic society to have access to information. Authors are given protection for their works in order to encourage production, and the ability to access information is protected in order to encourage a free flow of ideas. Both are necessary to meet the rationale for copyright law as stated in the Constitution: "To promote the Progress of Science and the useful Arts."

is easier said than done. Accordingly, copyright law is a continually developing doctrine, constantly reacting to new developments in technology.

You will not be surprised to hear that the original copyright law was a reaction to the development of the printing press. The rise of the ability to copy works quickly and cheaply and to distribute them widely, quickly, and cheaply, led to the need to protect the right of the creators of those works. (Does that sound familiar? How often have you heard it said that the Internet creates problems for authors because of the ability it gives us to copy works quickly and cheaply and to distribute them widely, quickly, and cheaply?)

WHEN DID COPYRIGHT BEGIN?

As is true for much of American law, copyright law finds its roots in the British legal system. Before mass publishing began, the majority of the British population was illiterate and uneducated. Those authors and artists who produced works did so not for mass consumption, but for the very limited aristocratic class. They were rewarded by the patronage system: Rather than being paid for each work they produced, they were supported by aristocrats, many of whom were interested in acquiring artistic works that they could then dedicate to the monarch and so achieve recognition for themselves. (Gasaway and Wiant, 1994)

The invention of the printing press in 1476 and the rise of its use coincided with the reign of the Tudors, from 1485 to 1603. The printing press was a valuable tool for the Tudor period, which was marked by the Renaissance, an emphasis on education, and the rise of a middle class. Mass publishing became one more piece of the social mosaic. Although publishers and book vendors became wealthy from the new technologies, authors seldom saw much if any reward. Making matters worse for authors, the publishing industry thrived on piracy. (Ibid.) Copyright, however, was a response not of concern for authors' rights, but to the government's reaction to the power created by the printing press: The monarchy was terrified by the possibilities for political and religious rebellion created by the widespread dissemination of heretical writings.

The government's response was, in 1534, to require both a license and approval from official censors before anyone could publish a work. (Leaffer, 1995) In 1557, the Stationer's Company, a guild for publishers and book vendors, was created to fulfill the role of censor and was given a monopoly on publishing. Thus, a mutual benefit was created: The Stationer's Company provided the monarchy with a censorship tool, and in return, the members of the Stationer's Company received a publishing monopoly. (Patterson, 1991: 19–20) Only members of the guild could publish, and any member could publish only works to which he had purchased the publication right, as listed by the guild. The right to publish lasted into perpetuity. Thus, copyright originally had nothing to do with authors themselves or the creation of books but had to do only with the making and selling of books. (Ibid.: 21–22)

By the early eighteenth century, however, the 150-year-old guild's license to control publishing had expired and was not renewed (Leaffer, 1995), and the guild had suffered from years of rampant piracy as well (Gasaway and Wiant, 1994). The House of Commons seems to have grown tired of the monopoly powers wielded by the guild; in refusing to renew the license, it stated eighteen reasons for doing so, one of which was that the stationers were "empowered to hinder the printing [of] all innocent and useful Books; and have an Opportunity to enter a Title for themselves, and their Friends, for what belongs to, and is the Labour and Right of, others." (Ibid.: 17 and 249 n. 20 [citing 11 H.C. Jour. 305–06]) The members petitioned parliament for help and then became victims of the adage: Be careful what you ask for. The result was the first modern copyright law.

The Statute of Anne, officially titled "An act for the encouragement of learning, by vesting the copies of printed books in the authors or purchasers of such copies, during the times therein mentioned," was passed by Parliament in 1710. Note that the title itself conveys three major changes in the concept of copyright, each of which is reflected in the constitutional basis for U.S. copyright law: (1) the purpose: "for the encouragement of learning" in the Statute of Anne and "to promote the Progress of Science and the useful Arts" in the Constitution; (2) the object of protection: "by vesting the copies of printed books in the authors or purchasers of such copies" and "by securing . . . to Authors and Inventors the exclusive Right to their respective Writings and Discoveries"; and (3) a limitation on the duration of protection: "during the times mentioned therein" and "for limited Times." Where the Stationer's Company had owned perpetual rights to works it published, authors' rights in their own works were limited. Copyright in works already in publication was given a term of 21 years; newly published works were protected for 14 years, which term was renewable for another 14 years if the author was still alive. The Statute required registration with the Stationer's Company in order for a work to be protected. In later years, a requirement of posting a copyright notice on all registered works was added; at this point, "innocent infringement" became impossible. (Gasaway and Wiant, 1994)

Note that another major aspect of the Statute of Anne was that, by limiting the duration of copyright protection, it created a public domain for the first time. Prior to this, copyright protection had lasted for perpetuity. In addition, the Statute of Anne suggested for the first time the idea of the "first sale doctrine," discussed in more detail in Chapter 3. The modern first sale doctrine gives the owner of a particular copy of a work the right to dispose of that copy in any way he wishes or to display it publicly, exceptions to two exclusive rights of the copyright owner. Similarly, the Statute of Anne granted copyright owners the rights to print, publish, and vend, thereby limiting the author's or publisher's control of how a copy was used once purchased. (Patterson, 1991: 29–30)

Despite the revolutionary nature of the rights bestowed by the Statute of Anne, the law still was quite limited in scope. First, it applied only to written works. Thus, piracy remained a serious problem for artists. Eventually, as a result of great pressure from individual artists, Parliament passed the Engraver's Act of 1735, which gave the same rights to artists as those given to authors by the Statute of Anne. (Gasaway and Wiant, 1994)

HOW DOES THAT BRITISH HISTORY RELATE TO AMERICAN COPYRIGHT LAW?

Most of the original American colonies had adopted their own copyright statutes. Nonetheless, the framers of the Constitution considered the issue important enough to incorporate into the constitution of the new nation. The United States Constitution provides that "Congress shall have Power to . . . promote the Progress of Science and the useful Arts, by securing for limited Times to Authors and Inventors the Exclusive Right to their respective Writings and Discoveries." (U.S. Constitution, art. 1, sec. 8, cl. 8) Although no further guidance for establishing copyright law, such as defining what should be included in the "exclusive rights" granted to authors, is given in the Constitution, the wording of the copyright clause makes clear the intent (1) to further the public good, (2) by protecting the rights of authors, (3) for a limited time, thereby ensuring a public domain.

Passing the Copyright Act of 1790 was one of the first acts of the new Congress. The act was modeled after the Statute of Anne and granted protection to authors of maps, charts, and books for an original 14-year period, renewable for an additional 14 years if the author survived the first term. (Leaffer, 1995) Over the course of the nineteenth century, the scope of the Act was expanded by amendments to include protection for prints, musical compositions, dramatic works, photographs, artistic works, and sculpture. (Merges, 1997)

WHEN DID MODERN COPYRIGHT LAW ACTUALLY BEGIN?

The copyright statute was first overhauled in the early twentieth century. The Copyright Act of 1909 made several substantial changes to copyright law. First, it expanded the scope of copyright law to cover "all writings of an author." (*Copyright Act of 1909,*

Trends in Copyright Law

Looking at the development of copyright law reveals several trends, including the following:

- Increasing the term of copyright protection
- Expanding the types of works that may be copyrighted
- Reducing the formalities required to acquire copyright protection
- Growing complexity in the law as it attempts to respond to increasing complexity in technology
- To some extent, increasing recognition of the needs of "special" groups that represent users, such as libraries and educational institutions. This recognition is due solely to the actions of individuals and professional associations in taking active roles in the debate accompanying changes to the law. Special interest groups representing copyright owners have always been involved in creating copyright legislation, but the current trend of increased representation of users by special interest groups is a trend we direly need and welcome.

U.S. Code, vol. 17, sec. 4 [1909]) Second, it doubled the term of protection from two 14-year terms to two 28-year terms. (As under the previous act, the first term was renewable upon expiration of the first only if the author survived.) Third, whereas the previous act had established the beginning of protection at the moment of registration, under the 1909 Act protection began at the moment of publication. Like the original act, unpublished works were not protected. (Leaffer, 1995) Unchanged from the first act were the requirements of registration and deposit with the Library of Congress. (Gasaway and Wiant, 1994)

WHAT IS OUR CURRENT SOURCE OF COPYRIGHT LAW?

Like the original Copyright Act of 1790, the 1909 Act was amended several times to adapt to a changing world. Finally, in 1955, Congress authorized a revision of the Copyright Act—which, after 21 years of work, ultimately culminated in the Copyright Act of 1976. The fact that Congress worked on the revision for 20 years might lead one to believe that the resulting act would be concise, logical, and well crafted. Instead, the 1976 Copyright Act is a statute that courts, lawyers, and commentators sometimes have great difficulty interpreting and a statute whose interpretation has generated much debate. Very broadly speaking, these problems are the result of the manner in which the original act was created, the rapidity with which the world of information changes, and the number of amendments that have been made since 1976 in attempts to address both of these issues.

Professor Jessica D. Litman provides an excellent discussion about the unusual and awkward process that resulted in the 1976 Act. (Litman, 1987) Her article might be of particular interest to librarians, since she includes detailed explanations of how the fair use provisions evolved. I highly recommend it for anyone interested in understanding the legislative drafting process in general or the process that produced the 1976 Copyright Act specifically.

Lobbyists become involved in the drafting of all major legislation at some point. Lobbyists are people who meet with and work with members of Congress and their staff to explain their interests in a particular piece of legislation and to try to convince members of Congress that the legislation should be drafted to reflect those interests. Representatives and senators often depend on lobbyists to help them become knowledgeable about particular issues and how legislation might affect different constituency groups. The result of lobbying, then, is that members of Congress work together with people advocating special interests in drafting legislation. In the end, of course, it is Congress that must decide what interests to address and how. The American Library Association is an extremely active advocate and lobby for libraries and library users.

The 1976 Copyright Act, however, involved a more extreme process. Rather than working intimately with Congress in drafting the statute, special interest groups with economic interests in copyright law, such as authors, publishers, and the film industry, negotiated amongst themselves, found compromises acceptable to the various groups, and presented to Congress language for the statute that reflected those compromises. Congress then enacted those compromises. Congress itself was behind this process, essentially forcing the parties to negotiate compromises before it would consider their language for the statute.

Why this unusual process? Two major reasons, but certainly not the only ones, are the awareness of Congressional members of the depth and complexity of copyright law and their own inability to master such a huge body of law (which is a perfect example of why Congress relies on lobbyists), and Congress' concern about the possibility of enacting law that would make no one happy and create problems for everyone.

Why is this process a problem? Because it results in a law that is difficult to interpret and thus to apply. An established process exists for interpreting statutes when applying them to a given situation. Traditionally, courts (or anyone else attempting to interpret statutory law) look first to the "plain language" of the law: Is the law as it was written clear in its meaning? If not, the second step is to turn to the legislative history of the statute: Can we determine what Congress intended the law to mean? If this does not answer the problem, we turn to judicial interpretation: How have the courts applied the law in similar situations?

Litman argues that serious problems exist at each of these steps in the process of interpreting the 1976 Copyright Act. The law as it is written is extremely complex, with the language often not precise and various sections interdependent on each other. As for legislative history, it is difficult to determine Congressional intent when most of the bargaining happened between private groups. For these reasons, Litman suggests, courts continued to turn to either the 1909 Copyright Act or to familiar case law based on that act in attempting to interpret and apply the 1976 Act. As a result, the statute is complex and case law is convoluted, and often contradictory, interpreting that statute. Even though the new act was more favorable to copyright owners and less so to users than the 1909 act, the act does reflect a balance of special interests that took over 20 years to achieve. Because of the difficulty of interpretation, however, the courts have "undermined this balance . . . not systematically, but with unpredictable randomness." (Ibid.: 903)

On top of this, amendments to the Copyright Act seem to be made almost every session of Congress. It often appears that each successive revision is more complex than the previous, but this is also a reflection of the increasing complexity of the world in which copyright moves. Like both Copyright Acts before it, the 1976 act has been subject to a variety of amendments in attempts to adapt copyright law to an ever more rapidly changing world. Unfortunately, the current state of the Copyright Act suffers from even more complexity as a result of 25 years of often highly political amendments.

The rest of this book is devoted to discussing the intricacies of what currently is and is not covered by copyright protection and what exactly that protection means. The next chapter gives a broad overview of these issues. Here, I will simply describe some of the substantial changes made in the 1976 Act.

First, and perhaps most importantly, publication is not required to obtain copyright protection. A work is protected from the moment it is first "fixed in a tangible medium of expression." (*Copyright Act of 1976, U.S. Code*, vol. 17, sec. 102(a) [1999]) Second, the act changed the term of copyright law from two 28-year terms to life of the author plus 50 years. (For works made for hire, which essentially have corporate authors, and anonymous or pseudonymous works, the term was 75 years from publication or 100 years from creation, whichever is less.) (Ibid.: sec. 301)

The new act covered a broad range of subject matter. A nonexclusive list includes literary, musical, and dramatic works; pantomimes and choreographic works; pictorial, graphic, and sculptural works; motion pictures and audiovisual works; and sound recordings. (Ibid.: sec. 102) The rights of a copyright owner are specified as the right to reproduce, prepare derivative works, distribute copies, and publicly perform and display the work. (Ibid.: sec. 106) Specific limitations to these rights are also laid out, including, for the first time, an attempt to codify the fair use doctrine. (Ibid.: secs. 107–112) Until the 1976 act, fair use had been developed slowly by the courts. Fair use is discussed further in Chapter 3.

Important aspects of the law that did not change, and which later caused problems, include the requirement to place a copyright notice on a work.

WHAT SIGNIFICANT STATUTORY CHANGES HAVE OCCURRED SINCE 1976?

The Congresses writing the 1976 Act recognized the need to establish a flexible law that could be adapted to unforeseen changes in technology as painlessly as possible. A clear example of this attempt is the definition of "copies": "material objects . . . in which a work is fixed by any method *now known or later developed*, and from which the work can be perceived, reproduced, or otherwise communicated, *either directly or with the aid of a machine or device*." (Ibid.: sec. 101 [emphasis added]) Nonetheless, some changes in technology were so unforeseeable in 1976 that the act was only partly successful in meeting this goal.

Technology is one of two major forces behind amendments to copyright law. The other is the increasingly important international nature of copyright law. Even before the Internet, international law was a major concern for copyright. Think of all you've heard or read about bootleg CDs and cassette tapes made in Asia, imitation Rolexes sold in Times Square, and knock-off name-brand clothing. The Internet, of course, thrusts us up to an entirely new level, since everything that goes on the Internet is immediately international in scope.

How do governments deal with these issues, given that copyright law is not at all the same from country to country? Treaties. Treaties are agreements between governments stating that signatories will follow certain regulations specified in the treaties, subject to whatever penalties may be laid out in the specific treaty. In some cases, penalties involve lack of recognition of each other's goods; for example, a treaty may state that if a signatory does not meet the treaty requirements, its own authors' copyrights will not be recognized in other member countries. In other cases, penalties focus on trade regulations; if signatories do not abide by the rules of the treaty, they may be sanctioned with trade restrictions.

Two treaties have resulted in major changes to the 1976 Copyright Act: the Berne Convention for the Protection of Literary and Artistic Works (Berne Convention) and the Agreement on Trade-Related Aspects of Intellectual Property Rights (TRIPs). The United States joined both treaties to ensure greater international protection for its authors and inventors. The Berne Convention required that formalities such as requiring notice and registration be done away with. As a result, the Copyright Act was amended in 1988 to do away with the requirement of posting notice; registration is not required for other Berne Convention countries but is still required

> Q: What can I do to ensure that the rights of my library as an institution and my library users, as well as my rights as an individual, are acknowledged and addressed in future copyright law?
>
> A: First of all, you should have a general understanding of copyright law and how it affects your library, your users, and you. That's the purpose of this book. Next, you should keep up with what's going on in Congress and the courts concerning copyright issues. Finally, part of your duty as an information professional is to make your voice heard to decision makers. You can do this through the American Library Association among other organizations. Source 12 provides a list of ways in which you can keep abreast of issues and also discusses how you can be an active player in decisions that affect your institution and your users.

for U.S. authors in order to bring infringement suits. Joining TRIPs led to the Digital Millennium Copyright Act, discussed further in Chapter 5, which addresses a range of issues and problems created by the digital world.

Finally, another major change recently made to copyright law is the Sonny Bono Copyright Term Extension Act, passed in 1998, which extends the term of copyright by 20 years, to life of the author plus 70 years. For anonymous and pseudonymous works and works made for hire, the term is 95 years from first publication or 120 years from time of creation, whichever is shorter. (Ibid.: sec. 302)

CONCLUSION

One way to address gaps that develop over time in any law is to amend the law as each new issue presents itself. Sometimes this works well; at other times, the amendments become so numerous that the result is a piecemeal law, a hodgepodge of bandages. It has been argued that our current copyright law is rapidly approaching this point and is ripe for a new revision. The same problem that has led to this situation, however—the remarkably rapid pace of technological development—also argues against moving too soon in rewriting the law as a whole. Almost any professional working with the Internet on a regular basis would agree that we have a long way to go before the development of the Internet and its myriad possible uses "shakes out" enough to offer some consistency in the cyberworld. Rewriting the copyright statute in the midst of such a dramatic paradigm shift would be pointless.

Meanwhile, we must manage, and sometimes struggle, with the law in its current state, constantly asking ourselves what changes are necessary and worthwhile in a constantly changing arena. As information professionals, we also must keep in mind that part of our responsibility is to help others, especially those making our laws, to understand how to make these judgments and how to recognize the difference between knee-jerk reactions and well thought-out plans. A good example of both the difficulty in recognizing this difference and the crucial need for librarians to take part proactively in these discussions is seen in the emotional reaction to the easy availability of pornography on the Internet that has led to attempts to mandate filtering in libraries and educational institutions.

BIBLIOGRAPHY

Copyright Act of 1976, U.S. Code, vol. 17 (1999).

Gasaway, Laura N. and Sarah K. Wiant. 1994. *Libraries and Copyright: A Guide to Copyright Law in the 1990s.* Washington, D.C.: Special Libraries Association.

Leaffer, Marshall. 1995. *Understanding Copyright Law.* 2d ed. New York: Matthew Bender.

Litman, Jessica D. 1987. "Copyright, Compromise, and Legislative History." *Cornell Law Review* 72 (July): 857–904.

Merges, Robert P., et al. 1997. *Intellectual Property in the New Technological Age.* New York: Aspen Law & Business.

Patterson, L. Ray and Stanley W. Lindberg. 1991. *The Nature of Copyright: A Law of Users' Rights.* Athens, Ga: The University of Georgia Press.

U.S. Constitution, art. 1, sec. 8, cl. 8.

2
Overview

To recognize and understand some of the quagmires of copyright issues involving the Internet, you first should be familiar with a few basics of copyright law. Copyright is considered by many in the legal arena to be one of the more complicated areas of law. This chapter barely dips into the subject, giving you just enough to introduce the basic ideas behind copyright and to understand what your rights are and how to avoid violating the rights of others. Several excellent guides to copyright are available, many of them targeted specifically to librarians and educators. My favorites are listed in Sources 14 and 15.

WHAT CAN BE COPYRIGHTED?

Written words are only the tip of the copyrightable works iceberg. Anything that meets the following four requirements is eligible for copyright protection:

1. expression
2. an original work of authorship
3. with a modicum of creativity
4. (a) fixed in a tangible medium of expression, now known or later developed
   (b) from which the work can be perceived, reproduced, or otherwise communicated, whether directly or with the aid of a machine or device (*Copyright Act of 1976, U.S. Code*, vol. 17, sec. 101; *Feist Publ'ns, Inc. v. Rural Tel. Serv. Co., Inc.*, 499 U.S. 340 [1991])

This means that musical works, audio recordings, movies, artwork, photographs, dances, dramatic works, and even architecture can be copyrighted.

Let's take a closer look at each requirement and what it means in the cyberspace arena.

Expression

Copyright protects expressions, as opposed to ideas. Einstein could copyright the book *Meaning of Relativity*, in which he explains his discovery, or expresses his idea, but he could not copyright the actual idea of relativity. The fundamental purpose of copyright law is to encourage the dissemination of ideas. If one could copyright ideas, one person would have almost total control over the use of that idea for years. Aside from the impracticality of this notion, our society fears the potential results of limiting access to knowledge rather than providing means by which one can build on knowledge. In comparison, by protecting the expression of ideas, the creator of the idea is rewarded for making his idea available to the public, where society can then benefit from it.

Original Work of Authorship

"Original" does not mean something that no one has ever thought of before. Original, for copyright purposes, simply means that the work was created by the author, not something copied from another source. Thus, the idea of telling a tragic story of star-crossed lovers has been around at least since Ovid told the story of Pyramus and Thisbe, but each original telling of that idea can be copyrighted—even had they all been written at the same time, Ovid could have copyrighted his story, and Shakespeare could have copyrighted *Romeo and Juliet*, and Irving Shulman could have copyrighted *West Side Story*.

Modicum of Creativity

Even if a work is created by the author and has not been copied from elsewhere, it must exhibit a "modicum of creativity." Although "modicum" is nowhere defined, it turns out to be pretty minimal. Facts themselves cannot be copyrighted, since they are, by definition, not subject to different modes of expression. I can say that it was extremely hot yesterday, you can say yesterday was a scorcher, Jane can say it was so hot she thought she would faint. These expressions may be based on fact, but they are not facts. But there's only one way to say it was 102 degrees outside; this is a fact.

However, the actual presentation of facts may exhibit the "modicum of creativity" necessary to be copyrightable, because, as the United States Supreme Court stated in a landmark case concerning the creativity requirement, "the author typically chooses which facts to include, in what order to place them, and how to arrange the data so that readers may use them effectively." (*Feist Publ'ns, Inc. v. Rural Tel. Serv. Co., Inc.*, 499 U.S. 340 [1991])

Thus, a white pages phone book would not be copyrightable, because the author has listed everyone in a given area rather than using his discretion to choose who to list and has listed them in the most obvious order and arrangement (alphabetically). In contrast, the *Physicians' Desk Reference (PDR)* is copyrightable. Although all of the information it contains is factual, the authors chose what to include, how to organize it, and how to present it. The facts contained in the *PDR*, however, are not themselves copyrightable.

Fixed in a Tangible Medium of Expression

The entire phrase from Section 102 is ". . . fixed in any tangible medium of expression, now known or later developed, from which [the works] can be perceived, reproduced, or otherwise communicated, either directly or with the aid of a machine or device." The phrase "now known or later developed" often is cited as proof that Congress intended to write copyright laws that would be applicable throughout unpredictable changes in technology. Nonetheless, the fixation requirement has become problematic and caused great controversy when applied to the cyberworld.

Consider, for example, email. Email seldom is intended to be permanent and often is used for communications that would have been by phone ten years ago. Most people tend to think of email as being rather ephemeral. However, even when the individual recipient of an email deletes it as soon as she has read it, several copies have been made during the short life span of the message. Many systems create a copy of a message in a "sent mail" folder when the sender transmits it. Copies are made during the transmission of the message. A copy is made when the message arrives on the recipient's server. In some systems currently being used, the recipient creates a copy on her own computer by downloading the message from the server. Each of these copies resides in a tangible medium—a hard drive, a server, a floppy disk. Thus, even though most users may not intend email to be around long enough to take advantage of it, email certainly is copyrightable matter.

This sounds reasonable. But what happens when one simply browses the Web? The pages viewed are fixed in a tangible medium, residing on a server. One can download images and pages. But even when the user does not download them, copies are made in our RAM when we access a page. More certainly than email, RAM is intended to be temporary storage. Yet courts have held that a copy made in RAM is "fixed in a tangible medium of expression" for purposes of copyright law. This has immense implications for Web users; can a user infringe copyright law simply by browsing the Web? Such issues will be discussed in more detail in Chapter 7.

HOW DO I GET COPYRIGHT PROTECTION?

Very few formalities are required to copyright a work. If the work meets the above requirements, it is copyrighted at the moment of fixation. There is no requirement to publish a work in order to copyright it. There is no requirement to display any type of notice, such as © or "Copyrighted by ABC Press." An author is not required to list his work, or to deposit a copy of his work, with the United States Copyright Office or anyone else in order to receive copyright protection.

The lack of formal requirements also has substantial implications for copyright in cyberspace. The bottom line: You cannot tell by looking at a work whether or not it is copyrighted. For this reason, it is very important to assume that everything you see is copyrighted, unless you know otherwise. Note, however, that one large category of works is exempted in the Copyright Act from copyright protection: those produced by the federal government. No work created by the United States government may be protected by copyright. (*Copyright Act of 1976, U.S. Code*, vol. 17, sec. 105 [1999])

As an author, there are reasons to register your copyright and to display notice. First, it gives other users notice that your work is copyrighted. It is less likely that your rights will be violated. Second, you must register your work with the Copyright Office to be able to file a federal claim of copyright infringement, should your rights be violated. In addition, should you as the copyright owner file a lawsuit, registration entitles you to claim statutory damages of up to $30,000 per work, or if the infringement is intentional, up to $150,000, instead of claiming actual damages and profits (the court decides what amount to award, based on what it considers to be "just") as well as to recover attorneys' fees if you win the suit. (*Copyright Act of 1976, U.S. Code*, vol. 17, sec. 504 [2000])

WHAT RIGHTS DO I GET BY COPYRIGHTING MY WORK?

Four basic categories of rights are created by copyright protection. The author of a copyrighted work has the *exclusive* rights to:

1. reproduce, or make copies of, the work
2. prepare derivative works based on her work (such as writing a sequel or making a movie of a book)
3. distribute copies of the work to the public
4. publicly display or perform the work

In addition, the right to perform a sound recording by means of digital audio transmission was added in 1995. (*Copyright Act of 1976, U.S. Code*, vol. 17, sec. 106 [1999])

That these rights are exclusive means that no one other than the copyright owner has the legal right to make copies or to distribute copies of the work (or to prepare derivative works or publicly display or perform the work) without the permission of the copyright owner. There are, however, important limitations on these rights, which are described below and discussed throughout the book.

These rights last for the lifetime of the author plus an additional 70 years after his death. Like so much else in copyright law, the duration of the rights has changed periodically as the copyright statute has been revised. The result is that different works have different copyright life spans, depending on when they were created or published. See Source 2 for an overview of the duration of works created or published at different times.

Each of these rights applied to the Internet leads to different results and issues than in the real world. As alluded to above, there is some debate over what even constitutes a copy in cyberspace. Do end users make copies when they simply browse the Web? If so, does that mean each time a user looks at a Web page she potentially infringes the copyright of that Web page? There are also questions about what constitutes a derivative work. Some copyright owners have argued in court that a derivative of their work is created when their work is linked via frames because their Web page now appears quite differently than they intended. What about distribution and display? Does accessing a Web page constitute distribution of that page? Does linking to a page constitute distribution? Does viewing the Web in a public place, like a library, constitute public display of the page? If so, who is responsible for that display, the end user, the library, the Internet service provider, or the original author of the page?

None of these questions has an easy or straightforward answer. (Otherwise, there would be no need for this book.) All of them are important questions, the resolution of which will affect all Internet users. Each will be discussed further in relation to particular types of Web usage.

ARE THERE LIMITATIONS OR EXCEPTIONS TO THESE RIGHTS?

There are several limitations to the above stated rights. Probably the single most important limitation for libraries is that of fair use. Fair use will be discussed in some depth in Chapter 3. For the moment, it is important to know that what constitutes fair use is not clearly defined and that it is a defense. This means that it is difficult to know in advance what constitutes fair use. It is not enough to say that any use made by a library or for noncommercial purposes is covered by fair use. This is made clear by the fact that other exceptions specifically for libraries are included in the statute, such as limited exceptions for reproduction, including but not limited to photocopying; if all library uses were considered fair use, there would be no need for these exceptions.

One exception that is particularly important to libraries, although libraries are not specifically mentioned in this section of the statute, is the first sale doctrine, found in Section 109. (Ibid.: sec. 109) (see Source 1) This rule states that the owner of a particular lawfully made copy is entitled to dispose of that copy however he wishes without the authority of the copyright owner. This exception allows libraries to lend books to users and to sell old copies at book sales without violating the law. Another exemption, Section 109(c), allows the owner of a particular lawfully made copy to display publicly that copy. (see Source 1) This exception allows libraries to create exhibits using copyrighted works.

Another limitation on rights of which librarians should be aware is the ownership of copyrights in works made for hire. A work made for hire is "a work prepared by an employee within the scope of his or her employment." (Ibid.: sec. 101) Unless there is an express agreement otherwise, the employer owns the copyrights in such a work. This means that, absent an agreement to the contrary, the institution for which you work owns the copyrights in those beautiful Web pages you sweated over to create. In academia, for example, it is common for the institution to own copyright in the works made by its staff employees, though not faculty. Traditionally, faculty members usually own the copyright in their works, although the issue is currently being debated in academia. In addition, most experts recognize that for certain categories of works, such as online courses created at the request of the institution, it is appropriate for the institution to own at least the rights necessary to use the course.

Some of the most recent copyright legislation limits not the rights of copyright owners but the liability of information service providers. Why should this be important to libraries? Because under this section of the copyright law, an information service provider (ISP) is defined as "a provider of online services or network access, or the operator of facilities therefor." (Ibid.: sec. 512(k)(1)(B); see Source 1) Clearly, it seems that a library providing access to the Internet may be considered an ISP under the Copyright Act. This section, which will also be discussed in greater depth in Chapter 11, limits the liability of ISPs for the infringing activities of their users *if* the ISPs meet certain requirements. Without it, or for ISPs who do not meet the requirements, it is entirely possible for an ISP (read "library") to be held criminally liable when one of its users violates the copyright law.

HOW DO I AVOID GETTING IN TROUBLE?!

There are three categories of copyright violation: direct infringement, contributory infringement, and vicarious infringement. Direct infringement is the most obvious—if you violate one of the exclusive rights of the copyright owner, say by making copies of a protected article and distributing them to everyone attending your conference presentation on the topic, you have directly infringed and are subject to various remedies, including damages of up to $30,000 (probably not likely to be this high in the example just given).

It is very important to know that there is no knowledge requirement for direct infringement. This means that ignorance is no excuse. Pause for a moment to combine this with the above explanation that no copyright notice is required in order to protect a work. Together, this means that you can be held liable for violating the copyright of a work you did not even know was copyrighted in the first place. How to keep safe? Assume everything you see is copyrighted, unless you know otherwise.

Contributory infringement occurs when you knowingly induce, cause, or contribute to someone else's direct infringement. Does providing links on your library Web pages to other pages with infringing material, thereby "knowingly inducing" users to access the infringing page, constitute contributory infringement?

Vicarious infringement occurs when you have the right and ability to control the infringing activity and when you have an obvious and direct financial interest in the activity. Seldom will a situation occur in a library to which vicarious infringement may be applied.

WHAT HAPPENS TO ME OR MY LIBRARY IF WE ARE FOUND GUILTY OF INFRINGEMENT?

This is the subject of Chapter 10. For the moment, suffice to say that it is highly unlikely that you or your library would ever get to this point. First, as a general rule, should a copyright owner decide that you are infringing her work, she will almost always send you a cease and desist letter. At that point, first ask yourself whether your use truly is infringing—does it fall under one of the statutory exceptions? It is a fair use? If you decide it is not, you probably will either cease and desist in using her work, or work out an agreement to use it. Seldom do copyright infringement situations actually make it to the courtroom. If that should happen, however, it is possible that your use will be excused under an exception to the copyright law or the defense of fair use.

Should, against the odds, your library be found to have infringed a copyright, you are probably in a better position than most infringers. In a lawsuit for infringement, the copyright owner may choose to receive either actual damages that he has suffered as a result of the infringement plus any profits the infringer incurred, or statutory damages. Usually, the amount of statutory damages, or fines, for infringing are almost solely at the discretion of the judge. For "innocent infringement," a fine may be as little as $200. For intentional infringement, it may be as much as $150,000. (Ibid.: sec. 504)

However, an exception has been carved out for infringers who, based on reasonable grounds, believe that their use was a fair use under copyright law if the infringer was an employee of a nonprofit educational institution, a library, or an archive who was acting in the scope of her employment. Only the act of reproduction is covered by this exception. If the infringer fits this description, statutory damages are remitted. In most circumstances, actual damages and lost profits probably would be slight, so the effect of this provision is to protect library staff and educators who make photo-copies or other reproductions believing that their actions are allowed under fair use. Note that the infringer must have "reason-able grounds" for believing that the use was a fair use; the general belief that any and all copies made by library staff for any non-profit purpose might not be considered "reasonable grounds." On the other hand, basing actions on ALA and CONFU Guidelines (see Sources 3–8) is much more likely to be considered "reasonable grounds." (Ibid.: sec. 504(c)[2])

BIBLIOGRAPHY

Copyright Act of 1976, U.S. Code, vol. 17, secs. 101, 102, 105, 106, 504, 109(a), 109(c), and 512(k)(1)(B).
Feist Publ'ns, Inc. v. Rural Tel. Serv. Co., Inc., 499 U.S. 340 (1991).

3
Fair Use and Statutory Exceptions for Libraries

For librarians and other educators and public servants, the fair use doctrine may be one of the most confusing aspects of copyright law. Certainly it is one of the more complicated components of copyright law, according to almost anyone's standards. Unfortunately, it is human nature to try to simplify complex issues so that we can better understand and deal with them. In the world of fair use, this translates to dangerous and widespread assumptions. Too many people in various educational and nonprofit arenas assume that any uses of a copyrighted work made for educational purposes, or even more generally for noncommercial purposes, are fair use. Unfortunately, nothing in copyright law is that simple.

WHAT IS THE FAIR USE DOCTRINE?

Fair use is a judicially created doctrine, born not out of legislation, but in the courts. This implies that the courts began to recognize that in some cases carrying out the letter of the law violated the spirit of the law. In some situations, it is more fair to *not* follow the law. When would this be the case? Recall that the purpose of copyright law is "to promote the progress of science and the useful arts;" this can be considered the "spirit" of copyright law. When following the letter of the law negates this purpose, the letter of the law conflicts with the spirit of the law. To deal with such situations, the American legal system applies "rules of equity," which, very broadly stated, often means that the legal system will choose to apply the spirit of the law despite the fact that it conflicts with the letter of the law. Such is the origin of the fair use doctrine.

25

The fair use doctrine allows one to use copyrighted works without permission of the owner if the use meets specific criteria, which are meant to determine whether promoting the progress of science and the useful arts is better served by allowing the use, despite the copyright protection. A fair use may involve any of the exclusive rights of the copyright owner.

The tricky part comes in attempting to create a flexible doctrine. Obviously, making a determination like this can be a very subjective process. Knowing this, the courts, and later Congress, attempted to create a doctrine that will allow only those uses that really should be allowed in order to be fair and equitable. It would be extremely difficult to write a fair use statute in very specific terms, stating precisely what type of copying is and is not allowed, so that all copying meant to be allowed is, yet no one can take advantage of the language of the law. Thus, in attempting to be flexible and allow subjective decisions, the fair use doctrine is somewhat unclear at times.

Fair use originally was developed by the courts, long before it was codified in the 1976 Copyright Act. Although the general principle of fair use can be seen in British cases dating back to the eighteenth century, the milestone case that gave us our current vision of fair use was decided in 1841. The defendant in *Folsom v. Marsh* had copied letters written by George Washington for a biography on Washington, but, rather than copying from the original letters, he had copied from the reproduction of those letters in a multivolume biography written by the plaintiff. The Circuit Court of Massachusetts stated that:

> In short, we must often in deciding questions of this sort, look to the nature and objects of the selections made, the quantity and value of the materials used, and the degree in which the use may prejudice the sale or diminish the profits, or supersede the objects, of the original work. (*Folsom v. Marsh*, 9 F. Cas. 342 [C.C.D. Mass. 1841])

The courts relied on this statement for over 100 years until the very criteria cited here were codified in Section 107 of the Copyright Act of 1976. (see Source 1) The fact that fair use originally was developed by the courts, those who sat on the front line of deciding copyright infringement issues, and survived in the courts for many years, suggests that fair use is a doctrine born of a widely recognized and accepted need.

HOW ARE FAIR USE JUDGMENTS MADE?

The first thing to note is that fair use judgments are made on a case-by-case basis. This means there are no stringent rules that say, for example, as long as you copy less than 10 percent of a book, your use is fair. Each use is evaluated on its own. The guidelines for making this evaluation, however, are enunciated in Section 107 of the Copyright Act. (see Source 1) Additional guidelines, although not part of the law, are provided by other sources, such as the Conference on Fair Use, legislative history, and the American Library Association. (see Sources 3 to 9)

Types of Uses

The preface to Section 107 gives a nonexclusive list (other factors as well as those listed may be considered) of illustrative uses that may be considered fair use: criticism, commentary, news reporting, teaching, scholarship, and research. (see Source 1) This list serves only as an example of the types of uses likely to be determined to be fair. It is nonexclusive, so other uses also may be considered fair. Just as importantly, it does not mean that those uses listed will always be fair.

WHAT IS THE CASE-BY-CASE ANALYSIS BASED ON?

The primary part of determining whether a particular use is a fair use is applying four factors set out in Section 107. The case-by-case analysis of these four factors must be made for every claim of fair use, including uses of the type listed within the statute, such as teaching, scholarship, and research. The court also may consider other factors, but that seldom happens.

Factor 1: Purpose and Character of the Use

The purpose and character of the use factor looks at (1) whether the use is commercial or for a nonprofit educational purpose and (2) whether the use is transformative. Nonprofit educational uses are more likely to be fair uses, because they are more likely to support the purpose of copyright law and less likely than commercial uses to harm the copyright owner. A transformative use is one that changes the original work in some way as opposed to flat-out copying it. If a use "adds something new, with a further purpose or different character, altering the first with new expression, meaning, or message," the use is more likely to be fair. (*Campbell v. Acuff-Rose Music*, 510 U.S. 569[1994]) This, too, can be traced back to the question of balancing the purpose of copyright law—to promote the public good—with the interests of the copyright owner. An exact copy of a work is more likely to mean a lost sale to a copyright owner, whereas a transformative use is more likely to further the advancement of the arts.

The case from which the "transformative" language comes serves as a good example of both what is meant by a transformative use and the tension between that and a commercial use. In that case, a rap music group, 2 Live Crew, had recorded a parody of "Pretty Woman," a classic Roy Orbison song. The group used the original music and repeated the phrase "pretty woman," but otherwise used entirely different lyrics. The Supreme Court noted that creating transformative works, because they are new works, furthers the purpose of copyright law. It then turned to the discussion of parodies specifically, which are a good example of a transformative use, and explained how parodies may further the public good: "It can provide social benefit, by shedding light on an earlier work, and, in the process, creating a new one." Thus, even a commercial use may be a fair use if the use serves a public good with which copyright law is concerned.

Note that a transformative work very well may be a derivative work as well. Fair use allows uses that otherwise would infringe any of a copyright owner's rights, including the right to create derivative works. However, creating a derivative work creates a new avenue for exploitation of the exclusive rights. Allowing others to create derivative works deprives the copyright owner of those opportunities. Thus, some potential conflict exists between the two considerations under this factor: A commercial work is less likely to be fair use, but a transformative work is more likely to be fair use.

Factor 2: Nature of the Copyrighted Work

In determining the nature of the protected work, courts usually consider whether the work is factual or creative. Recall that a work must be original and show a "modicum of creativity" to be protectable by copyright. Pure facts cannot be protected. However, many factual works, such as a biography, or even a collection of statistics, include much original, creative work as well as facts. In a biography, original work would include the language the author chooses to tell the story. In a statistical collection, the selection

> Q: Aren't all library and educational uses considered to be fair use?
> A: No! Fair use is determined by the application of four criteria to any and every case in which a defendant claims his use is fair. Nonprofit institutions, libraries, and educational institutions get no break per se. Many uses by the groups will be fair, but only because their uses tend to be more likely than many to meet the requirements of fair use. It is important to understand that there are no guarantees under the fair use doctrine. Decisions of fair use are made on an individual, case-by-case basis.

and organization of the facts may be sufficiently original to allow copyright protection. Protecting factual works encourages the publication and dissemination of hard knowledge. At the same time, however, our society considers the ability to access and use works of hard knowledge to be more important to education and society, thus to the progress of science and the arts, than the ability to access and use purely fictional works. So, courts are more likely to judge use of a factual work to be a fair use than use of a purely fictional work. Courts also tend to give stronger protection to works created for entertainment purposes.

Courts also consider whether a work is published or unpublished. Usually, an unpublished work will be given stronger protection than a published work. The purpose is to preserve the right of first publication for the author. One could argue that this is a case of giving more importance to the author's rights than to the public access to works. On the other hand, one could argue that an author needs such protection to encourage him to produce works. Without such protection, another party potentially could "scoop" the author, so that even if the use otherwise would be fair, such as for commentary purposes, the author still is in danger of losing valuable compensation for his work. Such was the situation in the defining case concerning unpublished materials, *Harper & Row, Publishers, Inc. v. Nation Enterprises*. (471 U.S. 539 [1985]) The Supreme Court ruled that publication by *The Nation* of a relatively small portion of an unpublished biography of Gerald Ford, in which Ford discussed his pardon of Richard Nixon, was not a fair use. The holding focused on the unpublished nature of the work.

In *Harper & Row*, the reporters responsible for the story apparently had gotten access to the manuscript through questionable means. In comparison, the Second Circuit Court of Appeals held that use in a biography of significant portions of J.D. Salinger's unpublished letters was not a fair use, despite the fact that they were publicly accessible in the special collections of various librar-

ies. (*Salinger v. Random House, Inc.*, 811 F. 2d 90 [2d Cir. 1987])
Again, the court focused on the unpublished nature of the works,
interpreting *Harper & Row* as stating that no use of unpublished
works could be fair use. The same court two years later, however,
found uses of a smaller amount of personal letters and journals to
be a fair use. (*Wright v. Warner Books, Inc.*, 953 F. 2d 731 [2d Cir.
1991])

Congress finally stepped into the debate in 1992 and amended
Section 107 to add, "The fact that a work is unpublished shall not
itself bar a finding of fair use if such finding is made upon consideration of all the above [fair use] factors." (*Copyright Act of 1976*,
U.S. Code, vol. 17, sec. 107 [1999]) In other words, Congress emphasized again that no single factor is determinative and that judgments of fair use are to be made on a case-by-case basis.

Factor 3: Amount and Substantiality of the Portion Used in Comparison to the Work as a Whole

As you might guess, the smaller the portion of the work used, the
more likely the use will be considered fair. No distinct guidelines
are given, however, for what that ratio should be. (However, in the
context of copies made for classroom copying, nonbinding guidelines are provided in the House Report on the Copyright Act; see
the discussion below.) In addition, even taking proportionately tiny
portions of a work may constitute infringement if the portion taken
is important enough to the work as a whole.

The rationale behind making a smaller portion more likely to
be a fair use is that different proportions will be appropriate for
different uses. The inquiry is: Has the user taken more than is
necessary to meet her needs? Many librarians write book reviews
for publication in professional journals. Consider in this context
how your needs vary. If you are commenting on the author's political views in general, you might not need to actually quote any of
the text, or you might quote only a few lines to make the point of
the vehemence of his views. On the other hand, if you are commenting on a poet's use of repetition, you might need to quote several lines of a poem to make your point.

Even taking a very small portion of a very large work, however, may not satisfy the fair use analysis if the portion taken is
"the heart" of the work. Going back to the case above in which *The
Nation* quoted from the unpublished Ford biography, the Supreme
Court held that copying only 300 words of 200,000 was not allowable, because the words taken constituted "the heart of the book,"

Q: Aren't the fair use criteria well enough established that I can tell which of my uses will be fair and which won't?

A: There is no guarantee under fair use. The criteria used to judge fair use are subjective. There are no concrete guidelines, such as any use for research purposes is fair, or any copying of less than 5 percent of a book is fair. Each determination is made based on the facts of that specific case.

that is, the material about Ford's pardon of Nixon. (*Harper & Row, Publ'r, Inc. v. Nation Enter.*, 471 U.S. 539 [1985]) The Court gave the following explanation for this judgment:

> A *Time* editor described the chapters on the pardon as "the most interesting and moving parts of the entire manuscript." The portions actually quoted were selected by Mr. Navasky as among the most powerful passages in those chapters. He testified that he used verbatim excerpts because simply reciting the information could not adequately convey the "absolute certainty with which [Ford] expressed himself," or show that "this comes from President Ford," or carry the "definitive quality" of the original. In short, he quoted these passages precisely because they qualitatively embodied Ford's distinctive expression. (Ibid.)

Note that the very same rationale could be used by the author to argue that he needed precisely the portion of the work that he took in order to convey his point. This is a prime example of the complexity associated with fair use determinations, due in large part to the subjective nature of the determination. In this case, the fact that *The Nation* scooped Harper & Row, the book publisher, may have played a subjective role in the Court's final holding of infringement.

Factor 4: Effect on the Potential Marketplace

The inquiry here is: How great was the effect of the use on the potential market for or value of the work? The rationale behind this factor relates directly to the purpose of copyright: If the copyright owner's ability to sell his work is impaired significantly, so is the incentive basis for copyright protection.

Several aspects of this factor should be noted. First, the focus is on *potential* market harm, not actual harm. In other words, would unrestricted and widespread use of the type the defendant has made harm the marketability of the work?

It is also important to note that the defendant need not actually be selling copies of the work to harm a potential market. *Harper & Row*, discussed above, is a good example of that. The defendant magazine was not distributing copies of the original work—recall that only very small portions of the work had even been copied—but the importance of the pieces copied were held likely to damage the market for the entire work, since the copied portions were considered to be the portions of most interest to the buying public. Thus, even though copies may be used for nonprofit purposes, the possibility of market damage still exists.

Pulling It All Together for Libraries

As you may have noticed, the four fair use factors interrelate. Nonetheless, it is important to analyze each factor separately from the others. *American Geophysical Union v. Texaco* (60 F. 3d 913 [2d Cir. 1994]), with which many librarians are already familiar, is a good example of how the factors interrelate. It also provides a look at how subjective and individual each fair use analysis is. In that case, the argument focused on the behavior of one scientist as an example of the type of behavior common within the corporation of Texaco. Issues of a journal, *Catalysis*, to which Texaco held three subscriptions, were circulated to scientists at that particular Texaco facility. The scientist in question, Chickering, copied articles he thought might be of use later and kept them in a file for the sake of convenience.

In considering the first factor, purpose and character of the use, the court noted that Chickering had made the copies for his own convenience and had never even used five of the seven articles copied. It then acknowledged that photocopying those articles could serve other purposes, such as allowing Chickering to carry the article with him into the lab to avoid risk of damaging the original journal; had such purposes dominated, the court said, the first factor might tilt in favor of Chickering. Because the copying was done for "archival purposes," superceded the original rather than transformed it, and utilized Texaco's efforts to develop profitable products, the plaintiff publishers won the first factor test. (Note that the court uses "archival purposes" in the sense of filing away for future use, as opposed to the library jargon use of "archival" to refer to preservation of works.)

The court held the second factor, nature of the work, to favor the defendant Texaco, based on the predominantly factual nature of the work.

The third factor, amount and substantiality of the copied por-

---

Q: What are the exceptions for libraries in copyright law?
A: As opposed to fair use, several exemptions to copyright law exist for library uses that are explicitly and clearly stated. Those include the first sale doctrine, limited reproduction by libraries, and limited copying for classroom purposes.

---

tion compared to the work as a whole, was held to favor the plaintiffs, since the articles were copied in their entirety. Notice that the court looked at each *article* as an individual work, not a journal *issue* or *volume*. As the court noted, each article was individually authored and enjoyed individual copyright protection as an original work of authorship. Compare this, however, with Section 108(d), which states that one limitation to an author's exclusive rights is the right of libraries to make one copy of an "article or other contribution to a copyrighted collection or periodical issue" for interlibrary loan purposes. (*Copyright Act of 1976, U.S. Code,* vol. 17, sec. 108(d) [1999]; see Source 1)

Finally, we come to the fourth factor, effect on the potential market for the work. This is where the fun starts and is the portion of the fair use analysis of most interest to librarians. The court began by noting that there is "neither a traditional market for, nor a clearly defined value of," individual journal articles. (Ibid.) Rather than personally marketing their journal articles, authors sell their rights to publishers who produce and market the work in exchange for royalties paid to the author. In academia, however, authors are much more likely to be motivated by nonfinancial rewards, such as prestige, than financial rewards. The profits made from journals, then, act as an incentive for publishers to produce and disseminate the information; such dissemination is the author's incentive for writing. Thus, the court rationalized, "evidence concerning the effect that photocopying individual journal articles has on the traditional market for journal subscriptions is of somewhat less significance than if a market existed for the sale of individual copies of articles." (Ibid.)

The court's attention then turned to "the significance of the publishers' establishment of an innovative licensing scheme for the photocopying of individual journal articles." Even though the plaintiff publishers had not established their own mechanism for direct sale and distribution of individual articles, "they have created, primarily through the CCC [Copyright Clearing Center], a workable market for institutional users to obtain licenses for the right to produce their own copies of individual articles." (Ibid.) In one of the most significant statements in the case, the court stated that the right to seek payment for a particular use can be related to the ease with which such a payment may be made. In other words, were there no CCC, the court might have given this factor to the defendants; even if the plaintiffs had some sort of ethical right to payment, if there was no realistic way for the user to make that payment, the use is more likely to be fair.

Finally, the court noted that its holding applies only to "the institutional, systematic, archival multiplication of copies," not to copying for personal use. (Ibid.)

WHAT OTHER STATUTORY PROTECTIONS ARE AVAILABLE FOR LIBRARIANS?

Section 108: Library Photocopying

Section 108 of the Copyright Act provides limited rights to libraries to reproduce works, which includes but is not limited to photocopying for purposes such as providing interlibrary loans and archiving. Section 108 is somewhat long and detailed and is reproduced in Source 1. What follows is a brief overview of the major subsections.

Section 108(a) establishes the criteria for what qualifies as a library or archives and paves the way for interlibrary loan services. It states that a library or archives, or any employee acting within the scope of her employment, may "reproduce no more than one copy . . . of a work . . . or distribute such copy" *if* the following conditions are met: (1) The copies are not made for commercial advantage; (2) the library's collections are open to the public *or* available to persons doing research in a specialized field other than those affiliated with the institution; *and* (3) the copy or distribution includes a notice of copyright on the copy or, if no notice is found on the work, a legend stating that the work may be protected by copyright.

Sections 108(b) and (c) allow copies to be made for purposes of preservation and replacement. A library fitting the description in 108(a)(2) above may make up to three copies of an unpublished work for purposes of preservation or to deposit in another library or archives for research uses *if* the following conditions are met: (1) The item being copied is currently in the library's collection; *and* (2) any digital copy must not be otherwise distributed in a digital format nor made available to the public in digital format beyond the premises of the library. Up to three copies of a published work may be made for the purpose of replacing a copy that is damaged, deteriorating, lost, or stolen, or to replace an obsolete format, *if* (1) "the library or archives has, after a reasonable effort, determined that an unused replacement cannot be obtained at a fair price;" *and* (2) any digital copy must not be otherwise distributed in a digital format nor made available to the public in digital format beyond the premises of the library.

Sections 108(d) and (e) address libraries' right to make copies for users. A library may make a copy of no more than one article from a journal issue, or no more than one "other contribution" to a copyrighted collection, or "a small part of any other copyrighted work" *if* the following conditions are met: (1) The copy becomes the property of the user; (2) the library has had no notice that the copy will be used for anything other than "private study, scholarship, or research"; *and* (3) the library prominently displays a copyright warning according to requirements issued by the Copyright Office at the place where orders of copies are taken and places a warning on forms used by patrons to order copies.

Finally, the allowances of Section 108 apply only to the "isolated and unrelated reproduction or distribution of a single copy . . . of the same material on separate occasions." The allowances do not apply when the library or an employee is aware that the copying is being done for purposes of "related or concerted reproduction or distribution of multiple copies . . . of the same material," whether or not the copies are made at the same time and whether or not intended for aggregate use by a group or for use by individual members of a group. Neither does Section 108 apply to instances of systematic copying or distribution of single or multiple copies or copying intended to act as a replacement for a subscription or purchase by anyone, including another library. In addition, Section 108 does not apply to copies or distribution of a musical, pictorial, graphic, or sculptural work; motion picture; or other audiovisual work other than those dealing with news, the only exceptions being copies made for archival or replacement purposes and graphics that are a part of other works.

In 1998, Section 108 was amended to include an additional exemption. Section 108(h) allows a library or archives to reproduce, distribute, display, or perform a work that is in the last 20 years of its copyright term for purposes of preservation, scholarship, or research. The library first must determine "on the basis of a reasonable investigation" that none of the following still apply: (1) The work is still "subject to normal commercial exploitation"; (2) a copy can be obtained at a "reasonable" price; or (3) the copyright owner provides notice that either (1) or (2) applies. It is interesting to note that this exemption, which applies only to a work during the last 20 years of its copyright term, was part of the Digital Millennium Copyright Act, which was working its way through Congress at the same time as the Sonny Bono Copyright Term Extension Act, which extended copyright protection by 20 years. Section 108(h) was a nod to libraries and other groups who argued that extending the term by 20 years would have an adverse effect on fair use applications such as scholarship, research, and preservation.

Classroom Copying

The House Judiciary Committee included in its report to Congress on the 1976 Copyright Act an "Agreement on Guidelines for Classroom Copying in Not-For-Profit Education Institutions with Respect to Books and Periodicals" (Congress is fond of long titles; see Source 9). The guidelines are the result of a series of meetings of three groups addressing the interests of educators, publishers, and authors: the Ad Hoc Committee of Educational Institutions and Organizations on Copyright Law Revision; the Authors League of America; and the Association of American Publishers. During the many years of drafting the copyright revisions, most of the discussion about Section 107 involved questions of classroom reproduction, especially photocopying. Members of the Judiciary Committee recognized that educators needed more certainty than was provided by the somewhat broad fair use exception and asked the three groups to meet independently to agree on permissible educational uses of copyrighted material. Although those three groups were able to reach agreement, it should be noted that the American Association of University Professors and the Association of American Law Schools strongly criticized the guidelines as being too restrictive on multiple copying for classroom use, especially at the university and graduate levels. (House Report, 1976)

The purpose of these guidelines is to "state the minimum standards for educational fair use." The guidelines go on to warn that things may change in the future, including how much copying will be permissible for educational purposes, as well as what types of copying may and may not be permissible. Finally, the guidelines emphasize that they are not meant to limit permissible copying; copying beyond that described in the guidelines may meet fair use. Unfortunately, however, courts at times seem to interpret the guidelines as a maximum limit.

The complete text of the guidelines is in Source 9. In a nutshell, the guidelines suggest that for research purposes, or for use in teaching or preparation for teaching, one copy may be made by or for a teacher of: a book chapter; a journal article; a short story, short essay, or short poem; or a chart, diagram, drawing, cartoon, or picture from a book, periodical, or newspaper. Multiple copies for classroom use may be made by or for a teacher, as long as they do not exceed more than one copy per student, and so long as they meet specific requirements for brevity, spontaneity, and cumulative effect, and include a notice of copyright.

The brevity requirements limit the number or percentage of words and graphics (such as charts or graphs) copied from a single work. The spontaneity factor requires that the copying be initiated by the teacher and that the decision to use the work be so close in time to the moment it will be used as to make it unreasonable to expect to be able to request and receive copyright permission in time. The cumulative effect test states that the copying must be for use only in one course; restricts the amount of material that may be copied in one term from the same author, collective work, or periodical volume (except for current news); and limits the total amount of copying per course per term. Finally, the guidelines require that each copy must contain a notice of copyright, and they prohibit copying for the purpose of replacing collective works or books; copying of "consumable" works, for example, workbooks and exercises; repeated copying from term to term by the same teacher; and charging students more than actual cost for the copies.

First Sale Doctrine

The first sale doctrine literally allows libraries to function. Recall that one of the exclusive rights of a copyright owner is the right to distribute copies of his work. Think about what libraries do; they distribute copies of works to the public for free. Yes, lending is a form of distribution. The first sale doctrine, codified in Section 109 of the Copyright Act and reprinted in Source 1, states that once an individual copy of a work has been sold, the owner of that particular copy may sell or otherwise dispose of that copy without the permission of the copyright owner. (*Copyright Act of 1976, U.S. Code,* vol. 17, sec. 109(a) [1999]) Without this exception, libraries could not loan books nor resell them in the ever popular annual book sale. The first sale doctrine also allows the owner of a particular copy to display publicly the work. (Ibid.: sec. 109[c]) Recalling that the right to public display is also an exclusive right, the exception in Section 109 allows libraries to create displays of their materials to attract and inform users about collections.

The first sale doctrine does not apply to the rental, lease, or lending of computer programs or sound recordings for the purpose of direct or indirect commercial advantage. (Ibid.: sec. 109(b)(1)[A]) Nonprofit libraries lending computer programs for nonprofit purposes may, however, lend copies of software but must include a copyright warning on the packaging of the copy being lent. (Ibid.:sec. 109(b)(2)[A]) The wording of the warning is prescribed by the Registrar of Copyrights. (See 37 C.F.R. sec. 201.24 for the required wording.) This subsection of the Copyright Act also specifically states that the "transfer of possession" of a computer program "by a nonprofit educational institution to another nonprofit educational institution or to faculty, staff, and students" does not constitute commercial use and thus is allowed under the first sale doctrine. (*Copyright Act of 1976, U.S. Code*, vol. 17 sec. (109(b)(1)(A) [1999]) Nonprofit libraries and nonprofit educational institutions also are allowed to rent, lease, or lend copies of "phonorecords," which would include any sound recording such as cassette tapes or CDs as well as traditional disks (Ibid.) These exceptions do not apply to for-profit libraries or to the resale of computer programs, such as at a library book sale.

Note that under the first sale doctrine, video stores may rent videos to the public, but record stores may not rent CDs. An interesting story lies behind this difference. Obviously, the motivating factor for excepting computer programs and sound recordings from the first sale doctrine is the ease with which such items may be copied and redistributed. The software and music industries were afraid of losing sales. Given the ease with which videotapes may be copied, why would the movie industry not have supported a similar exception for videos?

The movie industry, as it turns out, did fear the invention of videotapes and VCRs in their early days. As generally happens, the industry went after the big guys: VCR manufacturers. The charge was contributory copyright infringement, because VCRs were used by consumers to tape movies and shows off of television. In the end, the Supreme Court found that consumers who taped at home for showing at home used taping for "time-shifting" purposes, that is, to tape a show in order to watch later at a more convenient time. This, the Court said, was a fair use. (*Sony Corp. of Am. v. Universal City Studios, Inc.*, 464 U.S. 417 [1984]) A few interesting details about this case: First, the Court did not address the issue of "library-building," or recording movies and shows to create a personal library, although it was raised by the plaintiffs; second, the decision as five to four, which means we came within one justice's vote of essentially outlawing VCRs!

WHAT IS THE BOTTOM LINE?

As you now realize, defenses to copyright infringement, even for good guys like libraries, who have absolutely no interest in profiting from actions of infringement, are complicated and uncertain. As your head spins, I would like to leave you with a few very basic thoughts to keep in mind always:

- There is great debate over whether fair use should be considered a right or a defense. If a right, it belongs to users and guarantees that users can proactively go out and engage in activities that constitute fair use. If a defense, it is simply an exception to the rights granted to copyright owners and an exception to the duty of users to respect those rights. Professor Laura Gasaway sums up the debate well by comparing an affirmative right to a privilege, the granting of a favor. (Gasaway, 2000) In practice, which view one chooses determines the approach one takes: Do you demand that your rights be respected, or do you act defensively?

- Fair use is decided on a case-by-case basis. There are no hard and fast rules. This means that one can never be 100 percent certain, no matter what the circumstances, that any given situation will be excused as fair use. On the other hand, Section 108 provides exceptions for specific library uses so that one knows anything that comes within the explicit criteria laid out there does not constitute infringement. Despite those specifics, Section 108 seems to be concerned that libraries will believe that they must limit their actions to only those specifics—it explicitly states that nothing in Section 108 "in any way affects the *right* of fair use." Many interpret this as encouragement to take advantage of fair use and not shy away from the uncertainty of it. In addition, keep in mind that although the Copyright Act may not lay out specific acts that do or do not constitute fair use, such acts are established in case law. An example is the use of VCRs to tape TV programs for home viewing, discussed above.

- In contrast to fair use, the rights in Section 108 (library reproduction and copying for preservation and replacement purposes) and in Section 109 (the first sale doctrine) are *exceptions* to the exclusive rights of copyright owners. They provide solid limits of what may and may not be done. The upside is that you know in advance what you can do safely. The downside is that if you do not follow the rules, you will not have much to stand on should you be charged with infringement.

BIBLIOGRAPHY

American Geophysical Union v. Texaco, Inc., 60 F.3d 913 (2d Cir. 1994).

Campbell v. Acuff-Rose Music, 510 U.S. 569 (1994).

Copyright Act of 1976, U.S. Code, vol. 17 secs. 107, 108(d), and 109 (1999).

Folsom v. Marsh, 9 F. Cas. 342 (C.C.D. Mass. 1841)

Gasaway, Laura. 2000. "Fair Use: A Right or A Privilege?" *Information Outlook* 4 (November 2000): 39–40.

House Committee on the Judiciary, *Copyright Act of 1976*, 94th Congress, 1976, H. Rept. 1476.

Harper & Row v. Nation Enter., 471 U.S. 539 (1985).

Salinger v. Random House, Inc., 811 F.2d 90 (2d Cir. 1987).

Sony Corp. of Am. v. Universal City Studios, Inc., 464 U.S. 417 (1984).

Wright v. Warner Books, Inc., 953 F2d 731 (2d Cir. 1991).

4
Internet Basics

If you choose to skip over this chapter now, keep it in mind as you read through the rest of the book. If you come across something that just does not seem to make sense ("why would simply browsing the Web be considered making copies?"), come back and see if your question is answered here.

HOW DOES INFORMATION TRAVEL OVER THE INTERNET?

Network of Networks

We've all heard the Internet referred to as "a network of networks." It is important to keep in mind the implications of this quite accurate description. A network may be as small as a handful of computers or as large as hundreds or even thousands of computers. What makes a network, however, is some type of central control over the machines, software, and connections contained on it. A network at a major university, for example, may link thousands of computers in hundreds of different departments. Each department may use different types of software, depending on their needs. However, if all of those activities are controlled from a central computing center, this is a network. This is a simple example, of course; in reality, in such a large institution, each department probably connects to both a university network and its own network. The salient point is that a network has some kind of central control and administration.

Compare this to the "network of networks" description of the Internet. A web is a very appropriate analogy. Picture the three-dimensional models of molecules used in science classes, the ones that look like spheres of Tinkertoys. Each of these models is a network of computers, each interconnected with each other, but within a contained, if somewhat complicated, environment. Now picture hundreds—no, thousands—of those models all tossed together into a huge container, tangled up in miles of string. That's the Internet. If you trace a combination of string and structures long enough, you can find a connection between any two pieces. However, there is no overall organization of the pieces, and the entire glob was not planned as a whole. It just happened.

Packet-Switching

Information travels across the Internet via a process called "packet-switching." Even what seems to be a small piece of information, such as a brief e-mail message, is broken into even smaller pieces and numbered accordingly before being sent across the Internet. Each "packet" is sent over the network individually and may travel a route different from that traveled by the other packets to reach the same destination, where they will be reassembled according their assigned numbers. This allows the system to take advantage of the various routes available to it at any given time. Each packet can be sent along the first available route that can handle its size. This means that the information does not have to wait for an available route large enough to handle the entirety, which could take much longer. Once the packets all reach the destination, they are reassembled so that the recipient sees the same entire email or picture or Web page as did the sender.

Professor Trotter Hardy of the College of William and Mary School of Law suggests that to understand the importance of the packet-switching system, we should compare it to the traditional telephone system, which is based on "circuit-switching." (Trotter, 1998) A "circuit" is the particular path of physical wires over which a phone conversation will be carried. Typically, several physical wires run between various locations. These wires meet at various switching stations across the country. When a phone call is made, it goes to a nearby switching station, where the switch determines on which outgoing wire the call should be routed. That outgoing wire then may go to another switching station, which again must find an available outgoing wire, and so on. The various wires chosen by the switching stations form an end-to-end path called a "circuit." That path remains constant for the duration of the phone call, regardless of whether anyone is actually speaking.

The disadvantage of this mechanism, compared with the Internet's packet-switching process, is that it "wastes" the resources

of the circuit when there are pauses in the conversation, because
the wires are not being used at that point, yet the call in process
prevents anyone else from using them. Although the packet-switching process originally was developed when the Internet was part
of the Department of Defense network to allow information transmission to continue in the face of protracted missile attacks, it now
serves a different valuable purpose. The capacity of the physical
connections used by the Internet has not kept up with the continu-
ing exponential growth in Internet use. The packet-switching process allows that somewhat limited system to be used to its greatest advantage in transferring information as rapidly as possible.

Arrival

Like the circuit system, each packet may travel across several lines
and through several computers before reaching its destination.
Thus, one piece of information, an email message or a graphic from
a Web page, will be broken into several pieces, each of which may
travel a different route in its journey. Along the journey, each packet
goes through several computers, called "routers," each of which
makes the decision of how to send it most efficiently on the next
leg of its journey. If one route fails, the router will send a copy of
that packet through an alternative route. Finally, all of the packets arrive at their destination.

Upon arrival, the packets are reassembled in the end-user's
RAM, hard drive, or other storage device, depending in part on
whether the end-user has requested that the information be downloaded or "saved." When you are simply browsing the Web, your
computer, in effect, asks the computer hosting a site to send to
your computer copies of all the files associated with the page you
are viewing. A simple page without minimal graphics may exist in
only one file. A page with lots of graphics may include a separate
file for each graphic. Each file will be broken into packets, each of
which are numbered, and sent out on their various journeys across
the Internet. They will arrive at your computer, which will reas-
semble them and hold them in its RAM so that you can view
the page.

Storage: What Exactly Is RAM, and How Is It Different from My Hard Drive?

RAM stands for "random-access memory." It physically exists separately from your hard drive, on its own chip. RAM is used as temporary storage and allows you to work more rapidly, because it

stores what you are currently working on so that you can access it immediately rather than having to continually access it from your hard drive. For example, as I write this page, the sentences I am typing exist in RAM. I view the copy that is in the RAM. When I click on "save," the page is saved to my hard drive. At that point, there are two copies—one on my hard drive and one in my RAM. When you browse the Web, a copy of each page that you access is made in your RAM. When you view that page, you actually are viewing the copy that exists in your RAM.

When you turn off your computer, or close an application, the information you have been using is erased from RAM. If you have not saved it to a long-term storage device, such as a hard drive, floppy disk, or CD-ROM, it is gone for good, as most of us know from personal experience.

WHAT IS THE SIGNIFICANCE OF COPYRIGHT IN THIS PROCESS?

Why is the above discussion important for copyright purposes? Because it means that, potentially, several copies of each and every piece of information travelling across the Internet are made during the transfer of the information. Copies also may be made upon arrival at the end-user's computer. The end-user himself then may cause additional copies to be made. Because the copyright owner of each piece of information accessed on the Web is the only person who has the legal right to make copies of that information, some very important implications for copyright exist in the very way the Internet works.

In Route

The packet-switching process used by the Internet means that at least one copy of the information being transferred is made simply so that it can make the journey. More than one copy may be made; for example, if a packet "gets lost" during the journey, another copy of it will be made and sent through a different, hopefully more successful, route.

"But do these packets really count as 'copies?'" you ask. You are right—it does sound like a stretch, for a few reasons. First, because the information is broken into pieces, there is no one copy of the entire page or email message or graphic existing at any given time during the journey. Each packet is only one small portion of the data. But traditionally, an entire work does not have to be copied to constitute infringement. Indeed, a very small portion of the work may be considered infringing if it is found to encompass "the heart" of the work.

"Nonetheless," you say, "implying that these packets might infringe copyright seems ridiculous." Again, you are right. Perhaps the best place to find support for this argument is in the definition of "copies" in the Copyright Act. A copy is a "material object . . . in which a work is fixed . . . and from which the work can be perceived, reproduced, or otherwise communicated, either directly or with the aide of a machine or device." (*Copyright Act of 1976, U.S. Code* , vol. 17, sec. 101 [1999]) Is a packet "fixed" in a "material object"? A work is "fixed" when "its embodiment . . . is sufficiently permanent or stable to permit it to be perceived, reproduced, or otherwise communicated for a period of more than transitory duration." (Ibid.)

As discussed above, each packet exists for only fractions of a second, sometimes slightly longer, which probably is not enough to meet the definition of "fixed." However, the physical wires containing it and along which it travels may be considered a "material object." Can each packet be "perceived, reproduced, or otherwise communicated"? One might have to work hard at it, but it might be possible. Even though each packet is only a jumble of ones and zeroes, those jumbles can be copyrighted as software, even though the software may not be "perceived" as we traditionally think of viewing or reading something.

"Okay, even if you could say a packet is technically a copy," you insist, "you can't say that simply using the Internet constitutes copyright infringement!" If only it were that simple. That it is not is, in a nutshell, the very reason you are reading this book. As will be discussed in following chapters, some courts have implied that some of the most basic functions of using the Internet may, by their very nature, constitute copyright infringement.

Such arguments have generated the attention of a variety of organizations and individuals. For example, the National Research Council is an agency of the National Academy of Sciences, which has a mandate requiring it to advise the federal government on scientific and technical matters. The Council recently published the results of a project designed to, among other things, make policy recommendations concerning Internet use issues. The Council recognized the problem of temporary copies such as those made in RAM during browsing and suggested that attempts should be made to determine when temporary copies should and should not be under the control of copyright owners and to adapt copyright law accordingly. (Computer Science and Telecommunications Board, 2000: 228–30) These are the issues with which we are now struggling.

End-User

Simply put, the end-user can make two different types of copies: RAM copies and longer-term storage copies. While there is little debate that copies on a hard drive or CD-ROM are considered copies as defined in copyright law, there is a great deal of debate about whether RAM copies are so considered. Let's review the components of a copy:

1. "material objects in which a work is fixed"—RAM is a material object, a small card or chip in your computer.
2. "from which the work can be perceived, reproduced, or otherwise communicated"—as explained above, RAM is what allows you to perceive a Web page, for example.
3. "embodiment . . . sufficiently permanent . . . to permit it to be perceived, reproduced, or otherwise communicated for a period of more than transitory duration"—aha! What, you ask, is "a period of more than transitory duration?" And an excellent question it is. It will be discussed in more detail in Chapter 7.

Making the Internet More Friendly—Caching

Copies also are made and used on the Internet with "caching." Caching is basically the use of temporary copies to increase speed and efficiency. Copies made in your RAM are cache copies. Not only do you view the Internet via copies in your RAM, but those copies may also be called up later during the same session. For example, if you go back to a page you viewed five minutes before, your browser is likely to call up the RAM copy rather than make a new connection to the server hosting the page and make a new copy in your RAM. This saves time and also avoids using limited network capacity when it's not necessary.

Caching also is used as a more intentional method of saving time and space. Some online services, such as America Online, cache copies of Web pages frequently accessed by their users. This means that they store copies of those pages on their own server. When a user calls up that page, instead of going to the host server, the browser gets that page from AOL's server. This results in quicker access for the user and lessened demand on AOL's capacity. An increasing number of services are doing this, including some libraries.

You may have guessed already at some of the problems inherent in this practice, including timeliness of the information contained on the cached pages. Caching is discussed further in Chapter 7.

WHAT ABOUT SPECIFIC WEB FUNCTIONS?

Linking

Anyone who has used the Web knows that hyperlinks are its heart. You may not realize, however, that there are two different types of links, inline links and out links. An out link is one that simply takes the user to another site on the Web. An inline link, in contrast, connects to an image, document, or other file at another site on the Web and pulls it into the page currently being viewed. In both cases, copies are made in RAM when the identified information is viewed. The implications for out links already have been mentioned above.

There is an additional implication for inline links: derivative works. The copyright owner has the exclusive right to make derivative works of his copyrighted work. A derivative work is defined as "a work based upon one or more preexisting works." (*Copyright Act of 1976, U.S. Code*, vol. 17, sec. 101 [1999]) This may include translations, sequels, versions in different media, such as making a movie from a book, and much more. When my copyrighted image, which I have placed on my Web page, is brought into a different context on your Web page, is that a derivative work? Possibly.

Framing

A specific form of this issue is framing. Frames basically allow more than one Web page to be viewed in the same browser "window." Sometimes it is obvious when this happens, such as lines or scroll bars around a frame, but sometimes it is not as clear. While an inline link may bring in only part of another page, such as a specific image, framing brings in the entire other page.

When my page, with the URL *www.gretchen.com*, brings your page, with the URL *www.yourpage.com*, into a frame on mine, a few things happen that might bother you. First, I control how your page is viewed within mine, including what surrounds it and the size at which it is viewed. Second, my URL continues to be displayed in the URL box on a user's browser, so the user might think that your page is actually part of mine, or that I created it.

As you can begin to see, framing creates its own set of copyright issues. These will be discussed further in Chapter 6.

All Those Copies Revisited

Not only are several copies of Web pages made during the simple process of using the Web, but the Internet suddenly has made a reality out of the potential for mass distribution of publications by everyone with access to a computer. Ten years ago, Ann probably would not have photocopied 50 copies of a new short story she just read to send to 50 of her best friends. At seven cents a page, plus postage and envelopes, Ann would end up spending quite a bit of time and money to copy and distribute that short story. But if Ann reads that story on the Web, it takes her five minutes max, and no expense unless she pays for her Internet access by time, to copy it, attach it to emails, and send it to 50 friends. Once again, the very nature of the Internet leads to some serious copyright issues.

BIBLIOGRAPHY

Computer Science and Telecommunications Board, National Research Council. 2000. *The Digital Dilemma: Intellectual Property in the Information Age*. Washington, D.C.: National Academy Press.

Copyright Act of 1976, U.S. Code, vol. 17 sec. 101 (1999).

Hardy, I. Trotter. 1998. *Project Looking Forward: Sketching the Future of Copyright in a Networked World*. U.S. Copyright Office.

5

Recent Legislation

Two pieces of legislation affecting copyright have been enacted recently, both of which have received a great deal of attention in the library community: the Digital Millennium Copyright Act (DMCA) and the Sonny Bono Copyright Term Extension Act (Sonny Bono Act), both of which amended the 1976 Copyright Act. A third legislative issue is raised by a failed proposed addition to the Uniform Commercial Code (UCC), a model code dealing with all sorts of commercial transactions, which most states adopt almost verbatim. The addition would regulate various aspects of licensing in the electronic environment, which would affect everything from "click-wrap licensing" to purchasing software for circulation in your library.

When the proposed addition to the UCC was not adopted, its supporters turned it into the Uniform Computer Information Transaction Act (UCITA), which is being addressed individually by each of the 50 states. At the time of this writing, only two states have passed some form of UCITA, but many more are studying the issue. UCITA was passed in Maryland, where it went into effect October 1, 2000. Virginia also passed it, but delayed enactment until 2001, pending the outcome of a study by the Joint Commission on Technology and Science concerning potential problems. In Delaware, Hawaii, Oklahoma, and Washington, D.C., UCITA has been introduced in at least one chamber of the legislature. It was introduced but tabled for now in Illinois and Maine. In Arizona, New Jersey, and Washington, UCITA is being studied by government agencies or the state bars. Finally, Iowa passed "bomb shelter" legislation, which is intended to protect its own citizens from the effects of other states passing UCITA.

What do these pieces of legislation mean for libraries and library users? The Sonny Bono Act is fairly simple, and, for the most part, the library community is not happy about it. The DMCA and

UCITA are not at all simple, but we will try to hit the highlights here well enough to make the major issues clear.

HOW DOES THE SONNY BONO COPYRIGHT TERM EXTENSION ACT CHANGE COPYRIGHT DURATION?

The duration of copyright has been lengthening progressively, and ever more rapidly, during the last 100 years. The original Copyright Act of 1789 gave copyright owners a 14-year term, renewable for another 14 years at the end of the term if the author was still alive. The 1909 Act increased that to two 28-year terms. Under the 1976 Act, the copyright term was expanded beyond the lifetime of the author for the first time, creating one term for the life of the author plus 50 years. For corporate, anonymous, or pseudonymous works or works for hire, the term was for 75 years from publication or 100 years from creation, whichever occurred first. In 1998, Congress passed the Sonny Bono Copyright Term Extension Act, which added another 20 years to the term, for a total of life plus 70 years. For corporate, anonymous, or pseudonymous works or works for hire, the term was 95 years from publication or 120 years from creation, whichever occurred first. (For a good discussion of the history of the act, which many believe Congress almost sneaked past, see Fonda, 1999.)

Why this continual increase in term duration? What does this mean for libraries? Many copyright scholars and attorneys argue that when protection is awarded long after the life of the author has ended, we move away from the original purpose of copyright law, which is to act as an incentive in encouraging the creation of works. This argument is applicable especially when the duration of the term is increased after death. After all, if you are not motivated to create a work by knowing that your rights in it will be protected not only throughout your lifetime, but also for two generations after your death, would adding another 20 years to that postmortem protection change your mind?

So who, then, is arguing for these extensions? Think about who benefits: obviously not the dead author. Arguably, the dead author's family, though the vast majority of works will not be wildly popular 70 years after the death of the author. More likely, the main beneficiaries are corporate authors. First, a corporation is much more likely to live for 100 or more years after publishing a work than is a human. Second, a corporate work, such as a movie, is more likely to be in demand 70 years after publication than is any given book. More specifically, the Sonny Bono Act was motivated by the impending expiration of the copyright on Mickey Mouse. "Ah, now the light bulb goes on," you say; "we're doing this to support the entertainment and publishing industries, not to motivate individual authors." That's what many believe.

Perhaps more clear is how this hurts libraries and other education- and information-based industries, including for-profit information businesses. It now takes 20 years longer for a work to fall into the public domain. A copyright owner now has an additional 20 years to charge for access to his work. During the debate over the Sonny Bono Act, representatives of the library community argued that the vast majority of works are neither commercially exploited nor easy to find long before the proposed life-plus-70 term would expire, thus there was no need for the extension. On the other hand, scholars and educators are much more likely to need access to those works, and the extension would only hurt this, the most likely, use.

In an attempt to satisfy the library lobby, a provision was included in the Act that allows a library, archives, or nonprofit educational institution "to reproduce, distribute, display, or perform in facsimile or digital form a copy . . . for purposes of preservation, scholarship, or research, if such library or archives has first determined, on the basis of a reasonable investigation, that" the work is no longer "subject to normal commercial exploitation" (which is nowhere defined), cannot be obtained at a "reasonable price," or if the copyright owner provides notice that either of these conditions applies. (*Copyright Act of 1976, U.S. Code*, vol. 17, sec. 109 [1999]) In other words, libraries, but not individual users, are exempted from some of the repercussions of the Sonny Bono Act. Nonetheless, the general movement toward extending copyright duration further and further[1] should and does alarm many librarians and educators. It threatens the balance of copyright law, and, arguably, does nothing to "promote the progress of science and the useful arts."

An example of how the Sonny Bono Act might affect individuals can be seen in a lawsuit that is currently challenging the constitutionality of the act. In an effort to encourage his teenage daughters to read and become more interested in classic literature, Eric Eldred began a project of providing on the Web the text of classics that are in the public domain, plus additional material of interest, such as timelines, illustrations, and biographies of authors. Eventually his project, Eldritch Press, expanded to include nonfiction works as well. Eldritch Press received praise and recognition from the National Endowment for the Humanities, the Nathaniel

Hawthorne Society, and the William Dean Howells Society. Then the Sonny Bono Act was passed. Some of the works Eldred had planned to put online, such as a specific version of a collection of Robert Frost poems, now had coverage extended by 20 years.

Eldred began stirring the waters and eventually got the attention of Lawrence Lessig, professor of law then at Harvard University, now at Stanford University. Lessig brought a lawsuit challenging the Sonny Bono Act and including nine plaintiffs in addition to Eldred, such as Higginson Books and the American Film Heritage Association. The lawsuit, filed in federal district court in the District of Columbia, challenged the act on three grounds: (1) that it violated the First Amendment right to free speech; (2) that the extension to cover works retrospectively was unconstitutional because it violated both the terms "limited times" and "to the author" in Article 1, section 8 of the U.S. Constitution; and (3) that it violated the public trust doctrine. The district court granted summary judgment to the government, which means that it dismissed the case without hearing it, basing its opinion on the documents filed by the parties. The court held that: (1) the act does not violate the First Amendment, because there is no First Amendment right to use the copyrighted works of others; (2) the retrospective extension of the act is within Congress' constitutional power, because the "limited times" period is subject to the discretion of Congress, and an author may agree in advance to transfer any future benefit Congress might confer; and (3) the public trust doctrine applies only to navigable waters. (*Eldred v. Reno*, 74 F.Supp.2d 1 [D.D.C. 1999]) As of this writing, an appeal is pending before the D.C. Circuit Court of Appeals.

WHAT EXACTLY DOES THE DIGITAL MILLENNIUM COPYRIGHT ACT DO?

Doubtless you have heard many references to the Digital Millennium Copyright Act. You may not realize that the DMCA is not simply an amendment to one part of the Copyright Act; rather, it includes several provisions on a range of topics within copyright. Some of those provisions are discussed throughout this book as they apply to those specific areas of copyright. Here, I will hit only the highlights.

Notwithstanding the general theme of this book, that no one has quite yet figured out how to apply copyright to the cyberworld, there is a great deal of awareness of the existence of this problem.

The DMCA was meant to address some specific pieces of the problem. Creating the DMCA was a long and arduous job, because many constituencies had very specific concerns, and those concerns often conflicted. It is worthwhile to note that some earlier versions of the DMCA were much less friendly to libraries and library and information users than was the version that passed. Through the hard work, over a long period of time, of hundreds of librarians, library supporters, and library organizations, many issues of concern to libraries were addressed. The library community may not be completely happy with the DMCA, but, overall, it is a good example of yet another success story of the library lobby, in which all librarians should play a role.

Limited Liability of Online Service Providers

This topic is discussed in greater depth in Chapter 11. The basic issue is whether libraries act as online service providers (OSPs) when they provide Internet access to their users and staff, and, if so, whether they may be held liable for what those users do or access while online. This portion of the DMCA, now Section 512 of the Copyright Act and reprinted in Source 1, allows individual libraries to choose whether they want to claim protection as an OSP under the safe harbors provided in the act. Certain responsibilities inure by virtue of claiming that protection, such as registration of an agent and developing notification and termination policies. However, benefits also inure to claiming OSP status, namely limitations on liability for what might be considered completely innocent acts, such as system caching, transient storage in the process of transmitting information on the Internet, and linking to infringing sights. The bottom line is that each library must make this decision for itself, and each library should indeed make a decision.

Updating Section 108 to Supplement Preservation and Replacement Options

The DMCA amended Section 108, which includes exemptions for library reproductions and was discussed earlier in Chapter 3, to allow more copies to be made for preservation and archival purposes and to allow libraries to use a variety of technologies in making such copies.

Anti-Circumvention Rules and Copyright Management Information

A major concern in the cyberworld is the ease with which information may be stolen and misused. In response to such concerns, the DMCA prohibits circumvention of technology that prevents access to a work. In other words, if Jimmy employs a certain type of technology to control access to his Web page, for example, to prevent others from accessing his page if they have not registered with him or paid a fee, under the DMCA, it is now explicitly illegal for anyone to try to get around that preventive technology. A limited exception gives libraries a right to "browse" items to which they are considering purchasing access.

The library community was extremely concerned that this provision would affect fair use at a catastrophic level, creating what has been called an exclusive "right to browse" or "right to read." In response, the final version of the DMCA included the anti-circumvention provision but delayed its implementation for two years, subject in part to a study to be conducted by the Librarian of Congress concerning the likelihood that users will be "adversely affected" in their ability to make noninfringing uses of copyrighted works.

The DMCA also prohibits the manufacture, importation, sale, or trafficking in anti-circumvention technologies. This concerns the library community, because even though libraries and nonprofit educational institutions are given the "browsing right" mentioned above to circumvent protection technologies, this prohibition would seem to ensure that the technologies necessary for libraries to implement this right would not be available.

More specific to copyright, the DMCA also prohibits the removal or alteration of copyright management information, or information that is intended to identify the work as protected by copyright, including the terms and conditions of that protection.

WHAT IS THE UNIFORM COMPUTER INFORMATION TRANSACTION ACT?

A new major challenge to librarians dealing with copyright in cyberspace is rapidly and powerfully rearing its ugly head even as I write. The Uniform Computer Transaction Information Act is a model law that, as of July 2000, has been adopted in some form in two of the 50 states. It is an incredibly complicated act, confusing for lawyers, lawmakers, and laypeople. The following explanation is a very tiny nutshell for a very big nut.

The Uniform Commercial Code is a body of model law intended to address problems and complications caused by the lack of uniformity in the laws among the 50 states addressing commercial issues such as sales of goods, leases, and so on. The UCC is written by two collaborating groups, each composed primarily of practicing lawyers, judges, and law professors: the American Law Institute (ALI) and the National Conference of Commissioners on Uniform State Laws (NCCUSL). Once these groups have completed the lengthy task of writing a new section of the UCC, they then proceed with a campaign to have it adopted by as many states as possible.

UCITA is the result of several years of work and debate by the ALI and the NCCUSL. It addresses the creation of, production of, and access to information. It was intended to be Article 2B of the Uniform Commercial Code. After much back-and-forth with the NCCUSL and a few postponements of formal votes to accept Article 2B, the ALI announced in April 1999 that it would not support the proposed Article 2B. Three months later, the NCCUSL adopted the proposal as UCITA. It is now making its round to state legislatures, each of which must decide individually whether to adopt a version of it.

UCITA presents many points of concern for libraries and library users. Perhaps the primary concern is that UCITA is a potentially very serious threat to the fair use doctrine as applied to any electronic information as well as a threat to the right of first sale. In general, the library community is concerned that UCITA, which would validate both shrink-wrap and click-wrap licenses, would replace copyright law with contract law, presenting the danger that information users could "click away" their fair use rights. In such a scenario, there would be no mechanism for maintaining the balance found in copyright law between the rights of authors and the rights of the public. The owner of the information would control all uses of it, potentially forever.

The American Library Association has been working together with the Association of Research Libraries, American Association of Law Libraries, Special Libraries Association, and the Digital Future Coalition to address the serious flaws in UCITA. Their participation in this process was instrumental in the ALI's decision to withdraw its support. However, many powerful industries, in particular the software industry, strongly support UCITA. It is imperative that librarians become involved in this issue in order to protect our library users and our libraries as institutions. Call your state library association to find out what is happening in your state and what you can do to help. For more information on UCITA, see the following resources:

Americans for Fair Electronic Transactions (AFFECT)
www.ucita.com

American Library Association. Intellectual Property and Copyright.
www.ala.org/washoff/ucita.html

Kunze, Carol A. The 2B Guide
www.ucitaonline.com

FURTHER RESOURCES

Lutzker, Arnold P. "Primer on the Digital Millennium: What the Digital Millennium Copyright Act and the Copyright Term Extension Act Mean for the Library Community." *www.ala.org/washoff/primer.html* (March 2001)
Association of Research Libraries. "Digital Millennium Copyright Act: Status and Analysis." *www.arl.org/info/frn/copy/dmca.html* (March 2001)

BIBLIOGRAPHY

Copyright Act of 1976, U.S. Code, vol. 17 (1999).
Digital Millennium Copyright Act of 1998, 105th Cong., 2nd sess., 1998.
Eldred v. Reno, 74 F. Supp. 2d 1 (D.D.C. 1999).
Fonda, Daren. 1999. "Copyright Crusader Eric Eldred Says the Latest Copyright Law Goes Too Far, Keeping Thousands of Creations Out of the Public Domain." *Boston Globe* (29 August, 1999): p.12 magazine.
Sonny Bono Copyright Term Extension Act of 1998, 105th Cong., 2nd sess., 1998.

NOTES

1. Representative Sonny Bono died only months before the act was passed. His widow, Mary Bono, argued before Congress in support of the act. In that argument she stated, "Sonny Bono wanted to see copyright last forever."

Part II:
Applying Copyright to Cyberspace

6
Hyperlinking and Framing

HOW DOES HYPERLINKING WORK?

"Hyperlinking is the essence of the World Wide Web; it makes the Web the Web! Can simply linking to someone else's page be an infringement of copyright?"

Usually, one thinks of hyperlinking as just clicking on blue text or a thumbnail image to connect us to another Web page. But there are actually a few different kinds of hyperlinking, or ways of using hyperlinks, and each of these categories raises its own copyright issues. Some are much more likely than others to raise copyright concerns. In addition to directly infringing, there is a strong argument that a Web page author can be held liable for contributorily infringing copyright by connecting to a page that contains directly infringing materials.

Types of Links

Hyperlinks can be divided into three broad categories. What typically is thought of as a hyperlink is an "out link." When the user clicks on the linked text or image, the Web page he is currently viewing is replaced with a new page. A subcategory, if you will, of out linking is "deep linking." Deep linking refers to connecting to a specific page buried within a site, rather than the site's homepage. For example, if your library homepage links to Thomas, the Library of Congress page providing in-depth information on Congressional legislation and other activities, at *thomas.loc.gov*, this is an out link, because you are going beyond your library site to another site. Most likely, you will link to the Thomas homepage at *thomas.loc.gov*. Perhaps, however, your library pages include a list of Web sites providing current news, so you decide to link to Thomas' Bills in the News page at *thomas.loc.gov/home/textonly.html*. This would be considered a "deep link," because it bypasses the Thomas homepage and goes straight a "deeper" page at that site.

Finally, there are "inline links." Instead of taking you to an entirely new page, an inline link pulls in an item from another page to display it within your page. Framing uses inline links, but adds a little oomph as well. An example of an inline link might be if I find a lovely image I want to include on my Web page, but because its file is so large, I do not want to store it on my computer. So instead of saving it on my own machine, I simply link to it at the site where it resides. A user may not be required to click on anything to be able to see the image; to her, it appears simply to be part of my page, and she cannot tell from viewing my page where the image resides.

In comparison, framing brings in an entire other page, but within the page currently being viewed. Perhaps the most common use of frames is within a site. For example, on its Web site a library might want to keep a constant table of contents, or list of links to pages within the site, on one side of the screen, or the top or bottom, even if the main information being viewed changes. This can be done by placing the same list repeatedly on each page, or it could be done by making a "frame" out of that list and linking to other pages within the "viewing" part of the frame. Using the picture frame analogy, which is apparently the source for the term, the list of pages would be the actual frame, and it would be constant. New pages being linked to would appear in the glass part of the frame, where pictures are viewed.

Figure 6–1 is an example of a page with a constant index on the left (the box listing the available research guides). Each time the user clicks on a research guide, an entire new page will load, which will include a repeat of that box index. Figure 6–2 is an example of placing such an index in a frame. When a user clicks on a page in the index, that page will load in the main window to the right, but the index will remain. In this case, you can tell that frames are being used, because the index has its own scroll bar. This is not always the case, however. Sometimes it is impossible to tell just by looking if frames are being used.

Now imagine Figure 6–2 with the same index on the left, but with the University of Houston Library Research Guide page in the right window. The URL at the top might remain that of the Garnet A. Wilson Public Library. Which library's page would you think you were in? Would you expect clicking on "online catalog" in the index to take you to the online catalog of the University of Houston Libraries or of Garnet A. Wilson Public Library? This is the

Figure 6–1
Sample Web Site Featuring an Index that is Repeated as an Element of Every Page.

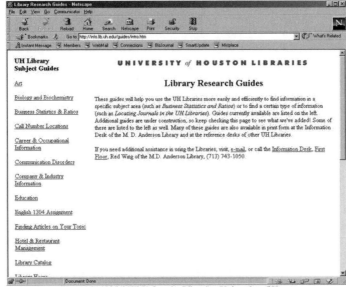

Copyright 1995-2000 University Libraries, University of Houston
Reprinted by permission of the University Libraries.

Figure 6–2
Sample Web Site Featuring a Contant Index in its own Frame Separate from Individual Pages.

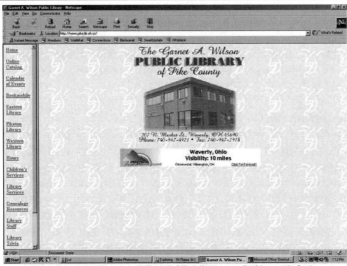

Copyright 2000 Garnet A. Wilson Public Library (used with permission)

potential problem created by using frames to link to pages beyond the hosting site.

Out Links

An out link (excluding deep links, discussed below) is probably the simplest type of link to dispose of from a copyright perspective. The most likely way in which problems will occur is by using protected images or text as your actual link. For example, if I want to create a Web page for my library providing information about current best sellers, I could run into trouble if I use as a link to other pages such information as any of the following: a copy of the copyrighted image from a book jacket; text either from the book or from a page to which I'm linking, such as a book review; or the trademarked logo of a publisher. Let's briefly consider each situation.

Copied Images as Links

The most likely to cause me trouble is the use of a copyrighted image as a link. Let's say I want to link to a page or pages about John Berendt's book *Midnight in the Garden of Good and Evil*. The photograph on the book jacket is both lovely and immediately recognizable to fans, so it would make a good image to use as my link. But wait! That photograph is copyrighted, and the right belongs to Jack Leigh. Will using it as a link on my page be a problem? If I do not have the owner's permission, it certainly could be. Simply by including the image on my page, I am making a copy (right #1). Arguably, I am distributing it to the public via the Web (right #2). By putting it within a context other than that which the copyright owner intended, I probably am making a derivative work with the photo (right #3). Arguably, I also am publicly displaying the work (right #4). What to do? Either seek permission from the copyright owner or do not use the image at all. Instead, use the title of the book.

Copied Text as Links

The possibility of infringing copyright by using text as a link is unlikely, primarily because when text is used as hyperlinks, usually only a few words are used, if that. In the example above, the obvious choice would be "Midnight in the Garden of Good and Evil." Although there is no quantitative minimum requirement for the amount of text used to infringe a copyright, an entire work need not be copied to constitute infringement. All that is necessary is copying a "substantial and material amount of . . . protected expression." (Leaffer, 1995: 290) How much is "substantial and material" is decided on an case-by-case basis—which is always a little frightening, because that means you cannot know beforehand whether or not you are doing something wrong.

The United States Supreme Court, rather unhelpfully, has held that the key is whether or not the "heart" of the work is taken. In *Harper & Row v. Nation Enterprises* (471 U.S. 539 [1985]), the Court held that taking as little as 300 copyrighted words, which then were published in a 2,250-word article, from a 200,000-word manuscript constituted infringement, because the taken words constituted "essentially the heart" of the book. This does not give us much of a standard to go on. As a practical matter, any text you use for linking purposes will probably be slight enough that it will not be an issue.[1] Keep in mind, though, that the eight-word "Frankly, my dear, I don't give a damn," is a lot more likely to get you into trouble than the twenty-word opening sentence from the same novel, "Scarlett O'Hara was not beautiful, but men seldom realized it when caught by her charm as the Tarleton twins were." (Mitchell, 1964)

Trademarked Logos as Links

Although this book is about copyright law, not trademark law, issues of trademark infringement do exist in regard to creating Web pages. These are described briefly in Chapter 9, but the discussion of trademarked images as hyperlinks bears repeating in this chapter.

Trademark protection and copyright protection are based on different rationales. The overarching goal of trademark is to avoid consumer confusion by misleading (that is, infringing) uses of trademarks. Thus, the standards of infringement are completely different.

"Oh," you might be thinking, "there's no way someone's going to confuse my library's Web pages with those of Nike just because I use the Nike swoosh to link to the Nike Web site, no matter how stupid they are." That seems obvious enough. However, there is this neat little branch of trademark infringement called "dilution." To be held liable for dilution, all you need to do is use the trademark to cause confusion as to your "affiliation, connection, or association" with the producer of the good. It has been argued that using a trademarked logo on a Web page causes dilution because it leads the user to believe that, in the example above, Nike sponsors or supports your library. So far, this argument has proved unsuccessful. Nonetheless, it is still a wide-open issue, as is most of Internet-related law. So take the simple, safe route: either get permission, or use a textual description ("Nike, Inc.") instead of a logo.

Deep Links

"Why would the level to which my page links have anything to do with whether or not I am infringing copyrights of the other page?"

Good question! It sounds totally illogical, yet a few suits based on this claim have been either filed or threatened by major companies like Ticketmaster (Schiesel, 1997) and Universal Pictures (Kaplan, 1999). The Ticketmaster case involved Microsoft's information service Seattle Sidewalk, which provides information about local events, including where and how to purchase tickets to such events. In that capacity, Seattle Sidewalk linked to Ticketmaster Web pages about specific events, rather than to Ticketmaster's homepage. Ticketmaster sued for both copyright and trademark infringement. The case was settled out of court, with part of the settlement being an agreement to keep the terms of the settlement secret.

The situation involving Universal Pictures never resulted in a lawsuit. Universal was upset by a young movie fan's Web site, Movie Link, that linked directly to trailers of Universal movies, rather than to the Universal homepage. When Universal threatened to sue, the Web author dropped his links to Universal's sites, stating that he had neither the money nor the power to go to court with such a well-funded entity.

So what were these cases all about? Shouldn't Ticketmaster and Universal Pictures be happy to have someone sending more business their way? There seems to be general agreement that the cases are about advertising dollars and a company seeking those dollars losing control over access to its own media products. There is a great deal of disagreement over whether it is legitimate to use copyright law to try to address this situation.

Most likely, Ticketmaster and Universal were concerned because the links on Seattle Sidewalk and Movie List allowed users to bypass the advertisements posted on their homepages and perhaps on pages in between the homepages and the destination pages as well. When users go directly to a deeper page, the homepage gets less hits, which means advertisers are either less likely to advertise at that site in the first place or not willing to pay as much as they would if all those users went through the page with their ads.

This is certainly a legitimate problem for the hosting page, and it represents one of those areas on which the Internet has put a new spin. Sure, you can turn down the volume or flip channels during TV commercials, but at the very least, the advertisers have no way of knowing when you do that. Software makes it very easy for Web sites to count the number of hits each page receives. Other options, such as placing ads on every single page, may not be very feasible. Of course, the Web host wants to control how users enter his site.

But is copyright law the appropriate mechanism for doing that? Probably not. In order to successfully claim copyright infringement, the harmed company would have to prove that one of its specific rights (reproduction, distribution, derivative works, public display/ performance) had been infringed. In situations like those discussed above, the facts would vary from case to case. If the Movie List Webmaster had downloaded copies of the movie trailers to his server, there might be a good claim for infringement of the repro- duction and distribution rights. But what if he simply linked to Universal's page? The outcome should not depend on the manner that a Webmaster decides is most economically feasible for him. Nonetheless, suits have been filed, and nothing has been settled. Even more frightening, some commentators think, is the fact that Microsoft as a defendant settled in the face of such a suit. If Bill Gates caves, they reason, there must be something to it.

On the other hand, in a more recent case on which appeal is currently pending, a federal district court in California denied a preliminary injunction to Ticketmaster against tickets.com, which deep-linked to information about specific events on Ticketmaster's Web pages. A ruling on preliminary injunction is not a decision on whether or not anyone is infringing; instead, it is a ruling based on the likelihood that the plaintiff will succeed on its charges at a later stage in the trial. Thus, a denial means that the court thinks it unlikely that the plaintiff will prevail in its arguments, which, in this case, suggests that the court thinks deep linking is not a problem.

HOW DO INLINE LINKING AND FRAMING WORK?

The problem with either inline linking or framing is the potential for creating a derivative work. Recall that the copyright owner has the exclusive right to create derivatives of his work. "Derivative work" is defined as "a work based upon one or more preexisting works, such as a translation . . . motion picture version . . . con- densation . . . or any other form in which a work may be recast, transformed, or adapted." (*Copyright Act of 1976, U.S. Code*, vol. 17., sec. 101 [1999]) Most courts have held that a derivative work must have some original expression of its own, though originality is usually a pretty low standard in the copyright world. So the question becomes, "Does bringing another image into your own page, or bringing other pages into your frames, constitute a derivative work?"

So far, there have been few if any verdicts. However, a few cases do give a peek at what future decisions might hold. In *Futuredontics, Inc. v. Applied Anagramatics, Inc.* (45 U.S.P.Q.2d (BNA) 2005 [C.D. Cal. 1998]), the defendant linked to the plaintiff's Web site, which displayed in a frame on defendant's site. The frame included the defendant's logo, information about the defendant, and links to the defendant's other Web pages.

The plaintiff argued that the defendant was violating its copyright by creating a derivative work, while the defendant argued that the frame should be considered a "lens" enabling users to view the information that the plaintiff posted on its own page. The defendant moved for the court to dismiss the case on the basis that it failed to state a claim, meaning that the complaint was not based on an actual legal problem.

The court denied the motion, stating that existing case law did not make clear whether the defendant had created a derivative work, and thus the plaintiff had sufficiently alleged a claim for copyright infringement. At the same time, however, the court refused to grant the plaintiff a preliminary injunction, stating that the plaintiff had failed to demonstrate probability of success on the merits that would give rise to presumption of irreparable injury, and that evidence submitted by the plaintiff was insufficient to establish irreparable injury or balance of hardships tipping sharply in its favor, both of which are required in order to grant a preliminary injunction. (Ibid.) On appeal of the denial of preliminary injunction, the Ninth Circuit agreed in an unofficial opinion, which means it carries no authoritative weight. (*Futuredontics, Inc. v. Applied Anagramatics, Inc.*, 152 F.3d 925 (9th Cir. 1998) [order denying preliminary injunction])

The point of the derivative works right is that the copyright owner is the only one who should be allowed to profit from a "recast, transformed, or adapted" version of his work. The advertisements are an important piece of the work in cases like those discussed here. *Futuredontics* suggests that simple user confusion as to whose page is being viewed may be an additional concern. By framing the work, with the resulting effect of making it more difficult than the copyright owner intended for the user to view advertising, the copyright owner may suffer financial harm. On the other hand, as mentioned above, there is usually an originality requirement for derivative works. Does framing someone else's page meet that requirement?

Consider the earlier example of Garner Public Library linking with frames to pages from the University of Houston Libraries. Certainly, the author of the U.H. pages never intended for them to be displayed with an index to another library's collections. Thus the work created, what the user views, seems to be a recasting or transformation of the original U.H. page.

This is just one more case in which current copyright law simply does not translate to the cyberworld. As a result, those who are harmed, or maybe just upset, by what others do in cyberspace can try to twist copyright law around until it fits their purposes. In some cases, this may be perfectly appropriate. In others, it starts to feel like copyright law is being used to accomplish purposes for which it was never intended. Have I mentioned yet that this is just one more reason for librarians to become involved in the legislative process? (see Source 12)

WHAT SHOULD I DO ABOUT USING DEEP LINKS AND FRAMES?

Generally speaking, two of the biggest concerns with deep linking and framing are the possibility of creating confusion as to whose site the user is actually viewing and the ability to interfere with another site's advertising or marketing actions. This means that libraries should try to avoid using frames or deep links in a manner that might cause confusion to the viewer.

Theoretically, one should be cautious about using deep links that might interfere with advertising. In reality, though, trying to avoid the use of any such links often would mean not using deep linking to commercial sites at all, since so many now include some form of advertising. Many copyright experts suggest that deep linking is not a problem for nonprofit libraries, but that other libraries should be somewhat cautious. (Melamut, 2000)

CAN THESE ACTIVITIES REALLY INFRINGE COPYRIGHT?

Not much has been established about whether various methods of linking and framing will directly infringe copyright. Just in case you are not perplexed enough, let's throw another wrench in the works. Aside from directly infringing copyright—that is, violating the copyright owner's rights yourself—one may also be held liable for contributory or vicarious liability. You contributorily infringe copyright if you knowingly and materially induce, cause, or contribute to someone else's direct infringement. If the contribution you make is providing equipment, that equipment must not have a substantial noninfringing use. Most courts have held that "knowingly" means that you must be aware of the other person's actions, but not necessarily that they are infringing. Vicarious infringement does not require that you know about the other person's actions. However, you must have the right and ability to control the infringing activity and an obvious and direct financial interest in the activity. How do contributory and vicarious infringement apply to linking and framing?

Perhaps the biggest question is, "Can I be held liable for linking to (or framing) someone else's page that includes infringing material?" You will not be surprised to hear that this issue has not been directly tried yet. At least one case has made the argument, which was dismissed by the court, but the situation was extreme enough that it is probably not a good general guideline. In addition, because the court was a district court, its opinions carry less weight than those of an appellate court. The plaintiff in *Bernstein v. J.C. Penney* (1998 U.S. Dist. LEXIS 19048 [C.D. Cal. 1998]) sued J.C. Penney for linking through a chain of links to a page that infringed Bernstein's copyrights in some photographs. Penney's pages promoted Elizabeth Arden perfume and included biographical information about Arden. The Arden page had a "for more information" link that led to (among other sites) the Internet Movie Database that led to (among other sites) the Swedish University Network, which posted infringing photographs of Elizabeth Taylor, spokeswoman for Elizabeth Arden. The court dismissed the complaint, which means that the case was thrown out of court, but did not explain its reasoning.

The important thing to keep in mind is that this was a case about linking three levels away: A→B→C (infringer). It seems unrealistic to expect or require A to investigate all of the sites to which B links. Consider how many "B level" links there are on A's site! However, it may not be as unreasonable to expect A to investigate each "B level" site to which it links. All sorts of issues are raised by this argument, of course, including "How do I know the page I'm linking to includes infringing material?" Recall, however, that contributory infringement does not require the infringer to know that the other person's activity is infringing, only to know about the other activity. By creating a Web page with links, you are inducing, contributing, or causing the user to access the pages to which you link; and you know (or at least have reason to know, which would probably count) that users are indeed linking to those pages. That's all that's required for contributory infringement, if those pages to which you link include infringing material.

"How can I possibly investigate every page to which my library links, let alone figure out whether or not they contain infringing material?!" you ask exasperatedly. In reality, you simply cannot. But use some common sense when you chose pages to which you link. Consider the following:

- How *likely* is it that the producers of this page would include infringing material? Of course, there's no guarantee, but a media mogul page, say Time-Warner, is much more likely to be aware of and careful to comply with copyright than a cottage-industry creating pages on a computer in someone's home.
- How likely is it that the material itself is infringing? Think "Napster." 'Nough said. If the source is offering only its own products, it's not nearly as likely to include infringing material as if it's offering everyone else's products as well. Keep in mind things like federal government documents, in whatever format, are not copyrighted.
- Are there copyright statements on the page? If there is a statement saying permissions have been granted, that's a good sign.

Also keep in mind that in the real world, what is most likely to happen should you link to pages with infringing material and the copyright owner becomes aware of it is that you will receive a "cease-and-desist" letter. If you cease, they almost certainly will desist in coming after you.

BIBLIOGRAPHY

Bernstein v. J.C. Penney, 1998 U.S. Dist. LEXIS 19048 (C.D. Cal. 1998).

Copyright Act of 1976, U.S. Code, vol. 17, sec. 101 (1999).

Futuredontics, Inc. v. Applied Anagramatics, Inc., 45 U.S.P.Q.2d (BNA) 2005 (C.D. Cal. 1998).

Futuredontics, Inc. v. Applied Anagramatics, Inc., 152 F.3d 925 (9th Cir. 1998); order denying preliminary injunction.

Harper & Row v. Nation Enterprises, 471 U.S. 539 (1985).

Hayes, David L. 1998. "Advanced Copyright Issues on the Internet." *Texas Intellectual Property Law Journal* 7:1 (Fall 1998): 1–103.

Kaplan, Carl S. 1999. "Is Linking Always Legal? The Experts Aren't Sure." *New York Times,* 6 August 1999.

Leaffer, Marshall. 1995. *Understanding Copyright Law*. New York: Matthew Bender.

Melamut, Steven. 2000. "Does Deep Linking Infringe Copyright?" *Information Outlook* 7 (September) 41.

Mitchell, Margaret. 1964. *Gone with the Wind*. New York: The Macmillan Company.

Schiesel, Seth. 1997. "Choosing Sides in Ticketmaster vs. Microsoft." *New York Times,* 5 May 1997.

NOTES

1. In the United States, titles per se cannot be copyrighted. The rationale behind this is that titles are usually too short to meet the originality requirement. In theory, a longer, more unique title could be copyrighted.

7
Browsing

Simply browsing the Web may have implications for five of the six exclusive rights of a copyright holder: reproduction, derivative works, public display, public performance, and digital performance of a sound recording. True, it does seem ridiculous that simply *using* the Web could infringe the copyrights of the creators of Web pages. If nothing else, wouldn't that be detrimental to the intentions of those Web authors? After all, why put material up on the Web unless you want other people to access it?

Viable arguments can be made that the functions involved in browsing the Web do in fact infringe copyrights if done without permission of the copyright owner. Viable arguments can also be made for an implied license in Web browsing, that is, that by putting information up on the Web, Web authors have given their implicit permission for others to at least browse the pages. There are problems associated with depending on the implied license argument, however, as we will see.

Even if our courts decide that a license to browse is implied by making information available on the Web, some cyberspace lawyers have argued that serious copyright implications still exist simply because of the potential of infringing copyrights via browsing. Recall that one of the most basic intentions of copyright law is to define and maintain a balance between the rights of authors and the rights of the public to have access to information. Giving control to authors over simply browsing the Web is akin to giving authors control over who reads their books. It has been referred to as creating an "exclusive right to read." Relying on defenses such as implied license or fair use does not take that control away from the author; rather, it says that the author has voluntarily relinquished the right to control who accesses his publications. Traditionally, an author has never had such a right in the United States.

Professor Raymond Nimmer, professor of copyright at the University of Houston School of Law, points out that creating a "right to read" is a shift in policy, which, "even if desirable, should occur because of an express policy choice rather than because new technology technically triggers concepts originally designed for a world of photocopy machines, recorders, and the like." (Nimmer, 1996: 4–30)

In other words, browsing may be the ultimate example of the inability of copyright law to keep up with technological developments, despite the clear intention of its authors to avoid such a situation. I would also hasten to add that Professor Nimmer's statement is just one more reason we as librarians should get involved in this discussion. We as a profession take pride in representing the needs of our users to our city councils, university presidents, and school boards. We must also improve our representation of our users at higher government levels to ensure that an "exclusive right to read" is not created, even if completely unintentionally. To learn more about what you can do, see Source 12.

HOW IS THE REPRODUCTION RIGHT IMPLICATED BY BROWSING?

Storage

RAM

Browsing the Web creates temporary copies of whatever is viewed and caches those copies either in RAM or on the computer's hard drive. If that material is copyrighted and no permission has been given, such copies could infringe copyright. The key question right now concerning RAM copies is whether those copies meet the requirement of being fixed for a period of time sufficient to allow the work to be "perceived, reproduced, or otherwise communicated for a period of more than transitory duration." This is likely to be one of those times when many people will throw up their hands exclaiming, "That's just legalese! Anyone who knows anything about the Internet knows that the whole purpose of RAM is to store information only temporarily." While that is true, it does not change the analysis of whether RAM copies might infringe copyrights. Indeed, at least two courts have held that RAM copies may indeed infringe copyrights.

In *MAI Systems Corporation v. Peak Computer, Inc.* (991 F.2d 511 [9th Cir. 1993]), the plaintiff manufactured both computers and operating systems to run them; it also provided maintenance for its hardware and software. MAI licensed its customers to use the software only for their own internal purposes. The defendant company maintained computer software for its clients. When Peak provided maintenance to a customer for MAI software, MAI sued, claiming that Peak had violated MAI's copyright in its software. When it performed maintenance on the software, the defendant turned on the computer, which created a copy of the software in RAM. The defendant proceeded to read an error log displayed from the RAM copy. The court held that the defendant created an illegal copy of the plaintiff's software when it loaded the software into the computer's RAM upon turning on the computer to perform maintenance. The court did not state as a matter of law that every RAM copy necessarily is fixed for copyright purposes. Rather, its decision was based on the fact that the use of the error log proved that the RAM copy could be "perceived, reproduced, or otherwise communicated." (Ibid.)

MAI did not involve use of the Internet, and the court's decision applied only to that specific situation. The court even pointed out that the defendant had not argued that the RAM copy was not fixed, implying that it would be open to hearing such arguments. A lower court, however, has addressed the issue of RAM copies made during browsing. (*MAI* was decided by the Ninth Circuit Court of Appeals, while *Intellectual Reserve* was heard by a federal district court. Appellate court decisions carry much more authority than those of district courts.)

Intellectual Reserve, Inc. v. Utah Lighthouse Ministry (75 F. Supp. 2d 1290 [D. Utah 1999]) was a case about contributory infringement, not direct infringement. The defendants had placed portions of the plaintiff's copyrighted works on their Web page. When the plaintiff ordered the defendants to remove the works, they did so but replaced them with a notice that the work was available elsewhere on the Web, gave URLs for those sites, and posted emails on their page encouraging users to go to those sites to access the works. The plaintiff then sued for contributory infringement, which charges the defendant with knowingly inducing, causing, or contributing to someone else's infringement. The court awarded a preliminary injunction to the plaintiff and, relying on *MAI*, specifically stated that in making a RAM copy while browsing, "the person who browsed infringes the copyright." (Ibid.: 1294) Although end-users were not parties to the action, the court's targeting of the simple behavior of browsing is potentially quite dangerous. The court has set the precedent that browsing the Web infringes the reproduction right when the user accesses pages containing infringing material.

Does Simply Browsing the Web Create Infringing Copies?
Technically, the answer to this question is "possibly yes." The act of browsing the Web creates copies of Web pages in your computer's temporary memory, even if you are unaware of it. The controversy created by this question centers on whether or not those copies are permanent enough to meet the statutory requirement of "fixed for more than a transitory period of duration." One line of cases has held that, at least in some circumstances, they are. If the page being viewed contains material that is copyrighted but that was incorporated into the page without the copyright owner's permission, and so is illegal just by being on the page, then the copies made on your computer are by definition also illegal.

If, however, you are viewing a page without infringing material on it, there are some defense arguments to the claim that the copies in your computer's temporary memory are infringing. The primary argument is that by placing the material on the Web, the author intended for people to access it; to do so requires the making of those temporary copies. In legal parlance, the author has given an "implied license" to view his page by making it available on the Web, which includes making whatever copies are technically necessary.

It is also possible that a Web user infringes the copyrights to publicly display or perform a work when she browses the Web in a public place like a library. A library may meet the definition in the Copyright Act of a public place, and a good argument can be made that viewing materials on the Web is a display or performance. Again, there is a strong argument that the author has given users an implied license to view his pages in a public place, like a library, by making the material openly available on the Web. In addition, individual work stations are not likely to be considered "public" places.

What specifically can be done about this problem? Recall that the *MAI* court invited arguments that a RAM copy is not fixed for more than a transitory duration. "Transitory duration" is not defined in the copyright law. One could argue that, because a RAM copy disappears when the browser is closed or the computer turned off, it is only transitory. On the other hand, one court has specifically stated that the fact that one can control how long a copy exists in RAM by turning off the power supports the argument that it is fixed for more than a transitory duration.

Another approach is to create legislation specifically addressing this issue. Indeed, following the *MAI* decision, the copyright law was amended to state that making a copy on a computer is not infringement when done solely for the purpose of providing maintenance. Perhaps Congress should pass a statute specifying that copies made automatically only for the purpose of browsing the Web are not infringing. Some people are concerned, though, with the implication that new laws must be made continually to address each specific change in technology. After all, the current copyright law clearly was written with the intention that it would address future technology changes. The best support for this is in the definition of copies in Section 101: "material objects . . . in which a work is fixed *by any method now known or later developed.*"

The National Research Council addressed the situation in a recent report issued by its Computer Science and Telecommunications Board, *The Digital Dilemma*. The Council is an agency of the National Academy of Sciences, which has a mandate requiring it to advise the federal government on scientific and technical matters. *The Digital Dilemma* presents the results of a project designed to, among other things, make policy recommendations concerning Internet use issues. The Board recognized the problem of temporary copies such as those made in RAM during browsing and suggested that attempts should be made to determine when temporary copies should and should not be under the control of copyright owners and to adapt copyright law accordingly.

In addition, the Board explicitly stated its concern with developing a system of piecemeal exceptions, suggesting a process that would ultimately result in "a more general-purpose and flexible rule." (Computer Science and Telecommunications Board, 2000, 228–30) Furthermore, the Board went so far as to suggest that "the notion of copy may not be an appropriate foundation for copyright law in the digital age," precisely because the making of copies is an integral part of so many computer functions. The report recommends to Congress exploring the possibility of constructing a new basis of copyright law based on the constitutional goal of promoting the progress of science and the useful arts. Instead of asking whether a copy had been made, the key question would be whether the use at issue was consistent with the constitutional goal. (Ibid.: 230–32).

Caching on the Hard Drive
Similar questions arise in regard to caching by a computer hard drive. Depending on how your browser is set up, "temporary" copies of files you access while browsing the Web may be made on your computer's hard drive rather than in RAM. The most important difference for our purposes is that hard drive cache is stored indefinitely. Typically, much more space is allotted to hard drive caches than is available in RAM. Your hard drive usually contin-

---

Can My Library Be Liable If Our Users Actually Are Violating Copyright Simply by Browsing the Web?

If your users can be held liable, then technically the library itself could also, under the theory of contributory liability, which requires knowingly and materially inducing, causing, or contributing to someone else's direct infringement. It is highly unlikely, however, that this would happen. Theoretically, a library could be held vicariously liable, though that would be an even longer shot. There is no requirement that the library know about the infringing activity in order to be held vicariously liable, but it must have the authority and ability to control that activity as well as have an obvious and direct financial interest in the activity. Although the library as an institution, and some individual at some level, has the authority and ability to control whether or not patrons use library computers to browse the Web, it is highly questionable whether libraries have the authority or ability to prevent users from accessing infringing pages. In addition, most libraries probably would not meet the last requirement of having an "obvious and direct" financial interest in their users browsing the Web. So the bottom line is technically yes, but in the real world, almost surely not.

---

ues to cache until it fills, then will delete files as necessary to allow space for caching new files. Unlike RAM, it is not emptied each time an application is closed. Also unlike RAM, it is simple to call up a directory of your cached files and view them on the spot. Although the issue of infringing copies cached on a hard drive has not been raised in a courtroom yet, if RAM copies can infringe copyrights, it seems even more certain that cached copies would do so. Whatever "transitory" may be, certainly cached copies, which can potentially last for years, are not it.

Downloading and Printing

The issues with downloading into long-term storage—on your hard drive, a floppy disk, CD-ROM, and so on—vary somewhat from the issues of RAM and cached copies. Downloading a file from the Web undoubtedly creates a copy of that file, as does printing. If this is done without permission of the copyright owner, and barring fair use and other exemptions, it infringes the copyright. However, downloading is not inherent in simply using the Web. While one can argue that limiting a user's right to create RAM copies limits his ability to use the Internet and thus creates the "exclusive right to read," the same argument cannot be made for downloading. The only reason to download or print a file is to come back to it later for a particular use. Control over this type of activity is precisely the kind of control copyright traditionally gives authors.

We can analogize by saying that giving an author control over RAM copies is equivalent to allowing the author to say, "You may have found my book on the shelf in a bookstore or library, but you can't read it unless you ask me first." Clearly, this was never an intention of copyright law. On the other hand, giving an author control over downloading and printing is equivalent to allowing the author to prevent one person from buying a copy of a book and then passing it around to all of her friends to make their own photocopies so they do not have to buy it. Control over this type of activity is unquestionably an intention of copyright law.

How do you know when you can and cannot legally download or print a page or a file? Most often, you simply do not. If you are downloading files such as software from a site that offers these files to the public, likely there is a usage policy posted. Your usage may be restricted, such as to noncommercial purposes or for a limited time. Sites offering free graphics may allow unlimited use but require you to credit the copyright owner. Some pages offer a "print-friendly" display, which is a good sign that the authors are happy for you to print from their site.

However, most pages simply do not make clear what is copyrighted and what is not, or what the author has given the user permission to do with copyrighted material. Not only that, but it may be that some of the information on a page you are looking at is itself infringing copyright.

Consider your reason for downloading or printing a page or file. Is it just for the sake of convenience? Do you want to use a graphic on your own Web page? Do you want to share a story you've found with friends? Then consider your alternatives. If you want to use something you've found on the Web for your own publications, whether online or print, contact the author of the page. Do not assume that the author is also the copyright owner. Instead, ask where that person obtained the file you want to use. Continue to trace it until you have located the original source. Then ask for permission to use the item. If you want to share a story or article with friends, send them the URL rather than the file. This will also take up less room in their email boxes. If you just want to continue to refer to the page, bookmark it.

In reality, of course, it is highly unlikely that a Web page author will come after individuals for copying from his page or printing it out for their own personal use. However, it is possible that a Web page owner who does not wish to have his page, or part of it, copied will discontinue making his files available if he feels his rights are being encroached upon. In other words, in addition to legal concerns, there is an issue of common courtesy involved.

HOW IS THE DERIVATIVE WORKS RIGHT IMPLICATED BY BROWSING?

The copyright owner of a work has the exclusive right to create derivatives of that work. A derivative work is defined in the Copyright Act as

> A work based upon one or more preexisting works, such as a translation, musical arrangement, dramatization . . . motion picture version . . . abridgment . . . or any other form in which a work may be recast, transformed, or adapted . . . [including] editorial revisions, annotations, elaborations, or other modifications, which, as a whole, represent an original work of authorship. (*Copyright Act of 1976, U.S. Code,* vol. 17, sec. 101 [1999])

Obviously, under this definition, were you to download someone else's copyrighted page, modify it in some ways, and repost it, all without her permission, you would be infringing that person's derivative works right. There is also the potential for less obvious, and more questionable, creation of derivative works in simply browsing the Web.

The most common is use of frames on Web pages. The basic argument is that using frames causes other people's pages to be presented in a manner and context different from that designed by the author. Does this really create a derivative work? At least two cases have claimed it does. Note, however, that both cases come from district courts, whose decisions are not nearly as authoritative as those of higher appellate courts. In *Futuredontics v. AAI* (1998 U.S. Dist. LEXIS 2265 (C.D. Cal. 1998), the court denied a motion to dismiss, thereby allowing the derivative works infringement argument to go forward. *The Washington Post Co. v. Total News, Inc.* (No. 97 Civ. 1190 [S.D.N.Y. filed Feb. 20, 1997]) was settled out of court, so the issue was not addressed by the court. However, the defendant agreed in the settlement to discontinue the use of frames in connection with the plaintiff's pages. These cases, and copyright issues concerning framing in general, are discussed further in Chapter 6.

Another possibly problematic use is translators that translate

Are You Saying My Library Could Be Sued Simply for Providing Access to the Internet?
Technically, yes, it could be, but realistically, it is not very likely. Even if you were sued, it is not clear yet what the outcome would be. The bottom line is that this area is just too new. Even though the Copyright Act of 1976 was written with the specific intention that it be flexible enough to apply to changing technology, that is simply not working. Chances are, no one would sue you in the first place. If she does, a defense of either implied license or fair use (or both) might get you off the hook. There is also a "safe harbor" for libraries who wish to designate themselves as Online Service Providers under Section 512 of the Copyright Act (see more in Chapter 11). But that does not resolve the biggest issue—the fact that we just cannot answer this question today. If this scares you a little, as it should, and you want to have a voice in creating the answer, see Source 12 to find out what you as an individual professional librarian, library worker, or library supporter can do to ensure that this ridiculous possibility never comes to pass.

entire Web pages from one language to another. At the site *www.babelfish.com*, for example, you can type in the URL of any Web page, and Babelfish will quickly translate it into the language of your choice, showing the page in its original form otherwise. Translations are clearly considered to be derivative works under U.S. copyright law. If you as the user type in the URL of the page to be translated, are you creating that derivative work? Or is Compaq, the owner of Babelfish? None of these questions have yet been raised in court. It is important to note, however, that case law makes clear that copyright law is concerned with publishing and distributing unauthorized translations, not translation for personal use. So, assuming they are accurate, Babelfish and its kind are wonderful tools, given the international nature of the Web. Should a user utilize Babelfish to translate a page and then post the new translation on his own site, however, he might have a problem.

Another "cybertoy" is Third Voice, a browser utility that allows users to post virtual Post-its on any Web page they choose. Any other user running Third Voice can see those comments (if they are "public"; Third Voice also allows users to create their own user groups, in which posted annotations are visible only to group members). Users can comment on other posted comments, creating a layered discussion on one Web page, and include hyperlinks in the postings. Postings range from political comments on political sites, to flames, to seemingly random profane comments and links to porno pages.

Some Web page authors are concerned that novice users will think the postings are designed to be part of the page. (But, one wonders, would novice users be using Third Voice without realizing what it does?) On the one hand, one could argue that because Third Voice changes both the appearance and content of a page, it creates a derivative work of that page. On the other hand, not all viewers see the changes, or some viewers may see some of the comments but not all. And the "changes" do not actually alter the code of the pages, so it is possible for everyone to view the original page, simply by turning off Third Voice. Jonathan Zittrain, executive director of the Berkman Center for Internet and Society at Harvard Law School, uses the analogy of making changes on a transparency through which one then views the original work, as opposed to changing the work itself. Whether or not the results of Third Voice constitute derivative works is still up in the air. However, a very vocal group of Web site hosts, Say No to TV, may ensure that the answer is soon addressed in the courts.

Somewhat similar to both Third Voice and Babelfish are Shredder *(www.potatoland.org/shredder)*, a Web site that transforms the pages of URLs typed in by users, and funksolegrind *(www.channel. org.uk/sHrd/)*, software that must be downloaded. Both Shredder and funksolegrind work like twisted Web browsers, distorting pages into what looks at times like surreal images, at other times just garbage. Also in the game are filters that filter out various types of advertisements on Web pages. The techniques used range from preventing pop-up windows from popping up to muting sound recordings to "decaffing" Java script.

Some of the same questions are raised by these Web page "transformers" as by Third Voice. On the one hand, they take control away from the author of how her work is being perceived. On the other hand, they do not alter the work for everyone viewing it. As a matter of fact, this is even more true for programs like the Shredder and for advertisement filters, which affect only viewers on one machine or network. However, a Web page author could argue that, in a setting like a library, an individual user does not have the choice of how to view Web pages, rather that it is being forced on him. This might support an argument for infringement. Again, it is not known yet how the law will shake out on this issue. Given the strong feelings, as well as deep pockets, involved, however, we can expect to hear more, possibly from the courts or legislators.

HOW ARE THE PUBLIC DISPLAY AND PERFORMANCE RIGHTS IMPLICATED BY BROWSING?

A copyright owner has the exclusive right to display and perform the copyrighted work publicly. To do so is defined as

> (1) to perform or display [a work] at a place open to the public or at any place where a substantial number of persons outside of a normal circle of a family and its social acquaintances is gathered; or
> (2) to transmit or otherwise communicate a performance or display of the work to a place specified by clause (1) or to the public . . . whether the members of the public capable of receiving the performance or display receive it in the same place or in separate places and at the same time or at different times. (Ibid.)

An exception to this rule is allowed under the First Sale Doctrine: "The owner of a particular copy lawfully made . . . is entitled . . . to display that copy publicly . . . to viewers present at the place where the copy is located." (Ibid.: sec. 109[c])

To "display" a work is defined as "to show a copy of it," including by means of various technological devices. (Ibid.: sec. 101) To "perform" a work is "to recite, render, play, dance, or act it . . . to show its images in any sequence or to make the sounds accompanying it audible." (Ibid.) A library certainly seems to fit the definition of a public place. Does this mean that users viewing Web pages in a library constitute a "public display" or "public performance"? The argument can certainly be made that users are "showing" a copy of the page they view.

Although showing the page to others may not be their intention, librarians are well aware that this can be the result; witness the hair pulling and teeth gnashing over how to deal with patrons viewing pages that other patrons find offensive. Likewise, viewing a video or listening to an audio clip on the Web seems to meet the definition of showing images in sequence or making sounds audible. More likely, though, is that individual stations would be considered private spaces in the context of triggering public performance rights, while auditoriums, meeting rooms, and classrooms are more likely to be considered public spaces. The only court cases yet to address the issue of public display and performance on the Internet have dealt with defendants who themselves posted infringing material to the Internet, not with users.

ISN'T THERE SOME KIND OF PROTECTION FOR BROWSERS?

"I understand the arguments, the reasoning, the logic," you're thinking, "but are you really suggesting that anyone, either individuals or institutions, would be held liable for simply using the Web?" Of course the idea sounds ludicrous. The point is that it is theoretically possible. In real life, and especially in areas presenting new and unresolved legal challenges, the way the law works is often like this: Although it seems quite clear that Sue has wronged Anne, because there is little law established in the area, Anne's attorneys will be creating new law in their prosecution of this case; because so few straws currently exist, Anne's attorneys will have to grab at whatever straws they can to find a basis for bringing the suit in the first place. This is the way new case law is created. In theory, it works well. In reality, one of the major dangers is that what works in Sue and Anne's particular case might have unreasonable implications in the big picture for the rest of us.[1]

Thus, until the law becomes more developed, either through the courts or through legislation, we must depend on already established protections. Unfortunately, these protections are not foolproof, primarily for two reasons. First, they were not developed to address the cyberworld, so there may be questions about how well they fit into that context. Second, they are primarily defenses. That means that while they might protect you from losing a case, they do not prevent charges being made against you in the first place. It means that you, as the defendant, bear the burden of making the argument and of doing so successfully. Simply naming a defense is not enough; you must convince the judge of its value over the value of the plaintiff's argument. This is just one more reason why the library profession and its members need to continue to work with legislators to create the legislation necessary to address these issues on the front end rather than rely on current legislation and case law to address them on the back end (see Source 12).

Implied License

An implied license is a license, or privilege, that is presumed to have been given based on another's actions rather than his words. Arguing that an implied license to browse has been given means arguing that the poster of a Web page impliedly licenses users to make whatever copies are necessary to allow them simply to view the material. Keep in mind that in using this argument, we are talking about legally browsing material legally posted to the Web.

We are not talking about viewing material illegally posted or about illegally viewing material, such as hacking your way through to a protected site.

As logical as the implied license argument seems, you probably have learned by now if you have read this entire chapter to this point, that nothing can be so simple in law. There are at least two areas of potential problems. First, the scope of an implied license is not clear. Has the author given permission only to make the RAM copies necessary to view a page, or also to cache a page on the user's server for future use, or also to print the page, or perhaps more? By definition, an implied license is not articulated in words. Thus, it is difficult to know what the author intended to allow be done with her pages, and it may become increasingly difficult to argue for each additional implied right.

Second, an implied license can be defeated by an express license. In other words, if a Web page author places a statement on her page saying, "Any Internet user has the right to view my page, but no one has the right to print it out without my permission," one cannot then argue an implied, or unstated, license to print the page. The author clearly has stated that this license does not exist. Express licenses then raise their own questions, including simply the practicality of widespread use. For example, think of the confusion generated if every Web page author placed a different express license on his page. As we know, most Web users are not copyright gurus. What if Tom places the following statement on his pages: "No one may make copies of this page without my permission." Tom seems to be unaware of the issues concerning copies in RAM. On the one hand, should he have reason to, he could argue that infringing copies have been made by simply viewing his page. On the other hand, the accused user could argue that even if this was what Tom intended by his statement, how could he, the accused user, know he was not allowed to view the page without first viewing it? Then again, innocence is not a defense to infringement. And so it goes, and goes, and goes. . . .

While it is true that the implied license defense may be strongest when applied to a charge of infringement by browsing, it is not strong enough to depend on it unreservedly.

Fair Use

Fair use is discussed more fully in Chapter 3. The fact that fair use requires a fact-specific and case-by-case analysis cannot be overemphasized. That said, the context of browsing may also allow for some of the strongest fair use arguments. Consider, for example, the factor of effect on the market. Arguably, browsing has no market effect. Again, this would not apply to someone hacking his way into a site that requires payment to enter. On the other hand, in some cases, one could argue that some users may choose to read a Web page instead of purchasing a print copy of the same material, which would create a market effect. Then again, that user could argue that by not restricting access to the page in some way, including paying to access it, the author impliedly allows browsing even at the expense of losing a purchase of a printed equivalent.

WHAT DOES THIS MEAN FOR OUR LIBRARIES?

In all likelihood, user browsing is not much threat for libraries for several reasons. Libraries may choose to designate themselves as protected Online Service Providers under Section 512 of the Copyright Act, discussed in Chapter 11. Even without such protection, it is unlikely, though not impossible, that a library would be the target of such a suit. The bottom line, however, is that there is very little libraries can do until the issue of browsing is further decided, either by the courts or by Congress. Libraries can, however, limit the caching they do to the very minimum necessary.

BIBLIOGRAPHY

Copyright Act of 1976, U.S. Code, vol. 17, secs. 101 and 109 (1999).
Futuredontics v. AAI, 1998 U.S. Dist. LEXIS 2265 (C.D. Cal. 1998).
Intellectual Reserve, Inc. v. Utah Lighthouse Ministry, 75 F. Supp. 2d (D. Utah 1999).
MAI Syst. Corp. v. Peak Computer, Inc., 991 F.2d 511 (9th Cir. 1993).
Nimmer, Raymond T. 1996. *Information Law.* St. Paul: West.
The Washington Post Co. v. Total News, Inc., No. 97 Civ. 1190 (S.D.N.Y. filed Feb. 20, 1997).

NOTES

1. A great example of this is the infamous holding in *MAI v. Peak Computers* that a copy in RAM can infringe copyright. Although this arguably was reasonable in that particular case, carried to the extreme it is not only ridiculous, but simply disastrous. However, in this kind of

situation in which the area of law is so new that it is almost non-existent, it is often difficult, if not impossible, for a judge to specify limitations on his holding. In considering judicial opinions in which the holding seems outrageous, it is important to keep in mind the greater context of the situation.

8
Using Digital Images

If I can't tell from looking at image on the Web whether or not it's copyrighted, how do I know when I can download it to use for my own purposes? Can I make digital copies of items my library owns for our Web pages? Isn't there something about being able to make digital copies for preservation purposes? If I have permission to use an image on a Web page, can I "doctor it up" a little to make it more suitable for my purposes or to improve on it?

All of these questions address some of the ways in which librarians may encounter copyright problems as they create Web pages for their libraries. As we go through each issue, keep in mind two bottom-line, basic rules:

1. Because a copyright owner is not required to include notice of copyright on his work in order to protect it, you cannot know by looking at an item that it is not copyrighted just because it does not have the © on it.
2. Legally owning a copy of a copyrighted work (like each book your library buys) does not give you, as the owner of that copy, the right to do whatever you want with that item. Most importantly, it does not give you, as the owner, the right to make copies of the item, technically even for personal use.

HOW DO I KNOW WHEN I CAN LEGALLY DOWNLOAD OR COPY AN IMAGE FROM THE WEB?

Congress did away with the copyright notice requirement in 1988— that is, in pre-Internet days. The lack of a requirement to identify copyrighted works as such translates to this in the cyberworld: You cannot tell by looking at a work whether or not it is copyrighted. If it has a © attached to the work (or if there is a full copyright notice, such as "copyright 1999 Joe Smith"), most likely it is copyrighted. On the other hand, the more commonly occurring lack of such a symbol or notice does not—repeat: does not—mean that the work is not copyrighted.

When does this create problems for librarians using the Web? Perhaps because they are often overworked and underfunded, librarians work hard to be efficient. An oft-heard phrase is, "don't reinvent the wheel." This means that if someone else has already done what you want to do, or taken steps toward it, you borrow her ideas or even actual works, or build on the foundation someone else has laid. As an instruction librarian, I constantly turned to my colleagues for examples of what they had done in certain situations, and we frequently shared instructional material with each other. Now the Web makes that so much easier. Many library instruction programs are creating digital resources and providing them on the Web, making it easy for patrons to access at any time, from any place. When she begins a new project and wants to see what others have done, all an instruction librarian has to do is surf the Web to see what kinds of materials others have created to teach how to search a certain database or how to conduct research in a certain subject area.

All of this is great, but what happens when we find pages we like, things others have done that we'd like to use? What if it's not just a colleague's Web page, but cute graphics from a totally unrelated page that would make your page so much more attractive to users? Aren't a lot of those graphics that we see repeatedly on the Web clip art anyway, thus free for anyone to use?

As we know, the copyright owner has the sole right to make copies of his work. Only when another person's use meets the fair use or other statutory exemptions can she legally copy that work. Thus, exceptions aside, copying a protected image from a Web page infringes the copyright in that image. Period. Even before anything is done with it. Is copying an image to use on a nonprofit, possibly educational, Web page, allowed under the fair use doctrine? The short answer is: There are no guarantees of what will be covered by fair use, despite many misconceptions that any nonprofit use is okay. For a more detailed explanation, see Chapter 3, which is devoted to the fair use doctrine. In some situations, your use might be acceptable. In others, it will not be.

What about clip art? Many, many Web sites provide free clip art to Web users. Clip art may be images, animations, and/or sounds. Some Web sites charge for using their clip art. Some sites may impose limitations on use, such as for noncommercial use only, or require the user to credit the site. But, you ask, how are these sites different from any other? How can I know that the clip art itself is not copyrighted? I'm sure you can foresee my answer: You cannot. The wise Web page designer will look for a copyright statement on the site at which the clip art he wants to use is located. Many have statements along the line of, "As far as we know, our site contains only works in the public domain and does not contain any copyrighted works." Of course, this is no guarantee, but it's as close as you can get. There's a whole lot of clip art out there. Take the time to find a site that at least seems to have made an effort to exclude infringing materials. It is certainly risky to use clip art from "Johnny's Favorite Junk" page, on which Johnny tells you that he's 12 years old, in the sixth grade, and loves *Star Wars* and Brittney Spears . . . and then provides you with pictures from the movie and of Brittney in concert!

WHEN I LEGALLY DOWNLOAD AN IMAGE, AM I LIMITED IN WHAT I CAN DO WITH IT?

Let's briefly revisit the various rights of copyright owners and discuss what the implications would be for using a legally acquired image on your Web pages. This is assuming that you have the right to copy the work from another source, whether a Web page or otherwise.

The Public Performance and Display Rights

The copyright owner has the exclusive right to display publicly any literary, musical, dramatic, pictorial, graphic, or sculptural works (*Copyright Act of 1976, U.S. Code* vol. 17, sec. 106(5) [1999]); and to perform publicly any literary, musical, dramatic works, motion pictures, and other audiovisual works. (Ibid.: sec. 106[4]) In addition, the copyright owner of a sound recording has the exclusive right to perform the work via digital audio transmission. (Ibid.: sec. 106[6])

Obviously, the next question is: Does putting a work on the Web constitute public performance or display?

Performance
"To perform" a work is defined as "to recite, render, play, dance, or act it, either directly or by means of any device or process." (Ibid.: sec. 101) Depending on the format of the work at issue, the performance right might be implicated. If the image you've copied is an animated John Travolta dancing to "Stayin' Alive" (or, even more clearly, a movie clip of the disco king), then to show the image is to perform it.[1] Arguably, "render" might cover any type of image, whether or not sound or animation is involved.[2]

Display
The Copyright Act defines "displaying" a work as "to show a copy of it, either directly or by means of . . . any other device or process." (Ibid.) Pretty clearly, then, to place a copy of an image on your Web page is to display that image.

The Public
But the trick comes in the qualifier: to *publicly* perform or display. The Copyright Act defines to perform or display a work publicly as

> (1)   to perform or display it at a place open to the public or in any place where a substantial number of persons outside of a normal circle of a family and its social acquaintances is gathered; or
> (2)   to transmit or otherwise communicate a performance or display of the work to a place specified by clause (1) or to the public . . . whether the members of the public . . . receive it in the same place or in separate places and at the same time or at different times. (Ibid.)

Certainly, a library is a place where "a substantial number of persons outside of a normal circle" of family and friends gather, and most libraries are open to the public. Thus, transmitting a display or performance to a library could meet the definition of a public display or performance. As discussed previously, however, individual workstations are not likely to be considered a public place, even though an argument to the opposite could be made.

But what about users who access your library's Web pages from home, or work, or a computer lab, or anywhere outside of the library? Is this a public performance or display? If the place in which the user accesses the pages is open to the public, or is a place where a substantial number of people gather, possibly so. But what about accessing the Web at home? The definition does say that it does not matter whether people receive the performance or display at the same place and time as others. But what if none of the places are "public" places? Could one argue that "place" means virtual place as well as physical? The House Report on the Copyright Act states that subscribers to cable TV would meet the definition of receiving a performance in a public place. Internet users would seem closely analogous to this example.

One federal district court has held that a party who posted infringing copies of *Playboy* photographs on a Web page that was accessible only to paying subscribers violated the copyright owner's right of public display because, "[t]hough limited to subscribers, the audience consisted of 'a substantial number of persons outside of a normal circle of family and its social acquaintances' *(sic)*." (*Playboy Enter., Inc. v. Frena*, 839 F. Supp. 1552: 1557 [M.D. Fla. 1993]) Under this reasoning, even if a library limits access to its pages—such as limiting access to currently enrolled students—placing the image in question on a library Web page would constitute public display or performance, but there is no general answer to this question yet.

Exceptions

The Copyright Act provides specific exceptions to the exclusive rights of public display and performance. The one most pertinent to our situation allows performance and display via transmission by nonprofit educational institutions if certain requirements are met. Note that most libraries, while nonprofit, are not educational institutions. In comparison, more recent amendments to the Copyright Act specify "nonprofit libraries." The requirements for qualifying for this exception are that the performance or display (1) be "a regular part of the systematic instructional activities of a governmental body or a nonprofit educational institution;" *and* (2) be *directly related to* and *of material assistance to* the teaching content of the transmission; *and* (3) the transmission be made primarily for reception in classrooms or by persons to whom the transmission is sent because of the persons' disabilities or other circumstances that keep them from attendance in regular classrooms. (*Copyright Act of 1976, U.S. Code*, vol. 17, sec. 110(2); emphasis added) This is a very limited exception, obviously targeted at traditional teaching rather than the broader function of libraries to disseminate information to the public. It might apply to library instruction transmitted only to classrooms (that is, "distance learning") or to individuals unable to attend classroom instruction; almost certainly, however, it would not apply across-the-board to the vast majority of library Web pages, no matter what the instructional content.

The Distribution Right

Finally, the copyright owner has the exclusive right to distribute copies of her work to the public. (Ibid.: sec. 106[3]) Whether placing a work on the Web constitutes public distribution is somewhat controversial. To begin with, is placing something on the Web, where others can come to your site to view or use it, distribution? Is that something a "copy" in the first place?

"Copy" is defined in the statute as a "material object . . . in which a work is fixed by any method now known or later developed, and from which the work can be perceived, reproduced, or otherwise communicated." (Ibid.: sec. 101) Although, as discussed above, the issue of whether copies existing in RAM constitute "copies" for the purpose of the Copyright Act has not been settled, copies existing on servers, hard drives, CD-ROMs, floppy disks, or other tools of long-term storage rather clearly meet this definition.

So, does placing a "copy" of an image on your Web page constitute a distribution to others? Compare it to sending out an email. In the latter situation, you are proactively giving out something. Once you create a Web page, you sit and wait for others to come to it. When they do, it is their acts of viewing the page, including any downloading or copying they might do, that create copies of the images on that page; your role at this point is quite passive. The statute says that the author has the right to distribute "by sale or other transfer of ownership, or by rental, lease or lending." Strong arguments have been made that when end-users view your site, they themselves may make copies in order to view your site, but that no "transfer of ownership" takes place, since the item you placed on your page is still there. True, the end-user may end up with a "copy" meeting the statutory definition, but that is in addition to the copy you still possess, not a transfer of that copy. A good analogy is making photocopies. Electrons are transferred from the original source to a blank piece of paper, which, by storing the electrons, creates a new copy. However, very few people would argue that this is a violation of the distribution right (though it could violate the reproduction right).

DOES THE RIGHT TO COPY AN IMAGE FROM A WEB PAGE INCLUDE THE RIGHT TO PUT IT ON MY WEB PAGE?

Technically, putting an image on a Web page may violate the rights of public performance and display. Distribution is more questionable. Realistically, if you have been given the right to copy an image from a Web page, the owner of that image probably assumes that you are likely to use it on another Web page. This is less true when you copy something from a printed work or from a film or audio recording. Nonetheless, assumptions are not a good thing on which to base decisions that might have serious legal implications. When you ask for permission directly from the copyright owner, tell him what you plan to do with the work. If a statement of permission is made with the work, look at it closely to see what exactly it is giving permission for. If it is only to copy, contact the copyright owner and ask specifically for permission to put on your Web page. Keep in mind, also, that if your use is allowed under the fair use doctrine or other exceptions to the copyright owner's exclusive rights, you do not need to seek permission in the first place.

DOES THE RIGHT TO COPY AND PLACE AN IMAGE ON MY WEB PAGE INCLUDE OTHER RIGHTS?

Say you come upon a page with a statement giving permission to anyone to copy the page or parts of it for her own use on her own Web pages, as long as it's not commercial and appropriate credit is given (this is not uncommon to see on educational pages). The image you really like is a little girl looking intently at a TV, but you need to replace the TV with a book. A couple of clicks and drags in Adobe Photoshop or some other digital design program, and you are done!

Let's pause a moment, though, to consider the legal implications of this action. A copyright owner owns the exclusive right to prepare derivative works. A derivative work is "a work based upon one or more preexisting works," in "any form in which a work may be recast, transformed, or adapted." One court has even held that cutting pictures out of an art book and pasting them on tiles creates a derivative work of those pictures. (*Mirage Editions., Inc. v. Albuquerque A.R.T.*, 856 F.2d 1341 [9th Cir. 1988]) Although many commentators view this as extreme, it is a good demonstration of how little "tweaking" it takes to create a derivative work.

In our situation, then, did replacing the TV with a book constitute creation of a derivative work? Almost certainly so. Was this infringement, assuming you did not have the author's permission? Again, almost certainly so. "There's this adorable dancing bear, but I can't stand the music he's dancing to. Can I change it?" Without permission of the copyright owner, probably not. "What about the cute-but-innocent cartoons of a naked Adam and Eve? Can I put clothes on them, so I can use them on a page for my children's program?" Likely, not without permission.

WHAT USES CAN I MAKE OF INFORMATION I FIND ON THE WEB?

It is very important to keep in mind that what you "can't" do assumes that (1) your use is not excused by the fair use doctrine or other more specific exceptions and (2) you do not have the author's permission. If you find a page that gives a permission statement, read it carefully to see if it allows you to do what you want to do— copy, post on your Web page, alter in any way. Most importantly, keep in mind that you can always assume the risk, knowing that many of the purposes for which you would be using the work would be allowed under fair use or other exceptions, or you can attempt to contact the author and get her permission to do whatever it is you want to do with the work. Just remember to get permission for exactly what you want to do, not just permission to generally "use" or to copy the work. Get permission the old-fashioned way, in print; email may or may not have the same legal status as a signed letter. See the discussion in Source 10 about seeking permissions, for additional important information about how to get author's permission, and for some caveats (that is, warnings) to keep in mind in dealing with the cyberworld.

CAN I PLACE IMAGES OF WORKS IN MY COLLECTION ON MY WEB PAGES?

An exception from infringement exists for digital copies made from print resources for the purpose of preserving or archiving the work. However, this is a very limited exception; depending on the nature of the work being digitized, various conditions must be met.

If the original work to be copied is an unpublished work, the copy being digitized must be currently in the library's collection, *and* the digital copy must *not* be distributed in its digital format nor made available to the public outside the premises of the library. (Ibid.: sec. 108[b]) If the digital copy is being made in order to replace a published work that has been lost, damaged, or stolen, or that is deteriorating, the library must first make a "reasonable effort" to determine that an unused replacement cannot be obtained at a fair market price, *and* the digital reproduction must *not* be made available to the public outside the premises of the library. (Ibid.: sec. 108[c])

We previously discussed the thorny issue of whether placing something on the Web constitutes public display or distribution. However, Section 108 more simply disallows making a digitized copy available to the public (unless the work is in its last 20 years of copyright coverage and meets the conditions put forth in 108[h]; see Source 1) Thus, a library should be able to place a digitized copy of a printed work within its collection, whether published or unpublished, on its own Web page that is available only within the library, but it would not be able to place the image on a page accessible outside of the library building. It is also important to keep in mind that these exceptions apply to copies made for preservation and replacement purposes only, not for purposes of providing easier access or creating copies accessible to multiple patrons at one time—in other words, not simply for the sake of convenience.

THE BOTTOM LINE

As always: Proceed with caution. Know the rules, be aware of your actions, and use common sense. Is your use likely to be considered a fair use? Should it be excused under one of the more specific exceptions to a copyright owner's exclusive rights? If not, use your research skills to try to find the information you need—is it copyrighted? Who owns the copyright? What can I do with it?—and act accordingly.

BIBLIOGRAPHY

Copyright Act of 1976, U.S. Code, vol. 17, secs. 101, 106, 108(b), 108(c), and 110(2) (1999).
Mirage Editions, Inc. v. Albuquerque A.R.T., 856 F.2d 1341 (9th Cir. 1988).
Playboy Enter., Inc. v. Frena, 839 F. Supp. 1552 (M.D. Fla. 1993).

NOTES

1. To be specific, remember that there are two different types of rights in a musical recording: the right in the musical work, that is, the right of the writer of the musical piece (in this case Barry, Maurice, and Robin Gibb); and the right in the sound recording (in this case RSO Records). This means that there are potentially two different copyright owners in a musical recording. The performance right applies only to the musical work (owned by the Bee Gees). However, the copyright owner in the sound recording (RSO Records) has the exclusive right "to perform the copyrighted work publicly *by means of a digital audio transmission.*" (sec. 106(6); emphasis added). Why the limited right? Short answer: Politics are behind almost every act of Congress! Rergardless, this surely would include transmissions of recordings via the Internet. Thus, for our purposes, performance of a recorded piece of music on the Internet would implicate rights in both the underlying musical work and the specific sound recording of the work.
2. "Render" is not defined in the Copyright Act. However, Webster's Ninth New Collegiate Dictionary defines "render" as "to transmit to another." (*Webster's Ninth New Collegiate Dictionary* (Merriam-Webster Inc., 1983): 997.)

9
Understanding Noncopyright Issues

Copyright, of course, is not the only law that applies to the Internet, nor is it the only law of which librarians should be knowledgeable concerning their use of the Internet. Some—certainly not all—other areas include censorship, especially concerning minors; filtering; privacy; defamation; and licensing issues, such as whether "clickwrap" agreements are valid. You have doubtless heard about laws that have attempted to address these areas, such as the Communications Decency Act (CDA), a portion of which was invalidated by the Supreme Court as being too broad; the Child Online Protection Act (COPA), which suffered a similar fate as the CDA; and the Uniform Computer Information Transactions Act (UCITA), a proposal put forth by the National Council of Commissioners on Uniform State Laws addressing online contracts, which some states have adopted as state law.

Another area of law that has implications for the Internet and that, for our purposes, is actually closely related to copyright, is trademark law. For that reason, I think it is important to discuss it here. It is important to note that, unlike copyright, trademark is governed by both federal and state laws. Here we will discuss only federal, which should be sufficient for this context.

HOW DOES TRADEMARK LAW COMPARE TO COPYRIGHT LAW?

The rationale behind copyright law is to encourage the production and distribution of works of art and science by protecting the rights of authors. In comparison, the rationale of trademark law is to protect the rights of a business owner to enjoy and benefit from the business he has earned as a result of investing in the goodwill and reputation of a trademark or trade name, and also to protect consumers from being misled by providing them a means for identifying the source of a good or service. For example, when you pick up a bag of Nutter Butter peanut butter cookies, you know not only that they will be of the same quality as in the last bag of Nutter Butter's, but also that, because they are produced by Nabisco, they will be of the quality that you associate with Nabisco. An obvious fringe benefit arises for the producers of goods and services when consumers continue to buy their products because of the knowledge about that product associated with the trademark.

A trademark is any word, name, symbol, device, or combination thereof that is used to identify and distinguish a good or service from that produced or sold by others by identifying the source of the good or service. Limitations apply to the types of words that may be used as trademarks and to the manner in which they are used. Unlike copyright law, an individual word or brief phrase can be protected by trademark law, although there are limitations on the types of words that can be trademarked.

In a nutshell, generic terms, such as "car," "restaurant," or "toy" cannot be trademarked. The rationale for this is that one company should not be able to control the use of the simple English word that describes the product that it and 100 other companies make. What would happen if Nabisco trademarked the word "cookie," so that no one else could use it in a commercial context to refer to, well, cookies? It would, for all practical purposes, take the word out of the daily English language. Descriptive terms, such as "raisin bran," can be trademarked only after they have achieved "secondary meaning," meaning that consumers have come to associate the term with a particular producer of the product so that, in the minds of consumers, it is distinguished from other types of raisin and bran cereals.

Trademarks must be used; one cannot "reserve" trademarks for years on end without using them in order to prevent others from using them. Keep in mind that a trademark is associated only with the type of good or service with which it is used. For example, Nabisco owns the trademark "Nutter Butter" for use with peanut butter sandwich cookies; if Ford decides it wants to create a new model car and name it the Nutter Butter, it can do so. Trademarks are also limited to geographic areas. Thus, there may be a "Joe's Pizza Shack" in Houston, one in Seattle, and one in New York City, with no association between them.

Both of these limitations make sense when you consider the purpose of trademark law: to avoid consumer confusion. No one is likely to assume that a car called the Nutter Butter has been made by Nabisco, and very few people will frequent Houston, Seattle, and New York City enough to assume that the Joe's Pizza Shacks are owned by the same Joe. This explanation is a great simplification; there are exceptions, such as, the geographic limitation incorporates areas in which the producer is likely to expand, so it would be more difficult for someone to open a Joe's Pizza Shack on Long Island than in Los Angeles. Again, consumers are more likely to be confused by the existence of the same good 30 miles apart than 3,000 miles apart. Once a trademark has been federally registered, however, the owner has rights to use it nationwide, excepting locations in which it has already been used by others.

WHAT DOES THIS MEAN FOR A LIBRARIAN CREATING WEB PAGES?

Trademarks may be violated in various ways: (1) infringement, (2) dilution, and (3) cybersquatting. A trademark owner has the exclusive right use his mark on his own goods and to prevent others from using the mark in a way that might confuse consumers. A trademark is infringed when the mark is used in connection with the sale, offering for sale, distribution, or advertising of any good or service in a context that is likely to cause confusion. (*Trademark Act of 1946, U.S. Code*, vol. 15, sec. 1114(1) [1999]) Dilution occurs when a "strong" mark is widely enough known that even when used on a dissimilar good or service, the uniqueness of the mark, and thus its value, is lessened, despite the lack of a likelihood of confusion. The diluting use must be a commercial use made in commerce. (Ibid.: sec. 1125(a)[1]) Cybersquatting, or cyberpiracy, occurs when someone registers a domain name that includes a trademarked name, the name of a famous person, or a name confusingly similar to either, with the bad-faith intent of profiting from the registration. The Anti-cyberpiracy Act prevents someone from registering the domain name *www.nike.com* with the intent of selling it to Nike for a huge profit. (Ibid.: sec. 1125[d])

A trademark may be used in many ways that confuse consumers other than stamping it on "bootleg" products. In the cyberworld, two common uses of marks are in URLs—the most common.com URLs use the trademarked name of the company owning the site: *www.nike.com*—and in images used to link to the pages of the trademark owner.

URLs

The limitations of trademark law, as well as the global nature of the Internet, have opened a huge can of worms concerning trademarked names in URLs. Remember the three different Joe's Pizza Shacks? There can only be one *www.joespizzashack.com.* Who gets it? Who gets *www.nutterbutter.com* —Nabisco or Ford? On a global scale, what about the Scottish hometown burger joint called McDonald's? As I said, this is a huge can of worms, and we will not go into it very deeply here, but it is good to be aware of some of the issues and how the Internet, once again, confuses our nice, neat legal systems. The short answer is that these problems are being addressed at several levels by various organizations and agencies, many of them international in scope.

As far as URLs go, let's stick with the basics. You are most likely to want to use a trademarked word or phrase in a deeper level of a URL, such as *www.library.edu/companyinfo/nike.* The courts dealing with this issue so far have held that in such a case, the word is being used only as part of an address, not to identify a good or service; in other words, it is not being used as a trademark. (*Data Concepts, Inc. v. Digital Consulting, Inc.*, 150 F.3d 620 [6th Cir. 1998]) So this kind of use is allowable.

However, using a trademark in the actual domain name of a page could cause you trouble. Recall the two ways in which you can violate a trademark: infringement and dilution. If your use of the mark is in connection with distribution of services, which is likely to be true for library Web pages, and your use of the mark is likely to cause confusion, you may be infringing. What if your library in the state of Washington has the largest collection of historical legal papers in the country related to the settlement of the West—can you use the URL *www.westlawlibrary.edu?* It is possible you might get by with that, under fair use or some other good argument, but, at the very least, you are ripe for a charge of infringement. What if your library was founded 100 ago by and named after the local philanthropist, Robert Lexis. Can you use the URL *www.lexislibrary.com?* Probably so. A use that is purely descriptive or geographically descriptive of the user's own goods or services is likely to get by as a "fair use."[1] But remember our fair use mantra: *There are no guarantees!*

The bottom line: Use for your domain name only words that logically identify you in the first place, but do not be afraid to use trademarked words that logically identify a path in your URL.

Metatags

Metatags are words that are placed in the HTML code of a Web page but that the user does not see. Used well, metatags can be a valuable tool in describing pages so that the user can more easily identify relevant pages when she looks for them with a search engine. Not surprisingly, some people abuse this tool. My favorite story is that of a pornographic Web page that, around tax time, repeated "IRS" and "Internal Revenue Service" many times in its metatags; when someone searched for the IRS page, a popular search at that time of the year, she often retrieved the porn site instead. What if you offer a variety of company information on your Web pages—can you use the trademarked company names, or perhaps other trademarks belonging to the company (say, "swoosh" for your page about Nike) in your metatags to help users more easily locate your page?

The analysis is similar to that of using trademarks in URLs. If you use trademarked terms as metatags in order to describe your own services, that's fair.[2] If you use a descriptive term to describe the content of your page, that's fair.[3] But if your library, Metropolis State College Library—engaged in a raging battle with the other academic library in town, University of Gotham Library, to attract the largest number of users and thereby guarantee its place as primary beneficiary in Mr. Potter's will—uses "Gotham Bats," the trademarked mascot of U.G., as a metatag, well, you are in trouble.[4]

The bottom line: Be honest; use for metatags only words that honestly describe the content of your page.

Words or Logos as Links

Using a trademarked logo as a hyperlink is the least litigated area so far of trademark infringement in cyberspace, so there is not much on which to base our analysis. A handful of cases have been decided, however. Arguably, using logos as hyperlinks goes beyond the "fair use" of a trademarked word or phrase as part of a descriptive pathway in a URL. Seldom, if ever, would it be more efficient to use an image of the Nike swoosh as a hyperlink rather than the word Nike, in the same way that it is more efficient to use to the word "nike" in your URL path instead of "that-national-athletic-shoe-store-that-starts-with-an-N-and-shows-inspiring-TV-commercials-of-athletes-overcoming-great-obstacles." That's a long URL!

Why would a trademark owner care if you use his logo rather than his company or product name? He wants to protect the value in that logo as opposed to the company name. Companies use symbolic images to identify their goods, because this can be much more effective than simply using the company name; consumers remember and react to images differently than to textual names. This is where dilution comes in. The argument is that your use of a trademarked logo may diminish the distinctiveness and value of that logo.

Let's say that Larry Flynt, infamous publisher of *Hustler* magazine, takes up an interest in fashion. He designs a Web page commenting on haute couture and providing links to the Web pages of designers like Chanel, Ann Taylor, and Ralph Lauren, the links being the designers' logos. Why might these fashion houses be upset? They might be afraid that people viewing Flynt's page will assume a connection between his product and theirs. Which would imply, even if subtly, a more likely connection to you: a printed word or a familiar logo that you often see on advertisements? Might you assume that the logo owner is advertising on the Web page? Wouldn't you be less likely to assume so if the name of the owner or her product is simply listed on the page? This is the type of concern and reasoning associated with dilution. Furthermore, in order to police the mark, the owner must make sure that it is being used to identify goods and services. If she does not take action, then she may have acquiesced to that use, that is, she may have impliedly given up her right to prevent that use. Enough acquiescence, and the trademark no longer serves its source-identifying purpose.

The bottom line: Do not use a logo as a hyperlink without permission if you can get by with using a word or phrase. Note that many pages give blanket permissions. Often, a page will say something like, "If you want to link to this page, use this logo." That's free advertising. Search engines are especially likely to do this. In these cases, permission to use the logo as a link has been granted.

BIBLIOGRAPHY

Brookfield Communications, Inc. v. West Coast Entertainment Corp., 174 F.3d 1036 (9th Cir. 1999).

Data Concepts, Inc. v. Digital Consulting, Inc., 150 F.3d 620 (6th Cir. 1998).

Playboy Enterprises, Inc. v. Welles, 47 U.S.P.Q.2d 1186 (BNA) 47 U.S.P.Q.2d (BNA) 1186 (S.D. Cal. 1998).

Trademark Act of 1946, U.S. Code, vol. 15, secs. 1114(1), 1115(b)(4), 1125(a)(1), and 1125(d) (2000).

NOTES

1. Statute 15 U.S.C. sec. 1115(b)(4), which states that the following constitutes a defense to trademark infringement: "the use of the name, term, or device charged to be an infringement is a use, otherwise than as a mark, of the party's individual name in his own business, or of the individual name of anyone in privity with such party, or of a term or device which is descriptive of and used fairly and in good faith only to describe the goods or services of such party, or their geographic origin."
2. *Playboy Enterprises, Inc. v. Welles,* 47 U.S.P.Q.2d 1186 (S.D. Cal. 1998), which holds that the defendant, a former Playboy Playmate of the Year was entitled to use the trademarked phrase "Playboy Playmate of the Year" as a metatag.
3. *Brookfield Communications, Inc. v. West Coast Entertainment Corp.,* 174 F.3d 1036 (9th Cir. 1999), which holds that use of the phrase "movie buff" as a metatag to describe a film enthusiast did not infringe the trademark "MovieBuff" whereas use of the word "MovieBuff" did infringe.
4. Ibid., which holds that the use of a metetag that is confusingly similar to the mark of a senior user is a form of infringement; *Playboy Enterprises, Inc. v. Calvin Designer Label,* 985 F. Supp. 1220 (N.D. Cal. 1997), which enjoins defendant from use of the plaintiff's trademarks "in buried code or metatags on their home page or webpages"; *Playboy Enterprises, Inc. v. AsiaFocus Int'l Inc.* 1998 WL 724000 (E.D. Va. 1998), which finds infringement by defendant's metatag use of plaintiff's trademark "Playboy."

10

Realizing Legal Liabilities

I'M THE GOOD GUY: WHAT CAN THEY DO TO ME?

Most likely, if a copyright owner decided that a library was infringing her copyright by posting something on the Web without permission, for example, her lawyer would contact the library or its governing institution with a threatening letter. The cease-and-desist letter would identify the alleged infringing action, provide support for the author's claim of copyright ownership, and insist that the librarian cease and desist his use of the work immediately, or else the copyright owner will file an infringement action against the library.

What do you do in this case? You immediately go to your institution's legal counsel[1] with the letter, whether or not you decide to remove the allegedly infringing work, and explain your side of the story. Maybe you were just unaware that you did something wrong, maybe you are uncertain if you've done something wrong, or maybe you are certain that you have not done something wrong. Whatever the case, there are three reasons you should consult legal counsel immediately: (1) to get her opinion on the legitimacy of your actions; (2) so that in case of any further developments, your legal counsel will be knowledgeable from the beginning; (3) so that the parent organization can help in making the decision about removal. You should make the decision about what to do together with your legal counsel. Your legal counsel should take the responsibility for replying. Nonetheless, it's always a good idea for you, as the most directly responsible person, to keep copies of all the communication concerning the issue.

How do I know if something on a Web page I'm accessing is copyrighted? How do I know if it's infringing?

You cannot be sure of either. But this does not mean you should never use other Web pages, or material from them, for your own uses. Take a commonsense approach. First, ask yourself: If I do use copyrighted work without getting permission, is the use likely to be a fair use or excused by other relevant exceptions? Then consider: If the material I use ends up being infringing material, or if I directly infringe myself, what is most likely to happen? As discussed previously, you almost certainly will receive a cease-and-desist letter from the copyright owner. You may respond with an argument that your use should be allowed under the fair use doctrine or another exception to the copyright owner's exclusive rights; or you may decide to suspend your use.

Should you choose to take the conservative approach, here are some suggestions:

- Contact the author of the page and ask him who owns the copyright to the part you want to use.
- Do not assume the author is the copyright owner. You might ask where he got the piece or if he created it himself.
- Once you have identified the likely copyright owner, ask for permission for your use.
- Obtain and keep a written copy, not an email printout, of the permission you have received.
- Include a notice of copyright on your page and a statement that you have received permission to use the item.
- If you can get by without the use, do so. For example, instead of sending a copy of a page to friends, send the URL so they can access it themselves.

WHAT KIND OF DAMAGES COULD A COURT ASSESS TO ME OR MY LIBRARY?

In most cases, you will determine that your actions are not infringing and convey this to the copyright owner; or you will cease and desist in your actions; or you will come to an arrangement of some sort with the copyright owner. Let's say that, for whatever reason, this does not work out so well, and the copyright owner decides he wants to pursue the problem in court. What are the remedies to which you or your institution would be subject?

First, a court may issue an injunction, which is basically a court order to cease and desist. (*Copyright Act of 1976, U.S. Code*, vol. 17, sec. 502 [1999]) An injunction may be either permanent, in which case you are ordered to refrain from use forever or take permanent corrective action; or temporary, in which case the court orders you to refrain from the action until the case is determined. Second, a court may order the impounding of allegedly infringing copies or the materials used in their making or distribution. (Ibid.: sec. 503) Although courts have impounded computers, usually this happens in cases involving issues such as child pornography, viruses, or fraud. Very seldom have computers been impounded in cases of copyright infringement.

Finally, the ugly stuff. An infringing person may be held liable for actual damages suffered and any profits gained by the infringer as well as statutory damages if the work was registered for copyright at the time the infringement occurred. (Ibid.: sec. 504[a]) The copyright owner may choose to recover statutory damages in lieu of actual damages. Statutory damages per work range from $750 to $30,000, the precise amount to be determined at the court's discretion. (Ibid.: sec. 504(c)[1]) Should the court find that the infringement was "willful,"—that is, knowingly, purposefully, intentionally—the court may award statutory damages of up to $150,000. (Ibid.: sec. 504(c)[2]) In addition, a willful infringer may be subject to criminal charges. (Ibid.: sec. 506) On the other hand, if the court finds that the infringement was innocent, it may reduce the damages to $200. (Ibid.: sec. 504(c)[2])

ARE THERE ANY EXCEPTIONS FOR THE "GOOD GUYS"?

"But, we really are the good guys," you're thinking. "Being fined at all just doesn't seem right." Congress agreed. The court must remit statutory damages to zero if the infringer believed and had reasonable grounds in believing that the use was a fair use *if* the infringer was an employee of a nonprofit educational institution, library, or archive acting in the scope of employment. (Ibid.)

Some of you clever employees of state institutions are thinking that this really does not apply to you or your institution, because state institutions and employees are immune to suit. This is an uncertain area at the time of this writing. Section 511 of the Copyright Act specifically states that states, their officers, and employees are not immune to suit under the Copyright Act, despite the Eleventh Amendment of the Constitution. (Ibid.: sec. 511; see Source 1) However, recent cases seem to be in the process of undoing Section 511. In 1999, in *Florida Prepaid Postsecondary Education Expense Board v. College Savings Bank* (527 U.S. 627 [1999]), the

United States Supreme Court heard a case concerning alleged patent infringement by a state agency. The patent statutes include provisions similar to Section 511 of the Copyright Act. Congress has the power to pass laws only as granted in the Constitution. When a federal law is challenged, it may be both challenged and defended based on various specific parts of the Constitution, depending on the situation. For example, we know that Congress' right to pass laws concerning copyright derives from Article 1, Section 8, Clause 8 of the Constitution. In *Florida Prepaid*, the Court held that Congress did not have the necessary authority under the Patent Clause (Art 1, sec. 8, cl. 8), the Commerce Clause (Art. 1, sec 8, cl. 3), or the Fourteenth Amendment (forbidding states from depriving persons of life, liberty, or property without due process of law) to abolish state sovereign immunity in the Patent Act.

Does this holding have any significance for copyright infringement? In 2000, the Fifth Circuit Court of Appeals, in part relying on the ruling in *Florida Prepaid*, held that Congress did not have the power under the Fourteenth Amendment to abolish state sovereign immunity for the purposes of the Copyright and Trademark Acts. (*Chavez v. Arte Publico Press*, 204 F.3d 601 [5th Cir. 2000])

So far, then, the Supreme Court has not specifically ruled on the constitutionality of the abrogation of sovereign immunity in Section 511 of the Copyright Act, but given the recent line of cases, many experts believe that the Court will eventually strike down Section 511. Should this happen, it would mean that state agencies again would enjoy sovereign immunity from charges of copyright infringement.

HOW LIKELY IS IT THAT A LIBRARY WOULD BE SUED FOR INFRINGEMENT?

So how worried do you really have to be? The likelihood that you or your institution actually will be sued in court is very slight. Chances are strong that the matter would be settled long before that point is reached, either because the use is excused or by your removing the allegedly infringing work from your Web pages, or by some more sophisticated negotiations. So why worry about the whole thing? Because getting to the latter point can be extremely time-consuming, expensive, and frightening. Because knowing what is legal and what is not, and knowing the defenses and exceptions that apply to you, give you more power to deal with potential problems. Because nothing in copyright is certain. And because in educational institutions, we have some responsibility to serve as role models for our students.

BIBLIOGRAPHY

Chavez v. Arte Publico Press, 204 F.3d 601 (5th Cir. 2000).
Copyright Act of 1976, U.S. Code, vol. 17, secs. 502, 504, 511 (2000).
Florida Prepaid Postsecondary Education Expense Board v. College Savings Bank, 527 U.S. 627 (1999).
U.S. Constitution, art. 1, sec. 8, cl. 3.

NOTES

1. Note that almost every institution governing a library will have legal counsel: the city, the university, the school district, the corporation. It's not a bad idea to find out who that person is and how to contact him just for general knowledge.

Part III:
Specific Library Applications

11

Liability and Libraries as Content and Internet Access Providers

WHY IS IT IMPORTANT TO UNDERSTAND THE VARIOUS TYPES OF INFRINGEMENT?

Infringing someone's copyright is extremely easy to do. So easy, in fact, that you can do it absolutely unknowingly. The variety of rights owned by a copyright owner, which were the basis of our discussion in Part II, is one reason infringement is easily achieved. Another reason is that copyright may be infringed indirectly as well as directly.

"So you're telling me," you ask, "that not only can I infringe a copyright without knowing it, but I can also infringe without even directly violating one of the owner's rights myself?!" Yes, that is what I'm telling you. "That doesn't seem fair," you respond. Which is exactly why it behooves you to be familiar with the various rights that are part of the "bundles" of copyright as well as the various ways in which you may infringe those rights, whether or not you are aware of your infringement and regardless of the amount of control you retain over the infringing activities.

CAN MY INSTITUTION BE LIABLE FOR SOMEONE ELSE'S ACTIONS ON OUR COMPUTERS?

What is most commonly thought of as copyright infringement is considered to be *direct infringement*: a volitional act that infringes one of the various rights of a copyright owner. It is important to note, as already stressed, that simply committing an act that violates one of the bundle of copyrights is, in itself, enough to infringe those rights and thus to be subject to the various remedies associated with infringement (discussed in Chapter 10). Copyright is a "strict liability" law, meaning that "ignorance is no excuse."

A person commits *contributory infringement* when she (1) "induces, causes or materially contributes to the [directly] infringing activity of another," (*Gershwin Publ'g Corp. v. Columbia Artist Management, Inc.,* 443 F.2d 1159, 1162 [2d Cir. 1971]) and (2) knows or has reason to know about the infringing actions. (*Cable/Home Communications Corp. v. Network Prods., Inc.,* 902 F.2d 829, 845 [11th Cir. 1990]) Note that, like direct infringement, it is not necessary to know that the acts are infringing, only that they are occurring.

Finally, one can commit *vicarious infringement* without any knowledge of the infringing activity if one "(1) has the right and ability to control the infringer's acts *and* (2) receives a direct financial benefit from the infringement." (*Religious Tech. Ctr. v. Netcom On-Line Communication Serv., Inc.,* 907 F.Supp. 1361, 1375 [N.D.Cal. 1995]) Thus, under the right circumstances, one can commit copyright infringement whether or not one knows that the act being committed infringes copyright or even whether or not one knows that the act is being committed.

HOW DO DIFFERENT TYPES OF INFRINGEMENT APPLY TO LIBRARY ACTIVITIES?

Libraries provide two different types of services via the Internet. First, they provide their patrons with access to the Internet, which means giving patrons the ability to use library equipment to access materials beyond the control of the library. Second, they provide content to their patrons when they create their own Web pages. For purposes of liability, this difference is important. The latter is the subject of most of Part II of this book. This chapter will discuss liability issues for libraries in their role as access provider, rather than as content provider. In this role, libraries also provide their staff with email and Internet services.

WHAT ARE THE LIABILITY IMPLICATIONS FOR LIBRARIES AS INTERNET ACCESS PROVIDERS?

The Digital Millennium Copyright Act added Section 512 to the copyright statute, which limits liability of online service providers (OSPs). (see Source 1) Do libraries qualify as OSPs under the act? Usually they do. However, very strict requirements must be met to take advantage of Section 512, both before and in response to allegations of infringement. In other words, although most libraries would qualify as OSPs, protection is not automatically granted. The Copyright Act does not protect a library unless and until it (a) takes specified action to indicate its desire to be protected by the act, which includes registering an agent (someone who will receive complaints) with the U.S. Copyright Office and (b) when accused of infringement, follows specific regulations in responding to the accusation. Because the latter could become quite burdensome, each library should consider seriously the trade-offs between complying with the act and not doing so. The same answer may not be appropriate for every institution. If a library does not comply with the regulations, Section 512 does not apply.

Section 512 is lengthy and complex. It can be found in its entirety in Source 1. What follows is a relatively brief summary of the high points that are probably of the most interest to librarians.

What Is a "Service Provider"?

"Service provider" is defined as "a provider of online services or network access, or the operator of facilities therefor," including "an entity offering the transmission, routing, or providing of connections for digital online communications, between or among points specified by a user, or material of the user's choosing, without modification to the content of the material as sent or received." (*Copyright Act of 1976, U.S. Code*, vol. 17, sec.512(k) [1999]) Note that the definition seems to emphasize the passive role of an OSP: The user must choose where he is going and the material he wishes to send or receive. The OSP simply provides the mechanism for the user to do this, and the OSP cannot modify the content of the material sent or received nor receive any benefit from doing so. Thus, a library fits this description to the extent that it provides the means for users to surf the Net. Section 512 would not apply to a library's creation of Web pages, posting content on the Internet, intercepting and modifying information, or controlling the users' actions.

Keep in mind, however, that the section was written with commercial OSPs in mind; therefore, some of the provisions will not apply to libraries and some will sound a little awkward in regard to libraries.

Exactly What Kind of Actions Are Covered?

Section 512 covers four types of Internet functions, for which an OSP under Section 512 will not be held liable:

(1) *transmitting, routing, or providing connections* for transmitting or routing, material through a system controlled by the OSP, including the intermediate and transient storage of the material as part of the transmission, routing, or provision of connections if:

- The OSP does not initiate the transmission;
- The transmission occurs through an automatic technical process without the OSP selecting material;
- The OSP does not modify the content of the material transmitted; *and*
- No copy of the material made by the OSP is maintained in such a way as to make it available to anyone other than the original user and is not kept for longer than is "reasonably necessary" to transmit the material.

(2) *system caching* for material made available by someone other than the OSP as long as the OSP abides by generally accepted industry standards concerning refreshing, reloading, or other updating.

(3) *placing infringing information on a system or network* at the direction of a user if

- The OSP does not have actual knowledge that the material is infringing or of facts that should make the infringement obvious;
- And does not receive a financial benefit directly attributable to the infringement; and
- The OSP must designate an agent to receive notifications of claims of infringement.

(4) *linking* to sites containing infringing material or using "information location tools," defined as including "a directory, index, reference, pointer, or hypertext link," if

- The OSP does not have actual knowledge that the material is infringing or of facts that should make the infringement obvious; and

- Does not receive a financial benefit directly attributable to the infringement.

What Are These Regulations?

Note that many of the activities listed above have their own specific requirements, such as the OSP must not have actual knowledge of infringing material, must abide by industry standards for refreshing, and so on. Additionally, to qualify for any protection under Section 512, an OSP must accommodate and not interfere with technological measures used by copyright owners to protect their works, such as digital watermarks; and must adopt and "reasonably implement" a policy providing for termination of subscribers and account holders who are repeat infringers. The latter is one of those sections that sound a little awkward when applied to libraries; it seems intended for OSPs that provide, for example, server space on which subscribers may post materials. Nonetheless, in some situations, this may apply to libraries as well. An "account holder" could be, for example, a member of the library staff who maintains pages on the library server. At any rate, it is an across-the-board requirement that must be met in order to qualify for Section 512 protection.

In addition, to qualify for the protection from caching and from posting information at a user's request, an OSP must "expeditiously" remove material or disable access to it when a claim of infringement is made. An attempt is made at protecting OSPs from false claims of infringement: Detailed specifications must be met by the person making the infringement claim, and anyone who knowingly makes a false claim is liable for any costs to the OSP as a result of that claim. Protection is also provided to OSPs for acting in good faith to remove or disable access to material that is subject of a claim of infringement *if* the OSP takes reasonable steps to notify a "subscriber" when material has been removed from the subscriber's page and, should that person provide a statement to the OSP that the material was removed as a result of mistaken identification, the OSP replaces the material.

Isn't There Anything Specific to Libraries?

Sort of. There is a provision for limitation on liability of nonprofit educational institutions. This is a very narrow exception, however. The gist of this section is that faculty and graduate students who are employed by the institution to teach or to research are not considered to be "the institution." In other words, the institution is not liable for the actions of those persons. This provision would apply to academic libraries in which librarians are considered members of the faculty. Three requirements must be met: (1) The person's actions must not involve the provision of online access to materials that were "required or recommended" for a course taught by that person; (2) the institution must not have received more than two notices within a three-year period of infringement by the person; *and* (3) the institution must provide to all users of its network or system information describing and promoting compliance with U.S. copyright law.

WHAT DO I HAVE TO DO TO BE COVERED BY THE ENTIRE SECTION 512?

Because there are so many specific requirements for each activity covered, you should read through the entire section to be sure you conform with each requirement. Especially because this is about statutory protection and lays out the requirements to obtain such protection, unlike what has been discussed elsewhere in this book, you should work with your institution's legal counsel to ensure that your library meets the qualifications and to be sure that your policies and actions are in concert with those of the institution as a whole. It is particularly wise to talk with your institution's legal counsel, because, should a claim of infringement be made against your library, it is that legal counsel who will be dealing with it. In addition, the institution must register an agent to receive complaints and must publish the email address of that person on the institution's Web site. It will also be published on the U.S. Copyright Office Web site.

The bottom line, should your institution choose to take advantage of Section 512:

- Do not select or modify the content of material received by your users.
- Do not maintain copies of material received by your users for longer than is necessary to perform normal Internet functions.
- Abide by industry standards concerning refreshing, reloading, and other updating.
- Designate an agent to receive notifications of infringement claims. Contact information for the agent must be made publicly available on your Web site and provided to the Copyright Office.
- If you have actual knowledge that your pages are linking to infringing material, disable those links.

- Ensure that your system can accommodate and not interfere with copyright protection technologies.
- Implement a policy to terminate subscribers or account holders who are repeat infringers.
- Should you receive notification (detailed requirements of what constitutes notification are provided in §512(c)[3]) of a claim of infringement, remove or disable access to the material, or investigate immediately to determine whether the material is indeed infringing.
- Notify the author of that page of the removal or of your decision not to remove the material because you have determined that it is not infringing.
- If the author provides the necessary statement (described in §512(g)[3]), reinstate the material or access to it.

BIBLIOGRAPHY

Copyright Act of 1976, U.S. Code, vol. 17, sec. 512 (1999).

Cable/Home Communications Corp. v. Network Prods., Inc. 902 F.2d 829 (11th Cir. 1990).

Gershwin Publishing Corp. v. Columbia Artist Management, Inc. 443 F.2d 1159 (2d Cir. 1971).

Religious Tech. Ctr. v Netcom On-Line Communication Serv., Inc., 907 F. Supp. 1361 (N.D. Cal. 1995).

12
Interlibrary Loan and Resource Sharing

One of the most valuable benefits the Internet provides is the ability to share information so easily, quickly, and cheaply. Certainly, electronic resources in general have been a great boon for resource-sharing projects. While it is pretty difficult for libraries hundreds of miles apart from each other to share a subscription to a printed index, the Internet allows libraries to share electronic databases quite easily, which results in tremendous savings for various types of consortiums and resource-sharing groups. Obviously, the Internet also makes it easy (and cheap) to send electronic copies of documents to people. So what a blessing to interlibrary loan (ILL) operations, which can now make digital copies of articles from print journals and send those copies to whoever requests them, right? Well, sort of. Like everything else in copyright, there are limits. "But even if I have to stick to the traditional limitations on the number of articles I can copy from one journal, at least I can take advantage of the fact that I can easily save a copy to send again, right?" Well, not exactly.

WHAT DOES THE COPYRIGHT ACT SAY ABOUT INTERLIBRARY LOAN?

At least two exclusive rights of copyright owners are implicated by interlibrary loan: copying and distribution. Of course, not all interlibrary loan involves copying. The distribution right, however, stands on its own; one need not distribute copies of a work to violate the distribution right. Lending of books is allowable only be-

121

cause of the first sale doctrine, delineated in Section 109 of the Copyright Act. (see Source 1) In a nutshell, the first sale doctrine says that once you purchase a copyrighted work, you have the right to redistribute that one copy that you own however you want, including selling it. The first sale doctrine is discussed further in Chapter 3.

Many interlibrary loans, however, involve copying a work, such as a journal article, and passing along that reproduction. This is a potential violation of both copying and distribution rights. Fortunately, Section 108 saves the day. Section 108(a) states that a library or archive, or any employee acting within the scope of her employment, may "reproduce no more than one copy . . . of a work . . . or distribute such copy" if the following conditions are met: (1) the copies are not made for commercial advantage; (2) the library's collections are open to the public *or* available to persons doing research in a specialized field other than those affiliated with the institution; and (3) the copy or distribution includes a notice of copyright on the copy or, if no notice is found on the work, a legend stating that the work may be protected by copyright.

Sections 108(d) and (e) limit this right further:

- A library may make a copy of no more than one article from a journal issue, or no more than one "other contribution" to a copyrighted collection, or "a small part of any other copyrighted work."
- The copy must become the property of the user.
- The library has had no notice that the copy will be used for anything other than "private study, scholarship, or research."
- The library must display prominently a copyright warning according to requirements issued by the Copyright Office at the place where orders of copies are taken.

Finally, the allowances of Section 108 apply only to the "isolated and unrelated reproduction or distribution of a single copy . . . of the same material on separate occasions." The allowances do not apply when the library or an employee is aware the copying is being done for purposes of "related or concerted reproduction or distribution of multiple copies . . . of the same material," whether or not the copies are made at the same time and whether or not intended for aggregate use by a group or for use by individual members of a group. Neither does Section 108 apply to instances of systematic copying or distribution of single or multiple copies or copying intended to act as a replacement for a subscription or purchase by anyone, including another library. In addition, Section 108 does not apply to copies or distribution of a musical, pictorial, graphic, or sculptural work; motion picture; or other audiovisual work other than those dealing with news, the only exceptions being copies made for archival or replacement purposes, and graphics that are a part of other works.

CONTU GUIDELINES

In response to the 1976 Copyright Act, which did not provide explicit, quantitative guidelines for interlibrary loan, the National Commission on New Technological Uses of Copyrighted Works (CONTU) developed guidelines to assist librarians in determining what is and is not allowable under the new law. (see Source 7) The Commission gathered together representatives of the various interested groups as they created the guidelines, so it is no surprise that the guidelines were and still are generally accepted by organizations representing librarians, publishers, and authors.

The guidelines apply to the copying of articles from periodicals published within the previous five years. The guidelines suggest that "such aggregate quantities as to substitute for a subscription to or purchase of such work," prohibited by Section 108(g)(2), will not be met if a library limits its interlibrary loan copying to:

- For any given periodical as a whole, as opposed to a specific issue:
  - Within any given calendar year
  - No more than five copies of an article or articles published within the previous five years.
- For any other work:
  - No more than five copies per year
  - During the entire period for which the work is covered by copyright.

In addition, requests must be accompanied by a statement that the borrowing library is complying with the CONTU guidelines; otherwise, the lending library is instructed to not fulfill the request. Finally, the borrowing library must keep records for three years of its activities.

HOW DOES THIS APPLY TO THE INTERNET?

The Conference on Fair Use included a working group on interlibrary loan and document delivery issues in the digital arena. After extensive discussion, the working group was unable to agree on guidelines for digital delivery of interlibrary loans. Thus, no guidelines have been issued specifically addressing interlibrary loan in the cyberworld. We must rely instead on the copyright statute and on the CONTU guidelines, both of which were written pre-Internet, and apply them as best we can to the digital environment.

Number of Copies

The issue of what constitutes a copy in cyberspace has been discussed already. Certainly this tricky issue raises its ugly head again in the ILL context. Would multiple distribution of one scanned copy create multiple copies? Or would it be considered repeated distribution of the same copy, comparable to repeated lending of the same book? For practical purposes, the answer does not matter, since both reproduction and distribution are limited to a single copy on an given "occasion."

Under Section 108(g), a library may make a single copy of a work on more than one occasion. (see Source 1) Under the CONTU guidelines, a library may borrow copies of the same item up to five times in five years. So why not save a copy once made/scanned?

Copy Must Become Property of the User

Another very important issue for digital copies is the requirement that the copy become the property of the individual user. Depending on the technology being used, the one and only digital copy of an item may not be transferred. Consider what happens when you email an attachment. You do not actually send the only copy of your file; rather, an additional copy is made and sent, and you still retain a copy on your computer. The requirement that the copy become the property of the owner technically cannot be met in some technological situations.

"Does this mean ILL activities should not use these technologies?" you ask. Keeping in mind that no law or guidelines supply the answer to this question, it would seem in the spirit of the law and the CONTU guidelines to destroy any copies made during filling a request that remain with the library. Quite clearly, a library may not keep "on file" a digital copy of an article it expects to distribute via ILL at a later time.

"How about, instead of emailing a requested item to a patron, providing a site on which the library would post digital images of requests, which patrons could then download?" you suggest. "We would restrict access, of course, to only the individual who requested that piece." This, again, runs into the problem of the copy becoming the property of the individual requestor. Theoretically, the library could leave an item online for a limited period of time and then destroy that copy. Tom could be sent a notice stating that his request is available at *www.illrequests.edu* for ten days only, at which point it will be deleted, and giving him his password of "ilovelibraries" that he will need to access the article he requested. In this scenario, Tom would be making his own copy if he chose to download a copy of the article. He might decide simply to read it online. Regardless, the library remains in possession of a copy, which clearly violates Section 108. Instead of destroying its copy as soon as another copy is sent out to the user, as in the email scenario, the library holds on to its copy for a specific period of time. This seems much further removed from keeping in the spirit of the law, especially given that other options are available.

It is possible that the analysis would change should one important aspect of this scenario change—the amount of time for which the item is kept online. Libraries commonly make photocopies of a work and then use the photocopy to fax to an ILL borrower. In these cases, obviously, the user receives one copy that becomes his property, but an additional copy is made in the process. Clearly, the lending library would not be allowed to file the photocopy to use at a later time for the same purpose. Presumably, then, the photocopy is destroyed. Analogizing this situation to our digital scenario, one could argue that leaving a digital copy online for a patron to access for a much shorter time period, such as a day or two, is similar to the photocopy made in the process of sending a fax. Providing access for a short period of time also encourages the user to make her own copy rather than depend on the digital copy for her actual use of the work, which she might be more likely to do given a longer period of access.

WHAT IS THE BOTTOM LINE ABOUT USING THE INTERNET FOR INTERLIBRARY LOAN ACTIVITIES?

The bottom line is that there are no specific guidelines or laws to direct us in how legally to make use of the Internet in interlibrary loans. We must follow the not-so-specific law and use guidelines written long before "Internet" was a word. On the other hand, one of my pet peeves is people who proclaim that the Internet has changed *everything*, so we must start from ground zero in creating new rules for its use. Seldom do we truly have to start all over from scratch. To some extent, applying the guidelines we already have is common sense: If you cannot borrow more than five copies of the same article in one year via photocopying and snail mail, then you certainly cannot receive electronic copies of the same article from more than five people in one year. The bottom line, then, is to know the rules, keep the rules in mind, and use common sense in trying to apply them to a new environment. And when you hear that new discussions are beginning about writing guidelines for ILL in cyberspace, get involved and represent the needs of your users to the decision makers.

BIBLIOGRAPHY

Copyright Act of 1976, U.S. Code, vol. 17, sec. 108 (1999).

Final Report of the National Commission on New Technological Uses of Copyright Works. 1978. Washington, D.C.: Library of Congress.

Lehman, Bruce A. 1998. *The Conference on Fair Use: Final Report to the Commissioner on the Conclusion of the Conference on Fair Use*. Washington, D.C.: Working Group on Intellectual Property Rights of the Information Infrastructure Task Force.

13

Electronic Reserve Systems and Class-Based Web Pages

The Internet opens an entire world of possibilities for offering reserves collections to patrons more efficiently for both them and librarians. If librarians can digitize items on reserve and offer access to them over the Internet, patrons can access them from anywhere they please, at any time. Even better, an unlimited number of patrons can access one item at any given time. We can make our patrons happier than ever and at less cost to us. So can we do this?

Similarly, many faculty and teachers have discovered the value of the Internet as a tool for disseminating works they once put on reserve or distributed as paper copies, and so forego using the library reserves service in the first place. Likewise, instruction librarians jumped on the Internet train as a means of providing students with access to materials previously handed out as photocopies. Are educators and librarians allowed to do this? What if a teacher or faculty member comes to you as her librarian and asks you to create or help with a page for her class, one that would contain digitized copies of items she used to photocopy and distribute in class?

The ability of libraries to provide traditional reserves services and of teachers to distribute photocopies of a work in class is based on the fair use doctrine (*Copyright Act of 1976, U.S. Code*, vol. 17, sec. 107 [1999]) and on limitations provided on certain types of performances and displays. (Ibid.: sec. 110) No limitations are written into the copyright statute specifically allowing library reserves or classroom copies. However, various sources, including the American Library Association, have provided guidelines for staying within the law while providing electronic reserves and making classroom copies, which can be transposed into the Internet environment. (see Sources 4 and 8)

HOW DOES FAIR USE APPLY TO RESERVES AND CLASSROOM COPYING?

Let's review the four fair use criteria and briefly apply them to both traditional and electronic reserves and classroom copying. (Fair use is discussed in much greater detail in Chapter 3.) Recall the basic rules of fair use analysis: (1) There are no clear-cut standards; rather, the analysis is made on a case-by-case basis; and (2) no single factor is determinative.

Purpose and Character of Use

This factor asks, among other questions, whether the use is for commercial purposes. This factor usually will weigh in favor of libraries and educators, as most libraries are nonprofit entities, and most of the uses associated with reserves and classroom copying are for nonprofit purposes.

Nature of the Copyrighted Work

With this criterion, the concern is whether the work is creative or factual and whether primarily for entertainment or scholarly purposes. Establishing fair use of a creative work is more difficult than of a factual work. In an academic library's reserves collection, there is likely to be a mix of creative and factual materials. Presumably, a court would weigh the fair use of these materials differently. The same is likely to be true of copies made for use in classrooms outside of the library. For library instruction uses, the concern is more likely to be with factual works, such as copying pages of research or reference materials in order to teach students how to use them. This is not to say that no use is allowed for creative and entertainment works or that every use is allowed for scholarly and factual works. Keep in mind that nature of the work is just one of the four fair use factors and that both CONFU and ALA guidelines provide guidance in determining what uses and how much use is likely to be considered fair. (see Sources 4 and 8)

Amount and Substantiality of Portion Copied

This factor, also, probably varies greatly. Professors often ask to make available on reserve an entire book or an entire article. Yes, one article may be considered a work as a whole, which makes sense if you consider that journal articles stand on their own and need not be read in context of the journal in which they are collected. Section 108(d), however, treats one article from a journal issue as okay for interlibrary loan purposes. By analogy, one could argue for the same treatment for reserves. At other times, only a portion of a work may be used; this is often the case in library instruction. Thus, whether this factor weighs in our favor will vary greatly from situation to situation.

Effect on the Potential Market for the Work

How this factor is measured is changing as technology changes and develops. In the print world, the question was akin to asking whether the copies being made were replacing what would otherwise be sales of an item. For example, a professor could not distribute photocopies of a textbook in order to save his students the cost of buying the book. Two changes in technology have begun to shift the focus of the question. First, with the Internet, copies can be distributed more easily, so that buying a hard copy in many cases becomes unnecessary in the first place. But that does not let us off the hook, because, second, with the establishment of collective licensing services like the Copyright Clearance Center, librarians have a way to pay for the use of materials, whether in paper or electronic format, even when they do not buy copies of them.

Courts now are beginning to take these technologies into account in evaluating the fourth fair use factor. For example, in response to a library's arguing that its copying and distribution of several copies of a journal article to faculty members does not have an effect on the market for the journal because it could not have afforded additional subscriptions anyway, the courts are listening to the publisher's response that it lost money because the market in licensing royalties was effected, since the library should have paid royalties for all those copies made. In other words, the copyright owner in such a case is asking the court to consider the market for royalties, as opposed to the market for the original work, which is what this factor traditionally has examined. Concerned that the availability of licensing services will lead to the argument that any use that could have had royalties paid through such a service will by definition be unfair, courts are still trying to sort out this issue. (*American Geophysical Union v. Texaco, Inc.,* 37 F.2d 881 (2d Cir. 1994); *Williams & Wilkins v. United States,* 487 F.2d 1345 [Ct. Cl. 1973]) Right now, then, it is possible that this factor would weigh against fair use in reserve or classroom copying situations if the copying could result in a loss of licensing fees and royalties to the copyright owners.

WHAT ARE THE LIMITATIONS ON THE PERFORMANCE AND DISPLAY RIGHTS?

We have already discussed the issues concerning what, in the cyberworld, constitutes a public performance or display. The only specific allowance made in the copyright statute for use of copyrighted materials in an educational environment concerns the performance or display of works. Section 110(2) allows the performance of a nondramatic literary or musical work, or the display of a work, via transmission[1] *if* (1) the performance or display is part of the "systematic instructional activities" of an nonprofit educational institution; *and* (2) it is "directly related and of material assistance to" the teaching content of the transmission; *and* (3) the transmission is meant for reception in classrooms or other places "normally devoted to instruction," or for reception by those who are disabled. (*Copyright Act of 1976, U.S. Code*, vol. 17, sec. 110(2) (1999); see Source 1)

Assuming that the material being "transmitted" through the Internet is part of regular instructional activities and is directly related to the instruction, the only serious problem here for providing Internet access to performances or displays of a work is the question of what constitutes places "normally devoted to instruction." In all likelihood, a library that is part of an educational institution would fit in this definition. Most likely, a student's home would not. Under this exception, then, it would seem that providing access to recorded performances or displays (which arguably includes anything placed on the Web) would be limited to access in educational institutions and libraries. However, it also seems likely that accessing such performances and displays at other sites would be considered under the fair use doctrine, which the following guidelines help us understand.

ARE THERE ANY GUIDELINES TO HELP US DETERMINE WHAT IS ALLOWED?

So where do we stand? Fair use is one of the trickiest parts of the entire, 50,000-plus words of the Copyright Act. You have seen why. Several guidelines are available to help librarians make decisions and set policies concerning use of electronic reserves and providing access to class materials, whether for a library class or other, on the Internet. It is important to keep in mind that these are only guidelines, not law. Even the guidelines put forth by Congress are not part of the law. In addition, it is important to keep in mind that these guidelines are *suggested minimum* standards to help make determinations of what constitutes fair use. They are not maximum limitations. Many uses that go beyond the numbers in these guidelines will be fair uses.

House Judiciary Committee

The House Judiciary Committee included in its report to Congress on the 1976 Copyright Act an "Agreement on Guidelines for Classroom Copying in Not-For-Profit Education Institutions with Respect to Books and Periodicals" (Congress is fond of long titles). (see Source 9) The purpose of these guidelines is to "state the minimum standards for educational fair use." Unfortunately, some courts seem to interpret the guidelines as a maximum limit instead of minimum standards. The guidelines go on to warn that things may change in the future, including how much copying will be permissible for educational purposes, as well as what types of copying may and may not be permissible. Finally, the guidelines emphasize that they are not meant to limit permissible copying; copying beyond that described in the guidelines may meet fair use.

The complete text of the guidelines is in Source 9. In a nutshell, the guidelines suggest that for research purposes, or to use in teaching or preparation for teaching, one copy may be made by or for a teacher of a book chapter; a journal article; a short story, short essay, or short poem; or a chart, diagram, drawing, cartoon, or picture from a book, periodical, or newspaper. Multiple copies for classroom use may be made by or for a teacher, as long as they do not exceed more than one copy per student, and so long as they meet specific requirements for brevity, spontaneity, and cumulative effect, and include a notice of copyright.

The brevity requirements limit the number or percentage of words and graphics (such as charts or graphs) copied from a single work. The spontaneity factor requires that the copying be initiated by the teacher and that the decision to use the work be so close in time to the moment it will be used as to make it unreasonable to expect to be able to request and receive copyright permission in time. The cumulative effect test states that the copying be for use only in one course; restricts the amount of material that may be copied in one term from the same author, collective work, or periodical volume (except for current news); and limits the total amount of copying per course per term. In addition, this test says that a faculty member cannot repeat copying of the same item from term to term. Finally, the guidelines prohibit copying for the purpose of replacing collective works or books; copying of "consumable" works, for example, workbooks and exercises; repeated copying from term to term by the same teacher; and charging students more than actual cost for the copies.

Let's apply these standards to using the Internet, either for electronic reserves or for a specific class project. The limits on how much of an item may be copied have implications on electronic reserves in that, in many cases, what a library keeps on reserve is the actual work required by a professor—the book or journal article she wants her students to read—rather than photocopies of that article. Placing a digitized version on the Web might violate this guideline. Strict limitations are placed on how much of one work may be copied, whether it be for purposes of making a single copy for the instructor's use or multiple copies for the students' use. If the instructor has placed on reserve a book out of which she wants her students to read one chapter, no problem. But if she wants the whole book read, there is a problem. Under these guidelines, one would not be able to make a copy of the whole book (that is, digitize it) to put on the Web. Likewise, one would have to be very careful with the limitations placed on making multiple copies for classroom use.

The greater potential problems, however, come with the requirements concerning copies per student, cumulative copying, and repeated copying. The argument could be made that when a teacher or librarian digitizes a work to place it on a Web site, he is making only one copy of the work. I have argued in previous chapters that the claim that a librarian in this situation is making multiple copies each time a user accesses a page is a poor argument indeed. Nonetheless, this might be a good time to look to the spirit of the law rather than the letter of the law.

To begin with, these guidelines are not law; they are meant to serve as suggestions and examples and to provide a minimum standard, not a strict definition. Secondly, the Judiciary Committee emphasized that "the conditions determining the extent of permissible copying for educational purposes" may change over time. Certainly, the Committee did not foresee, in 1976, the Internet! The "spirit" of the per-student restriction probably is intended to prevent use outside of the very specific use the teacher has in mind for her particular class. Similarly, the cumulative effects test requires that the copying be used only in one course in one term, and repeated copying for more than one term by the same instructor is forbidden. These restrictions support the spontaneity factor, which basically states that multiple copying may be done only when there is not time to obtain copyright permission from the copyright owner.

Boiling it down, here are some specific suggestions to consider when you digitize works to place them on the Internet either for reserve purposes or to create a Web page for a class (that line blurs in this context):

- Follow the guidelines.
- If your needs exceed what is allowed under the guidelines, and if there is time to seek copyright permission to make copies, do so. Discuss with the copyright owner the manner in which you wish to use the copies, that is, that you want to make the work available on the Web.
- Follow the restrictions in the guidelines concerning what portion of a particular work you may copy.
- Limit access to the materials to the single class for which they are intended. This usually will mean using password protection.
- When the course ends, take down the materials. Do not repost them without copyright permission.

ALA Model Policy Concerning College and University Photocopying for Classroom, Research and Library Reserve Use

In 1982, the American Library Association published a Model Policy intended to assist academic librarians, faculty, administrators, and legal counsel in implementing "the rights and responsibilities" of the 1976 Copyright Act. (see Source 8) The Model Policy provides guidelines for exercising fair use rights in the academic environment for classroom teaching, research activities, and library services. The Model Policy is based on an analysis of fair use rights and how they can be reflected by specific uses. It was a result of the joint efforts of ALA's legal counsel, the Copyright Subcommittee (ad hoc) of ALA's Legislation Committee, the Association of College and Research Libraries Copyright Committee, the Association of Research Libraries, and other academic librarians and copyright attorneys.

Sections of the Model Policy are available in Source 8. Section III.C. addresses photocopying for library reserves purposes. This section states that, at the request of a faculty member, a library may copy and put on reserve an entire article, an entire chapter from a book, or an entire poem, if the request is to have only one copy on reserve. If the request is to provide multiple copies on reserve, the following guidelines are suggested, along with the relevant sections of the copyright statute:

1. The amount of material should be reasonable in relation to the total amount of material assigned for one term of a course taking into account the nature of the course, its subject matter and level, 17 U.S.C. § 107(1) and (3);
2. The number of copies should be reasonable in light of the number of students enrolled, the difficulty and timing of assignments, and the number of other courses which may assign the same material, 17 U.S.C. § 107(1) and (3);
3. The material should contain a notice of copyright, 17 U.S.C. § 401;
4. The effect of photocopying the material should not be detrimental to the market for the work. (In general, the library should own at least one copy of the work.) 17 U.S.C. §107(4).

Conference on Fair Use (CONFU) Guidelines

The Conference on Fair Use was convened by the Working Group on Intellectual Property Rights of the Information Infrastructure Task Force. The goal of CONFU was to provide a forum to discuss the interests of copyright owners and users in the fair use context and, if appropriate, to develop guidelines to be used by educators and librarians. CONFU met several times from 1994 through 1998. However, the 93 organizations participating were unable to reach agreement on guidelines for several types of use, including electronic reserves.[2] Library representatives generally believed that the guidelines were too narrow, while publishing representatives believed they were too broad. As a result, many library organizations did not support the resulting guidelines that were issued. (see Source 4) Nonetheless, the guidelines are worth considering when you establish an electronic reserves policy. Just keep in mind that many uses that go beyond those delineated in the guidelines will be fair uses.

Georgia Harper, a leading expert in copyright in the higher education arena, suggests that, if anything, the guidelines are too conservative, and that if the issue is again put to a national body, guidelines more in favor of users are likely to prevail. (Harper, 2000) Thus, while there is no guarantee, and these guidelines are not official in any capacity, they do provide some fodder for thought. They are handy to have in that they apply specifically to the electronic environment, unlike the Judiciary Committee's guidelines. In addition, they seem to follow the Committee's guidelines in many ways.

The entire CONFU Guidelines are available in Source 4. Some of the most pertinent statements include:

- The total number of material included in electronic reserves systems for a specific course should be a small portion of the total assigned reading for a particular course. This is based in part on the fair use factor of amount and substantiality.
- On a preliminary or introductory screen, electronic reserves systems should display a notice stating that the making of copies of the material included may be subject to copyright law and cautioning against further electronic distribution of the material.
- Access should be limited to students registered in the course and to instructors and staff responsible for the course and the electronic system.
- Permission from the copyright holder is required if the item is to be reused in a subsequent term for the same course taught by the same instructor.

WHEN ALL ELSE FAILS, READ THE DIRECTIONS

Having been through the analysis of what might and might not be permissible uses of electronic reserves and providing class materials on Web pages, I should share the secret of the easy way to go about protecting yourself and your library: The Copyright Clearance Center will request copyright permission for materials to be used in electronic reserves systems. Of course, the Center is not able to obtain permission for everything ever published, but it is a good place to start. Because the issues discussed in this chapter have limitations, however, it is very important to understand them and to prepare a policy for how you intend to handle requests.

BIBLIOGRAPHY

American Geophysical Union v. Texaco, Inc., 37 F.2d 881 (2d Cir. 1994).

American Library Association. 1982. *Model Policy Concerning College and University Photocopying for Classroom, Research and Library Reserve Use.* Washington, D.C.: American Library Association.

Copyright Act of 1976, U.S. Code, vol. 17, secs. 107 and 110 (1999).

Harper, Georgia. (2000) *Copyright Crash Course* [Online]. Available: *www.utsystem.edu/OGC/IntellectualProperty/confu.htm* [August, 2000].

House Committee on the Judiciary, *Copyright Act of 1976*, 94th Congress, 1976, H. Rept. 1476.

Lehman, Bruce A. 1998. *The Conference on Fair Use: Final Report to the Commissioner on the Conclusion of the Conference on Fair Use.* Wash-

ington, D.C.: Working Group on Intellectual Property Right of the Information Infrastructure Task Force.
Williams & Wilkins v. United States, 487 F.2d 1345 (Ct. Cl. 1973).

NOTES

1. To "transmit" is defined as "to communicate . . . by any devise or process whereby images or sounds are received beyond the place from
   which they are sent." (Section 101)
2. For the record, organizations either endorsing or supporting the Fair
   Use Guidelines for Electronic Reserves Systems included the American Association of Law Libraries, Association of American University
   Presses, Music Library Association, and Special Libraries Association.
   Those opposing the Guidelines included various organizations supporting copyright owner interests and the Association Research
   Libraries.

14

Library Instruction and Distance Education

When I first began teaching library instruction classes, less than ten years ago, the only electronic tool we taught on a regular basis was the online catalog; all the other sources we taught were print-based. Our library subscribed to one or two Infotrac databases and to ERIC and PsycLit, all of which were on CD-ROM. The Web at that time was completely text-based; there were no graphics on the Internet. During the next two years, the Web as we now know it arrived. By the time I moved to a position as Coordinator of Library Instruction two years later, my new library relied more on electronic databases than on printed materials for many common research purposes.

One of my first projects was to join a team creating that library's first Web pages. Our instruction quickly became almost entirely electronic-based, and we developed an extensive program of classes specifically teaching users how to use the Web. Today, library users use databases accessed through the Web and material on the Web itself for research, the latter sometimes to the chagrin of librarians. Some of the most popular issues among instruction librarians concern how to teach use of the Web as a research tool as well as how to take advantage of it as a tool for teaching.

The arena of library instruction pulls together many of the copyright issues already discussed. Library instruction may involve distributing to students printed copies of Web pages, making slides from Web pages with tools like WebWhacker to use demonstrating Web pages in the process of teaching students how to use them, and sometimes providing distance learning—providing access outside of the classroom to instructional materials or sessions on the Web. These uses potentially may affect a copyright owner's rights of reproduction, distribution, public display or performance, and even creation of derivative works.

ARE THERE PROBLEMS WITH GIVING LIVE DEMONSTRATIONS IN THE CLASSROOM?

Demonstrating the Web during teaching, whether one is teaching how to search a database available through the Web or how to search on the Web itself, potentially invokes the copyright owner's rights of public performance and display. Such uses would have a strong argument of being excused by the fair use doctrine, but one need not even worry with that analysis, because under the copyright statute, demonstrating the use of the Web in a classroom setting for library instruction purposes is not a problem for nonprofit educational institutions. Section 110 of the Copyright Act allows "the performance or display of a work by instructors or pupils in the course of face-to-face teaching activities of a nonprofit educational institution, in a classroom or similar place devoted to instruction." (Section 110[1].)

IS THERE A PROBLEM WITH USING "CANNED" PRESENTATIONS OF WEB PAGES?

Many instruction librarians use tools such as WebWhacker to create "canned" demonstrations of Web pages. These tools allow one to capture images of Web pages and arrange them into what appears to be a live demonstration of the Web. The advantages to using this kind of demonstration instead of a live demonstration include not having to worry about slow connections or heavy traffic on the Internet and the ability to take your presentation off site. Why would demonstrating electronic "slides" of Web pages be any different from demonstrating the Web live? For copyright purposes, using electronic slides potentially invokes additional rights of the copyright owner. In addition to the display and performance rights discussed above, using electronic slides also involves the reproduction right, in copying the pages in the first place.

Might the reproduction of pages cause problems? The answer to this question draws on issues already discussed in different contexts. Certainly there is a good fair use argument, especially if you stay within published guidelines. Available guidelines do not specifically address this situation, however. The two that come closest are the Conference on Fair Use (CONFU) Guidelines for Digital Images (see Source 3) and the CONFU guidelines on Educational Multimedia. (see Source 6)

The Guidelines for Digital Images are meant to address the digitization of images for the creation of "databases of individual visual images from which images intended for educational uses may be selected for display." (CONFU Guidelines for Digital Images, 1998: 1.1 n. 4) The Guidelines for Educational Multimedia are meant to address multimedia projects that include the original work of educators or students in combination with copyright works in various media formats. (CONFU Guidelines for Educational Multimedia, 1998: 1.3) The two sets of guidelines are very similar—in fact, there is some repetition between them. Neither quite meets the situation of creating straightforward electronic slide presentations of electronic databases or Web pages, but both are meant to provide guidance in determining uses that should qualify as fair uses, so one can draw on both sets of guidelines to make inferences to apply to the situation of "canned" Web presentations.

The Guidelines for Digital Images say that an educator may compile digital images and display them on the nonprofit educational institution's secure network for classroom use, among other uses. The Guidelines also note that fair use "limits the number and substantiality of the images that may be used from a single source." Unhelpfully, the Guidelines do not expand on this point. The Guidelines on Educational Multimedia give more specific limitations, depending on the format used, but based on the Agreement on Guidelines for Classroom Copying in Not-For-Profit Educational Institutions from the House Judiciary Committee Report on the 1976 copyright revisions.

It is doubtful how useful these guidelines would be in the "canned" presentation situation, however. Realistically, in demonstrating databases, you will be using a very small number of the total potential Web pages included in the database. If the database contains 200,000 records, there are well over 200,000 potential Web pages that may be displayed from that database. Your use of a limited handful of pages is not likely to conflict with the amount and substantiality factor of fair use. What if you are demonstrating a particular Web site that includes only a half dozen pages? Although the numerical analysis may not help, your fair use position probably will remain strong as long as you copy no more than is truly necessary for your means. For example, if you want to show an example of Yahoo's organizational structure, you might copy four or five pages at different levels of the hierarchy, but you certainly would not attempt to copy all of Yahoo's pages within a given top-level category.

The Guidelines for Digital Images also state that credit must be given to the sources and a copyright notice displayed. This could be difficult, or at least tedious, when making electronic slides from Web pages. The Guidelines for Educational Multimedia allow the credit and copyright notice information to be combined and shown in a separate section of the presentation. Thus, the simplest option might be to include a slide containing credit and copyright notice information at the beginning or end of each section or of the presentation as a whole.

Both sets of guidelines contain time restrictions. The time restrictions in the digitized images guidelines specifically apply only to the digitization of newly acquired analog visual images, which does not include the situation with which we are concerned. (CONFU Guidelines for Digital Images, 1998: 2.4) The multimedia guidelines, however, state that "educators may use their educational multimedia projects created for educational purposes . . . for teaching courses, for a period of up to two years after the first instructional use with a class. Use beyond that time period, even for educational purposes, requires permission for each copyright portion incorporated in the production." Again, the type of demonstration with which we are concerned does not meet the definition of multimedia projects contained in the guidelines. Nonetheless, it could be argued that, in the absence of guidelines specifically designed for our situation, the multimedia guidelines should apply. On the other hand, the type of material with which we are concerned changes so frequently that one is not likely to be using the same "canned" demonstration for anything close to two years.

IS THERE A PROBLEM WITH ENHANCING ELECTRONIC PRESENTATIONS?

What if you want to do more than just create demonstrations involving screen captures from Web pages, such as including your own commentary or instruction within the electronic presentation or creating a presentation that involves not just demonstrations of online materials but also print materials, or a presentation that includes information about library hours or pictures from the library? As mentioned above, the Guidelines on Educational Multimedia apply to multimedia projects that incorporate an educator's "original material, such as course notes or commentary, together with various copyrighted media formats." (CONFU Guidelines for Educational Multimedia, 1998: 1.3; see Source 6) Such presentations are allowed under Section 110(1) (see Source 1), and the guidelines give more specific direction, such as the limitations on proportions of the work used, time restrictions, and requirement of providing credit and copyright notice, as discussed above.

WHAT ARE THE COPYRIGHT IMPLICATIONS FOR DISTANCE LEARNING?

In the library instruction context, distance learning includes providing live instruction to a remote site and creating electronic instructional sessions that may be accessed by students at their leisure. Under Section 110(2), the performance or display of a nondramatic literary work by or in the course of a transmission is not an infringement *if* the performance or display (1) is a regular part of the systematic instructional activities of a governmental body or a nonprofit educational institution; *and* (2) is directly related and of material assistance to the teaching content of the transmission; *and* (3) the transmission is made primarily for reception in classrooms or similar places normally devoted to instruction, for reception by persons whose disabilities or other circumstances prevent their attendance in classrooms, or for reception by officers or employees of governmental bodies as a part of their official duties. (17 U.S.C. sec. 110(2); see Source 1) Thus, transmission of library instruction classes that include demonstration of resources is not a problem if the transmission goes to a remote classroom. But what if you want to transmit the class to a nontraditional setting or provide access to your electronic class via computer at the convenience of the user?

The multimedia guidelines allow performance or display of an educator's multimedia project when assigned to students for directed self-study and for remote instruction to students enrolled in curriculum-based courses, as long as the transmission is provided over the educational institution's secure electronic network in realtime (that is, "live") or for after-class review or directed self-study. The network also must have technological limitations on access, such as password protection and must prevent the ability to make copies of copyrighted material. If the institution cannot provide the technology to prevent copies being made, the project can be provided for remote access only for a period of 15 days after the initial real-time remote use or 15 days after the assignment for directed self-study. (CONFU Guidelines on Educational Multimedia, 1998: 3.2) Under these guidelines, a library could provide access to a multi-media presentation on its network for an extended period of time only if it meets the above technological requirements. If it cannot do so, it can provide access only for 15 days. However, after that time, a copy may be placed on reserve. Students could check out a diskette, for example, containing the presentation.

The Guidelines on Distance Learning apply to situations other than ours: they apply only to live transmissions that include works or uses not covered under Section 110(2). (see Source 5)

DO VENDOR LICENSES ADDRESS USES MADE FOR INSTRUCTIONAL OR DISTANCE EDUCATION PURPOSES?

As our electronic environment becomes more advanced and omnipresent, librarians have become more sophisticated about licensing the use of electronic databases. Unfortunately, too many libraries still do not appreciate the importance and implications of the licenses they sign with vendors. Many libraries automatically sign the standard license provided without giving much thought to the contents of the license and whether the license truly meets the needs of the library. If you are sent a license that does not comport with the manner in which you intend to use a resource, talk to the vendor about it. Never sign something you have not read, and never sign a license with terms with which you know your library will not be able to comply.

That said, some vendor licenses may contain clauses addressing the use for instructional purposes of databases or information taken from databases, although this is not yet the norm. If your license addresses instructional situations, be sure to abide by the license. This may mean that you do not have to worry about the preceding analysis of what is and is not allowed, because your license will tell you explicitly what that particular vendor allows. On the other hand, if it is more restrictive than what you would like to be able to do, work with the vendor to come up with an agreement that is mutually acceptable.

BIBLIOGRAPHY

Copyright Act of 1976, U.S. Code, vol. 17, sec. 110.

House Committee on the Judiciary, *Copyright Act of 1976*, 94th Congress, 1976, H. Rept. 1476.

Lehman, Bruce A. 1998. *The Conference on Fair Use: Final Report to the Commissioner on the Conclusion of the Conference on Fair Use.* Washington, D.C.: Working Group on Intellectual Property Right of the Information Infrastructure Task Force.

15

Taking a Stand for Libraries and Library Users

Clearly, there are many unanswered questions in copyright that are important for librarians. How do I know how to behave when the answers aren't so clear? Should librarians be conservative and safe, or should we push the envelope? How do librarians work in their daily jobs to stand up for their rights and not be run over by publishers and other groups that are strongly pro-copyright?

This book takes a rather neutral approach on copyright. For the most part, the book is intended to give librarians a good overview of copyright law and how it affects them in the Internet environment. However, as is alluded to periodically throughout the book, the arena of copyright law never has been a neutral arena, and if anything, this is probably more true now than at any time since the days of the Statute of Anne. This chapter will briefly touch on the major problems for librarians and information users and what librarians can and should do about it.

WHY SHOULD LIBRARIANS GET INVOLVED IN WHAT IS ESSENTIALLY A POLITICAL ISSUE?

Various limitations on copyright, expansion on the rights of copyright owners, and concern for rights of users engender lengthy and ardent debate. Chief among these issues are fair use; various schemes that would create what Professor Litman refers to as an "exclusive right to read," such as "pay-per-use" database licenses; and, at the moment, the Uniform Computer Information Transactions Act.

The lengthy and ardent debates are not among librarians but between librarians and members of the commercial end of the information industry, primarily publishers. At a basic level, one could say that the objectives of librarians and publishers are at opposite ends of the information access spectrum: librarians want to ensure free access to information for everyone, and publishers make their living off making everyone pay for access. Obviously, this is oversimplified and exaggerated. Nonetheless, it makes the point.

Recall that the entire history of modern and American copyright has been an attempt to balance the interests of authors with those of users. Also keep in mind that American copyright is based on the Constitution, which guarantees rights to authors, but within limitations and for the motivational purpose of promoting the development of the arts and sciences. Publishers and other copyright owners are not "bad guys" because they want to get paid for their work; and librarians are not "bad guys" because they want to give people free access to property owned by others. The problem is in finding the middle ground, that which is most fair to as many parties involved as possible, and more importantly, that which does not damage the basic rights of either copyright owners or information users. The problem is finding the balance implied by the Constitution's grant of congressional power to promote the progress of science and the useful arts.

Right now, the tide seems to be running in favor of copyright holders. The Sonny Bono Copyright Term Extension Act is a good example; the Act and a critique of it are discussed in Chapter 5. Recall Representative Mary Bono's statement that Sonny Bono wanted copyright to last forever, that she had been told by her staffers that this would be unconstitutional, but that maybe Congress could do something about it anyway. The Sonny Bono Act is an excellent example of copyright law completely ignoring its foundation. In addition to the "limited time" restriction in the Constitution, the constitutional purpose of copyright is to motivate authors to write and to publish their works. It is highly unlikely that extending the duration of copyright protection from 50 years to 70 years *after the death of the author* would motivate an author who otherwise would not create.

The Uniform Computer Information Transactions Act (UCITA) is another good example. It is also discussed in more detail in Chapter 5. UCITA would become part of individual states' laws, not part of the Copyright Act. Nonetheless, its consequence would be to pre-empt copyright law with unnegotiated contract law, that is, to replace user rights under the copyright law, such as fair use, with agreements to give up those rights that users never have the opportunity to negotiate. Librarians are putting up a good fight against UCITA, as are a variety of consumer interest organizations, but it has already been passed by some states and is being addressed rapidly by many others, so far with quite mixed results.

Another example is found in the Digital Millennium Copyright Act (DMCA). While Section 1201(c) of the Copyright Act states that nothing in the DMCA shall affect fair use, and Section 1201(d) allows certain nonprofit libraries to "gain access" to a protected work for purposes of evaluating the work for possible acquisition, Section 1201(a) prohibits importation of equipment that allows circumvention of technologies preventing access to a copyrighted work. In other words, parts of the DMCA try to placate librarians by saying that fair use will not be affected by the act, but it goes on to prohibit the very technology that may be necessary to engage in uses that are indeed fair.

Currently, one of the most important problematic issues is the future of fair use generally. Fair use is implicated in the UCITA and DMCA issues mentioned above (UCITA would make legally binding nonnegotiated "click-wrap" and "shrink-wrap" licenses to which users must agree, with no chance to negotiate, and that may force the user to contract away his fair use rights), but the issue goes well beyond one or two specific pieces of legislation. As you know from reading Chapter 3, fair use is decided on a case-by-case basis. Behind this decision by Congress to appproach fair use case by case rather than to provide specific criteria for what does or does not constitute fair use was the recognition that what qualifies as "fair" will vary from situation to situation. Congress intended the fair use analysis to be flexible to allow for this. The downside, of course, to any program set up to be flexible is that it can flex in at least two directions.

At the crux of the larger fair use issue is the question briefly mentioned in Chapter 3: Is fair use an exception to an author's exclusive right, or is it a right of information users? Naturally, those who depend on fair use, such as librarians, insist that it is a statutory right, while those who oppose extensive fair use, such as publishers, insist that it is a very narrow exception. The Copyright Act itself is not clear. Section 107 is entitled "Limitations on exclusive rights: Fair use" (see Source 1), but Section 108 refers to "the right of fair use."

Professor Ray Patterson at the University of Georgia School of

Law, author of *The Nature of Copyright: A Law of Users ' Rights*, feels strongly about the right versus exception debate. He believes that based on Section 107, the fair use section of the Copyright Act, which does not refer to fair use as a "right," it is nonetheless reasonable to argue that fair use is a right. In an interview with Carrie Russell, Copyright Specialist for the American Library Association Office for Information Technology Policy, Professor Patterson minces no words in characterizing the debate: "Librarians should be as aggressive in protecting the right of fair use as the publishers are in seeking to destroy it . . . librarians are the last line of defense against the efforts of publishers to sacrifice the right of the people to know on the altar of profit." Lest your reaction is to consider this statement a bit extreme, he goes on to explain: "This statement is not as hyperbolic as it may seem. The conduct of the publishers indicates that their goal is to do away with free lending libraries, to transform copyright into a pay-per-use right. . . . To succeed, they must coopt librarians to be their licensing agents. Unless librarians refuse to be coopted, the publishers will succeed." (American Library Association, 2001)

HOW SHOULD LIBRARIANS GO ABOUT BEING AGGRESSIVE AND PREVENT BEING CO-OPTED?

First and foremost, librarians need to take a stand, remembering that they are not just representatives of their institutions, but, much more importantly, representatives of their users. It is part of our professional responsibility to represent the needs and rights of users to those making decisions that affect our users. One way to do this is to get involved in legislative issues, and this is discussed in detail in Source 12. However, your daily actions in your job also have an effect on these issues.

Although various guidelines meant to help determine whether specific uses are fair are discussed in this book (see Part III and Sources 3–9), remember that, not only is there disagreement concerning many of these guidelines, but all are meant to be minimal standards to assist in making fair use determinations. None were intended by the groups that developed them to be maximum limits. Thus, even with the use of specific guidelines, which were intended to help by giving more specific answers to fair use questions, there is no final answer as to whether a particular use will constitute fair use.

Advocates for librarians and information users believe that librarians must be assertive, as Professor Patterson stated, in exercising the fair use right. They are concerned that if librarians are conservative and limit themselves to the minimal uses put forth in guidelines, they are giving up the fight and limiting fair use forever to those standards. Being assertive means using individual judgment. It means going beyond the guidelines when it seems reasonable. Which, in turn, means asserting your rights knowledgeably, not blindly.

You will learn from this book and from many other sources how fair use decisions are made. Use this knowledge to make a determination of your own as to whether a use is fair. Work with your institution in exercising your fair use rights. More and more institutions have copyright policies for employees, faculty, and students to follow. Be aware, however, that those policies may themselves err on the side of caution and be overly conservative. Take advantage of the resources that are out there to help and support you, such as various library organizations and others listed in Source 13. Get involved in legislative and advocacy activities to give a louder voice to the needs of information uses, as discussed in Source 12.

Above all, remember that you are responsible for standing up for the rights of information users. And remember that you are not alone. As Professor Patterson said, "librarians are the last line of defense against the efforts of publishers to sacrifice the right of the people to know." (American Library Association, 2001)

BIBLIOGRAPHY

American Library Association. *Users' Rights in Copyright: An Interview with Ray Patterson*. Available: *http://copyright.ala.org/* [January 2001].
Patterson, L. Ray, and Stanley W. Lindberg. 1991. *The Nature of Copyright: A Law of Users' Rights*. Athens: University of Georgia Press.

Part IV
Copyright Information Sourcebox

Source 1

Selected Excerpts from the Copyright Act of 1976 (17 U.S.C. 101 *et seq.*)

SEC. 102. SUBJECT MATTER OF COPYRIGHT: IN GENERAL

(a) Copyright protection subsists, in accordance with this title, in original works of authorship fixed in any tangible medium of expression, now known or later developed, from which they can be perceived, reproduced, or otherwise communicated, either directly or with the aid of a machine or device. Works of authorship include the following categories:
(1) literary works;
(2) musical works, including any accompanying words;
(3) dramatic works, including any accompanying music;
(4) pantomimes and choreographic works;
(5) pictorial, graphic, and sculptural works;
(6) motion pictures and other audiovisual works;
(7) sound recordings; and
(8) architectural works.
(b) In no case does copyright protection for an original work of authorship extend to any idea, procedure, process, system, method of operation, concept, principle, or discovery, regardless of the form in which it is described, explained, illustrated, or embodied in such work.

SEC. 103. SUBJECT MATTER OF COPYRIGHT: COMPILATIONS AND DERIVATIVE WORKS

(a) The subject matter of copyright as specified by section 102 includes compilations and derivative works, but protection for a work employing preexisting material in which copyright subsists does not extend to any part of the work in which such material has been used unlawfully.

(b) The copyright in a compilation or derivative work extends only to the material contributed by the author of such work, as distinguished from the preexisting material employed in the work, and does not imply any exclusive right in the preexisting material. The copyright in such work is independent of, and does not affect or enlarge the scope, duration, ownership, or subsistence of, any copyright protection in the preexisting material.

SEC. 106. EXCLUSIVE RIGHTS IN COPYRIGHTED WORKS

Subject to sections 107 through 120, the owner of copyright under this title has the exclusive rights to do and to authorize any of the following:

(1) to reproduce the copyrighted work in copies or phonorecords;

(2) to prepare derivative works based upon the copyrighted work;

(3) to distribute copies or phonorecords of the copyrighted work to the public by sale or other transfer of ownership, or by rental, lease, or lending;

(4) in the case of literary, musical, dramatic, and choreographic works, pantomimes, and motion pictures and other audiovisual works, to perform the copyrighted work publicly;

(5) in the case of literary, musical, dramatic, and choreographic works, pantomimes, and pictorial, graphic, or sculptural works, including the individual images of a motion picture or other audiovisual work, to display the copyrighted work publicly; and

(6) in the case of sound recordings, to perform the copyrighted work publicly by means of a digital audio transmission.

SEC. 107. LIMITATIONS ON EXCLUSIVE RIGHTS: FAIR USE

Notwithstanding the provisions of sections 106 and 106A, the fair use of a copyrighted work, including such use by reproduction in copies or phonorecords or by any other means specified by that section, for purposes such as criticism, comment, news reporting, teaching (including multiple copies for classroom use), scholarship, or research, is not an infringement of copyright. In determining whether the use made of a work in any particular case is a fair use the factors to be considered shall include

(1) the purpose and character of the use, including whether such use is of a commercial nature or is for nonprofit educational purposes;

(2) the nature of the copyrighted work;

(3) the amount and substantiality of the portion used in relation to the copyrighted work as a whole; and

(4) the effect of the use upon the potential market for or value of the copyrighted work. The fact that a work is unpublished shall not itself bar a finding of fair use if such finding is made upon consideration of all the above factors.

SEC. 108. LIMITATIONS ON EXCLUSIVE RIGHTS: REPRODUCTION BY LIBRARIES AND ARCHIVES

(a) Except as otherwise provided in this title and notwithstanding the provisions of section 106, it is not an infringement of copyright for a library or archives, or any of its employees acting within the scope of their employment, to reproduce no more than one copy or phonorecord of a work, except as provided in subsections (b) and (c), or to distribute such copy or phonorecord, under the conditions specified by this section, if

(1) the reproduction or distribution is made without any purpose of direct or indirect commercial advantage;

(2 the collections of the library or archives are (i) open to the public, or (ii) available not only to researchers affiliated with the library or archives or with the institution of which it is a part, but also to other persons doing research in a specialized field; and

(3) the reproduction or distribution of the work includes a notice of copyright that appears on the copy or phonorecord that is reproduced under the provisions of this section, or includes a legend stating that the work may be protected by copyright if no such notice can be found on the copy or phonorecord that is reproduced under the provisions of this section.

(b) The rights of reproduction and distribution under this section apply to three copies or phonorecords of an unpublished work duplicated solely for purposes of preservation and security or for deposit for research use in another library or archives of the type described by clause (2) of subsection (a), if

    (1) the copy or phonorecord reproduced is currently in the collections of the library or archives; and

    (2) any such copy or phonorecord that is reproduced in digital format is not otherwise distributed in that format and is not made available to the public in that format outside the premises of the library or archives.

  (c) The right of reproduction under this section applies to three copies or phonorecords of a published work duplicated solely for the purpose of replacement of a copy or phonorecord that is damaged, deteriorating, lost, or stolen, or if the existing format in which the work is stored has become obsolete, if

    (1) the library or archives has, after a reasonable effort, determined that an unused replacement cannot be obtained at a fair price; and

    (2) any such copy or phonorecord that is reproduced in digital format is not made available to the public in that format outside the premises of the library or archives in lawful possession of such copy. For purposes of this subsection, a format shall be considered obsolete if the machine or device necessary to render perceptible a work stored in that format is no longer manufactured or is no longer reasonably available in the commercial marketplace.

  (d) The rights of reproduction and distribution under this section apply to a copy, made from the collection of a library or archives where the user makes his or her request or from that of another library or archives, of no more than one article or other contribution to a copyrighted collection or periodical issue, or to a copy or phonorecord of a small part of any other copyrighted work, if

    (1) the copy or phonorecord becomes the property of the user, and the library or archives has had no notice that the copy or phonorecord would be used for any purpose other than private study, scholarship, or research; and

    (2) the library or archives displays prominently, at the place where orders are accepted, and includes on its order form, a warning of copyright in accordance with requirements that the Register of Copyrights shall prescribe by regulation.

  (e) The rights of reproduction and distribution under this section apply to the entire work, or to a substantial part of it, made from the collection of a library or archives where the user makes his or her request or from that of another library or archives, if the library or archives has first determined, on the basis of a reasonable investigation, that a copy or phonorecord of the copyrighted work cannot be obtained at a fair price, if

    (1) the copy or phonorecord becomes the property of the user, and the

library or archives has had no notice that the copy or phonorecord would be used for any purpose other than private study, scholarship, or research; and

(2) the library or archives displays prominently, at the place where orders are accepted, and includes on its order form, a warning of copyright in accordance with requirements that the Register of Copyrights shall prescribe by regulation.

(f) Nothing in this section

(1) shall be construed to impose liability for copyright infringement upon a library or archives or its employees for the unsupervised use of reproducing equipment located on its premises: Provided, That such equipment displays a notice that the making of a copy may be subject to the copyright law;

(2) excuses a person who uses such reproducing equipment or who requests a copy or phonorecord under subsection (d) from liability for copyright infringement for any such act, or for any later use of such copy or phonorecord, if it exceeds fair use as provided by section 107;

(3) shall be construed to limit the reproduction and distribution by lending of a limited number of copies and excerpts by a library or archives of an audiovisual news program, subject to clauses (1), (2), and (3) of subsection (a); or

(4) in any way affects the right of fair use as provided by section 107, or any contractual obligations assumed at any time by the library or archives when it obtained a copy or phonorecord of a work in its collections.

(g) The rights of reproduction and distribution under this section extend to the isolated and unrelated reproduction or distribution of a single copy or phonorecord of the same material on separate occasions, but do not extend to cases where the library or archives, or its employee

(1) is aware or has substantial reason to believe that it is engaging in the related or concerted reproduction or distribution of multiple copies or phonorecords of the same material, whether made on one occasion or over a period of time, and whether intended for aggregate use by one or more individuals or for separate use by the individual members of a group; or

(2) engages in the systematic reproduction or distribution of single or multiple copies or phonorecords of material described in subsection (d): Provided, That nothing in this clause prevents a library or archives from participating in interlibrary arrangements that do not have, as their purpose or effect, that the library or archives receiving such copies or phonorecords for distribution does so in such aggregate quantities as to substitute for a subscription to or purchase of such work.

(h)

(1) For purposes of this section, during the last 20 years of any term of

copyright of a published work, a library or archives, including a nonprofit educational institution that functions as such, may reproduce, distribute, display, or perform in facsimile or digital form a copy or phonorecord of such work, or portions thereof, for purposes of preservation, scholarship, or research, if such library or archives has first determined, on the basis of a reasonable investigation, that none of the conditions set forth in subparagraphs (A), (B), and (C) of paragraph (2) apply.

(2) No reproduction, distribution, display, or performance is authorized under this subsection if

    (A) the work is subject to normal commercial exploitation;

    (B) a copy or phonorecord of the work can be obtained at a reasonable price; or

    (C) the copyright owner or its agent provides notice pursuant to regulations promulgated by the Register of Copyrights that either of the conditions set forth in subparagraphs (A) and (B) applies.

(3) The exemption provided in this subsection does not apply to any subsequent uses by users other than such library or archives.

(i) The rights of reproduction and distribution under this section do not apply to a musical work, a pictorial, graphic or sculptural work, or a motion picture or other audiovisual work other than an audiovisual work dealing with news, except that no such limitation shall apply with respect to rights granted by subsections (b) and (c), or with respect to pictorial or graphic works published as illustrations, diagrams, or similar adjuncts to works of which copies are reproduced or distributed in accordance with subsections (d) and (e).

SEC. 109. LIMITATIONS ON EXCLUSIVE RIGHTS: EFFECT OF TRANSFER OF PARTICULAR COPY OR PHONORECORD

(a) Notwithstanding the provisions of section 106(3), the owner of a particular copy or phonorecord lawfully made under this title, or any person authorized by such owner, is entitled, without the authority of the copyright owner, to sell or otherwise dispose of the possession of that copy or phonorecord. Notwithstanding the preceding sentence, copies or phonorecords of works subject to restored copyright under section 104A that are manufactured before the date of restoration of copyright or, with respect to reliance parties, before publication or service of notice under section 104A(e), may be sold or otherwise disposed of without the authorization of the owner of the restored copyright for purposes of direct or indirect commercial advantage only during the 12-month period beginning on

    (1) the date of the publication in the Federal Register of the notice of intent filed with the Copyright Office under section 104A(d)(2)(A), or

    (2) the date of the receipt of actual notice served under section 104A(d)(2)(B), whichever occurs first.

(b)

(1)

    (A) Notwithstanding the provisions of subsection (a), unless authorized by the owners of copyright in the sound recording or the owner of copyright in a computer program (including any tape, disk, or other medium embodying such program), and in the case of a sound recording in the musical works embodied therein, neither the owner of a particular phonorecord nor any person in possession of a particular copy of a computer program (including any tape, disk, or other medium embodying such program), may, for the purposes of direct or indirect commercial advantage, dispose of, or authorize the disposal of, the possession of that phonorecord or computer program (including any tape, disk, or other medium embodying such program) by rental, lease, or lending, or by any other act or practice in the nature of rental, lease, or lending. Nothing in the preceding sentence shall apply to the rental, lease, or lending of a phonorecord for nonprofit purposes by a nonprofit library or nonprofit educational institution. The transfer of possession of a lawfully made copy of a computer program by a nonprofit educational institution to another nonprofit educational institution or to faculty, staff, and students does not constitute rental, lease, or lending for direct or indirect commercial purposes under this subsection.

    (B) This subsection does not apply to

        (i) a computer program which is embodied in a machine or product and which cannot be copied during the ordinary operation or use of the machine or product; or

        (ii) a computer program embodied in or used in conjunction with a limited purpose computer that is designed for playing video games and may be designed for other purposes.

    (C) Nothing in this subsection affects any provision of chapter 9 of this title.

(2)

    (A) Nothing in this subsection shall apply to the lending of a computer program for nonprofit purposes by a nonprofit library, if each copy of a computer program which is lent by such library has affixed to the packaging containing the program a warning of copyright in accordance with requirements that the Register of Copyrights shall prescribe by regulation.

    (B) Not later than three years after the date of the enactment of the Computer Software Rental Amendments Act of 1990, and at such times thereafter as the Register of Copyrights considers appropriate, the Register of Copyrights, after consultation with representatives of copyright owners and librarians, shall submit to the Congress a report stating whether this paragraph has achieved its intended purpose of maintaining the integrity of the copyright system while providing nonprofit libraries the capability to fulfill their function. Such report shall advise the Congress as to any information or recommendations that the Register of Copyrights considers necessary to carry out the purposes of this subsection.

(3) Nothing in this subsection shall affect any provision of the antitrust laws. For purposes of the preceding sentence, "antitrust laws" has the meaning given that term in the first section of the Clayton Act and includes section 5 of the Federal Trade Commission Act to the extent that section relates to unfair methods of competition.

(4) Any person who distributes a phonorecord or a copy of a computer program (including any tape, disk, or other medium embodying such program) in violation of paragraph (1) is an infringer of copyright under section 501 of this title and is subject to the remedies set forth in sections 502, 503, 504, 505, and 509. Such violation shall not be a criminal offense under section 506 or cause such person to be subject to the criminal penalties set forth in section 2319 of title 18.

(c) Notwithstanding the provisions of section 106(5), the owner of a particular copy lawfully made under this title, or any person authorized by such owner, is entitled, without the authority of the copyright owner, to display that copy publicly, either directly or by the projection of no more than one image at a time, to viewers present at the place where the copy is located.

(d) The privileges prescribed by subsections (a) and (c) do not, unless authorized by the copyright owner, extend to any person who has acquired possession of the copy or phonorecord from the copyright owner, by rental, lease, loan, or otherwise, without acquiring ownership of it.

(e) Notwithstanding the provisions of sections 106(4) and 106(5), in the case of an electronic audiovisual game intended for use in coin-operated equipment, the owner of a particular copy of such a game lawfully made under this title, is entitled, without the authority of the copyright owner of the game, to publicly perform or display that game in coin-operated equipment, except that this subsection shall not apply to any work of authorship embodied in the audiovisual game if the copyright owner of the electronic audiovisual game is not also the copyright owner of the work of authorship.

SEC. 110. LIMITATIONS ON EXCLUSIVE RIGHTS: EXEMPTION OF CERTAIN PERFORMANCES AND DISPLAYS

Notwithstanding the provisions of section 106, the following are not infringements of copyright:

(1) performance or display of a work by instructors or pupils in the course of face-to-face teaching activities of a nonprofit educational institution, in a classroom or similar place devoted to instruction, unless, in the case of a motion picture or other audiovisual work, the performance, or the display of individual images, is given by means of a copy that was not lawfully made under this title, and that the person responsible for the performance knew or had reason to believe was not lawfully made;

(2) performance of a nondramatic literary or musical work or display of a work, by or in the course of a transmission, if

    (A) the performance or display is a regular part of the systematic instructional activities of a governmental body or a nonprofit educational institution; and

    (B) the performance or display is directly related and of material assistance to the teaching content of the transmission; and

    (C) the transmission is made primarily for

        (i) reception in classrooms or similar places normally devoted to instruction, or

        (ii) reception by persons to whom the transmission is directed because their disabilities or other special circumstances prevent their attendance in classrooms or similar places normally devoted to instruction, or

        (iii) reception by officers or employees of governmental bodies as a part of their official duties or employment;

(3) performance of a nondramatic literary or musical work or of a dramatico-musical work of a religious nature, or display of a work, in the course of services at a place of worship or other religious assembly;

(4) performance of a nondramatic literary or musical work otherwise than in a transmission to the public, without any purpose of direct or indirect commercial advantage and without payment of any fee or other compensation for the performance to any of its performers, promoters, or organizers, if

    (A) there is no direct or indirect admission charge; or

    (B) the proceeds, after deducting the reasonable costs of producing the performance, are used exclusively for educational, religious, or charitable purposes and not for private financial gain, except where the copyright owner has served notice of objection to the performance under the following conditions;

        (i) the notice shall be in writing and signed by the copyright owner or such owner's duly authorized agent; and

(ii) the notice shall be served on the person responsible for the performance at least seven days before the date of the performance, and shall state the reasons for the objection; and

(iii) the notice shall comply, in form, content, and manner of service, with requirements that the Register of Copyrights shall prescribe by regulation;

Sections 110(5) – 110(1) omitted

SEC. 302. DURATION OF COPYRIGHT: WORKS CREATED ON OR AFTER JANUARY 1, 1978

(a) In General. Copyright in a work created on or after January 1, 1978, subsists from its creation and, except as provided by the following subsections, endures for a term consisting of the life of the author and 70 years after the author's death.

(b) Joint Works. In the case of a joint work prepared by two or more authors who did not work for hire, the copyright endures for a term consisting of the life of the last surviving author and 70 years after such last surviving author's death.

(c) Anonymous Works, Pseudonymous Works, and Works Made for Hire. In the case of an anonymous work, a pseudonymous work, or a work made for hire, the copyright endures for a term of 95 years from the year of its first publication, or a term of 120 years from the year of its creation, whichever expires first. If, before the end of such term, the identity of one or more of the authors of an anonymous or pseudonymous work is revealed in the records of a registration made for that work under subsections (a) or (d) of section 408, or in the records provided by this subsection, the copyright in the work endures for the term specified by subsection (a) or (b), based on the life of the author or authors whose identity has been revealed. Any person having an interest in the copyright in an anonymous or pseudonymous work may at any time record, in records to be maintained by the Copyright Office for that purpose, a statement identifying one or more authors of the work; the statement shall also identify the person filing it, the nature of that person's interest, the source of the information recorded, and the particular work affected, and shall comply in form and content with requirements that the Register of Copyrights shall prescribe by regulation.

(d) Records Relating to Death of Authors. Any person having an interest in a copyright may at any time record in the Copyright Office a statement of the date of death of the author of the copyrighted work, or a statement that the author is still living on a particular date. The statement shall identify the person filing it, the nature of that person's interest, and the source of the information recorded, and shall comply in form and content with requirements that the Register of Copyrights shall prescribe by regulation. The Register shall maintain current records of information relating to the death of authors of copyrighted works, based on such recorded statements and, to the extent the Register considers practicable, on data contained in any of the records of the Copyright Office or in other reference sources.

(e) Presumption as to Author's Death. After a period of 95 years from the year of first publication of a work, or a period of 120 years from the year of its creation, whichever expires first, any person who obtains from the Copyright Office a certified report that the records provided by subsection (d) disclose nothing to indicate that the author of the work is living, or died less than 70 years before, is entitled to the benefits of a presumption that the author has been dead for at least 70 years. Reliance in good faith upon this presumption shall be a complete defense to any action for infringement under this title.

SEC. 303. DURATION OF COPYRIGHT: WORKS CREATED BUT NOT PUBLISHED OR COPYRIGHTED BEFORE JANUARY 1, 1978

(a) Copyright in a work created before January 1, 1978, but not theretofore in the public domain or copyrighted, subsists from January 1, 1978, and endures for the term provided by section 302. In no case, however, shall the term of copyright in such a work expire before December 31, 2002; and, if the work is published on or before December 31, 2002, the term of copyright shall not expire before December 31, 2047.

(b) The distribution before January 1, 1978, of a phonorecord shall not for any purpose constitute a publication of the musical work embodied therein.

SEC. 304. DURATION OF COPYRIGHT: SUBSISTING COPYRIGHTS

(a) Copyrights in Their First Term on January 1, 1978. (1)(A) Any copyright, the first term of which is subsisting on January 1,

1978, shall endure for 28 years from the date it was originally secured.

 (B) In the case of
  (i) any posthumous work or of any periodical, cyclopedic, or other composite work upon which the copyright was originally secured by the proprietor thereof, or
  (ii) any work copyrighted by a corporate body (otherwise than as assignee or licensee of the individual author) or by an employer for whom such work is made for hire, the proprietor of such copyright shall be entitled to a renewal and extension of the copyright in such work for the further term of 67 years.
 (C) In the case of any other copyrighted work, including a contribution by an individual author to a periodical or to a cyclopedic or other composite work
  (i) the author of such work, if the author is still living,
  (ii) the widow, widower, or children of the author, if the author is not living,
  {iii) the author's executors, if such author, widow, widower, or children are not living, or
  (iv) the author's next of kin, in the absence of a will of the author, shall be entitled to a renewal and extension of the copyright in such work for a further term of 67 years.

Sections 304(a)(2)(B) – 304(d) omitted.

SEC. 401. NOTICE OF COPYRIGHT: VISUALLY PERCEPTIBLE COPIES

(a) General Provisions. Whenever a work protected under this title is published in the United States or elsewhere by authority of the copyright owner, a notice of copyright as provided by this section may be placed on publicly distributed copies from which the work can be visually perceived, either directly or with the aid of a machine or device.

(b) Form of Notice. If a notice appears on the copies, it shall consist of the following three elements:

 (1) the symbol (AF) (the letter C in a circle), or the word "Copyright", or the abbreviation "'Copr."; and
 (2) the year of first publication of the work; in the case of compilations, or derivative works incorporating previously published material, the year date of first publication of the compilation or derivative work is sufficient. The year date may be omitted where a pictorial, graphic, or sculptural work, with accompanying text matter, if any, is reproduced in or on greeting cards, postcards, stationery, jewelry,

dolls, toys, or any useful articles; and

(3) the name of the owner of copyright in the work, or an abbreviation by which the name can be recognized, or a generally known alternative designation of the owner.

(c) Position of Notice. The notice shall be affixed to the copies in such manner and location as to give reasonable notice of the claim of copyright. The Register of Copyrights shall prescribe by regulation, as examples, specific methods of affixation and positions of the notice on various types of works that will satisfy this requirement, but these specifications shall not be considered exhaustive.

(d) Evidentiary Weight of Notice. If a notice of copyright in the form and position specified by this section appears on the published copy or copies to which a defendant in a copyright infringement suit had access, then no weight shall be given to such a defendant's interposition of a defense based on innocent infringement in mitigation of actual or statutory damages, except as provided in the last sentence of section 504(c)(2).

SEC. 501. INFRINGEMENT OF COPYRIGHT

(a) Anyone who violates any of the exclusive rights of the copyright owner as provided by sections 106 through 118 or of the author as provided in section 106A(a), or who imports copies or phonorecords into the United States in violation of section 602, is an infringer of the copyright or right of the author, as the case may be. For purposes of this chapter (other than section 506), any reference to copyright shall be deemed to include the rights conferred by section 106A(a). As used in this subsection, the term "anyone" includes any State, any instrumentality of a State, and any officer or employee of a State or instrumentality of a State acting in his or her official capacity. Any State, and any such instrumentality, officer, or employee, shall be subject to the provisions of this title in the same manner and to the same extent as any nongovernmental entity.

(b) The legal or beneficial owner of an exclusive right under a copyright is entitled, subject to the requirements of section 411, to institute an action for any infringement of that particular right committed while he or she is the owner of it. The court may require such owner to serve written notice of the action with a copy of the complaint upon any person shown, by the records of the Copyright Office or otherwise, to have or claim an interest in the copyright, and shall require that such notice be served upon any person whose interest is likely to be affected by a decision in the case. The court may require the joinder, and shall permit the intervention, of any person having or claiming an interest in the copyright.

(c) For any secondary transmission by a cable system that embodies a performance or a display of a work which is actionable as an act of infringement under subsection (c) of section 111, a television broadcast station holding a copyright or other license to transmit or perform the same version of that work shall, for purposes of subsection (b) of this section, be treated as a legal or beneficial owner if such secondary transmission occurs within the local service area of that television station.

(d) For any secondary transmission by a cable system that is actionable as an act of infringement pursuant to section 111(c)(3), the following shall also have standing to sue:

(i)   the primary transmitter whose transmission has been altered by the cable system; and

(ii)   any broadcast station within whose local service area the secondary transmission occurs.

(e) With respect to any secondary transmission that is made by a satellite carrier of a primary transmission embodying the performance or display of a work and is actionable as an act of infringement under section 119(a)(5), a network station holding a copyright or other license to transmit or perform the same version of that work shall, for purposes of subsection (b) of this section, be treated as a legal or beneficial owner if such secondary transmission occurs within the local service area of that station.

SEC. 502. REMEDIES FOR INFRINGEMENT: INJUNCTIONS

(a) Any court having jurisdiction of a civil action arising under this title may, subject to the provisions of section 1498 of title 28, grant temporary and final injunctions on such terms as it may deem reasonable to prevent or restrain infringement of a copyright.

(b) Any such injunction may be served anywhere in the United States on the person enjoined; it shall be operative throughout the United States and shall be enforceable, by proceedings in contempt or otherwise, by any United States court having jurisdiction of that person. The clerk of the court granting the injunction shall, when requested by any other court in which enforcement of the injunction is sought, transmit promptly to the other court a certified copy of all the papers in the case on file in such clerk's office.

SEC. 503. REMEDIES FOR INFRINGEMENT: IMPOUNDING AND DISPOSITION OF INFRINGING ARTICLES

(a) At any time while an action under this title is pending, the court may order the impounding, on such terms as it may deem reasonable, of all copies or phonorecords claimed to have been made or used in violation of the copyright owner's exclusive rights, and of all plates, molds, matrices, masters, tapes, film negatives, or other articles by means of which such copies or phonorecords may be reproduced.

(b) As part of a final judgment or decree, the court may order the destruction or other reasonable disposition of all copies or phonorecords found to have been made or used in violation of the copyright owner's exclusive rights, and of all plates, molds, matrices, masters, tapes, film negatives, or other articles by means of which such copies or phonorecords may be reproduced.

SEC. 504. REMEDIES FOR INFRINGEMENT: DAMAGES AND PROFITS

(a) In General. Except as otherwise provided by this title, an infringer of copyright is liable for either

(1) the copyright owner's actual damages and any additional profits of the infringer, as provided by subsection (b); or

(2) statutory damages, as provided by subsection (c).

(b) Actual Damages and Profits. The copyright owner is entitled to recover the actual damages suffered by him or her as a result of the infringement, and any profits of the infringer that are attributable to the infringement and are not taken into account in computing the actual damages. In establishing the infringer's profits, the copyright owner is required to present proof only of the infringer's gross revenue, and the infringer is required to prove his or her deductible expenses and the elements of profit attributable to factors other than the copyrighted work.

(c) Statutory Damages.

(1) Except as provided by clause (2) of this subsection, the copyright owner may elect, at any time before final judgment is rendered, to recover, instead of actual damages and profits, an award of statutory damages for all infringements involved in the action, with respect to any one work, for which any one infringer is liable individually, or for which any two or more infringers are liable jointly and severally, in a sum of not less than $750 or more than $30,000

as the court considers just. For the purposes of this subsection, all the parts of a compilation or derivative work constitute one work.

(2) In a case where the copyright owner sustains the burden of proving, and the court finds, that infringement was committed willfully, the court in its discretion may increase the award of statutory damages to a sum of not more than $150,000. In a case where the infringer sustains the burden of proving, and the court finds, that such infringer was not aware and had no reason to believe that his or her acts constituted an infringement of copyright, the court in its discretion may reduce the award of statutory damages to a sum of not less than $200. The court shall remit statutory damages in any case where an infringer believed and had reasonable grounds for believing that his or her use of the copyrighted work was a fair use under section 107, if the infringer was: (i) an employee or agent of a nonprofit educational institution, library, or archives acting within the scope of his or her employment who, or such institution, library, or archives itself, which infringed by reproducing the work in copies or phonorecords; or (ii) a public broadcasting entity which or a person who, as a regular part of the nonprofit activities of a public broadcasting entity (as defined in subsection (g) of section 118) infringed by performing a published nondramatic literary work or by reproducing a transmission program embodying a performance of such a work.

(d) Additional Damages in Certain Cases. In any case in which the court finds that a defendant proprietor of an establishment who claims as a defense that its activities were exempt under section 110(5) did not have reasonable grounds to believe that its use of a copyrighted work was exempt under such section, the plaintiff shall be entitled to, in addition to any award of damages under this section, an additional award of two times the amount of the license fee that the proprietor of the establishment concerned should have paid the plaintiff for such use during the preceding period of up to 3 years.

SEC. 505. REMEDIES FOR INFRINGEMENT: COSTS AND ATTORNEY'S FEES

In any civil action under this title, the court in its discretion may allow the recovery of full costs by or against any party other than the United States or an officer thereof. Except as otherwise provided by this title, the court may also award a reasonable attorney's fee to the prevailing party as part of the costs.

SEC. 506. CRIMINAL OFFENSES

(a) Criminal Infringement. Any person who infringes a copyright willfully either

(1) for purposes of commercial advantage or private financial gain, or

(2) by the reproduction or distribution, including by electronic means, during any 180-day period, of 1 or more copies or phonorecords of 1 or more copyrighted works, which have a total retail value of more than $1,000, shall be punished as provided under section 2319 of title 18, United States Code. For purposes of this subsection, evidence of reproduction or distribution of a copyrighted work, by itself, shall not be sufficient to establish willful infringement.

(b) Forfeiture and Destruction. When any person is convicted of any violation of subsection (a), the court in its judgment of conviction shall, in addition to the penalty therein prescribed, order the forfeiture and destruction or other disposition of all infringing copies or phonorecords and all implements, devices, or equipment used in the manufacture of such infringing copies or phonorecords.

(c) Fraudulent Copyright Notice. Any person who, with fraudulent intent, places on any article a notice of copyright or words of the same purport that such person knows to be false, or who, with fraudulent intent, publicly distributes or imports for public distribution any article bearing such notice or words that such person knows to be false, shall be fined not more than $2,500.

(d) Fraudulent Removal of Copyright Notice. Any person who, with fraudulent intent, removes or alters any notice of copyright appearing on a copy of a copyrighted work shall be fined not more than $2,500.

(e) False Representation. Any person who knowingly makes a false representation of a material fact in the application for copyright registration provided for by section 409, or in any written statement filed in connection with the application, shall be fined not more than $2,500.

(f) Rights of Attribution and Integrity. Nothing in this section applies to infringement of the rights conferred by section 106A(a).

SEC. 507. LIMITATIONS ON ACTIONS

(a) Criminal Proceedings. Except as expressly provided otherwise in this title, no criminal proceeding shall be maintained under the provisions of this title unless it is commenced within 5 years after the cause of action arose.

(b) Civil Actions. No civil action shall be maintained under the provisions of this title unless it is commenced within three years after the claim accrued.

SEC. 509. SEIZURE AND FORFEITURE

(a) All copies or phonorecords manufactured, reproduced, distributed, sold, or otherwise used, intended for use, or possessed with intent to use in violation of section 506(a), and all plates, molds, matrices, masters, tapes, film negatives, or other articles by means of which such copies or phonorecords may be reproduced, and all electronic, mechanical, or other devices for manufacturing, reproducing, or assembling such copies or phonorecords may be seized and forfeited to the United States.

Section 509(b) omitted

SEC. 511. LIABILITY OF STATES, INSTRUMENTALITIES OF STATES, AND STATE OFFICIALS FOR INFRINGEMENT OF COPYRIGHT

(a) In General. Any State, any instrumentality of a State, and any officer or employee of a State acting in his or her official capacity, shall not be immune, under the Eleventh Amendment of the Constitution of the United States or under any other doctrine of sovereign immunity, from suit in Federal court by any person, including any governmental or nongovernmental entity, for a violation of any of the exclusive rights of a copyright owner provided by sections 106 through 121, for importing copies of phonorecords in violation of section 602, or for any other violation under this title.

(b) Remedies. In a suit described in subsection (a) for a violation described in that subsection, remedies both at law and in equity) are available for the violation to the same extent as such remedies are available for such a violation in a suit against any public or private entity other than a State, instrumentality of a State, or officer or employee of a State acting in his or her official capacity. Such remedies include impounding and disposition of infringing articles under section 503, actual damages and profits and statutory damages under section 504, costs and attorney's fees under section 505, and the remedies provided in section 510.

SEC. 512. LIMITATIONS ON LIABILITY RELATING TO MATERIAL ONLINE

(a) Transitory Digital Network Communications. A service provider shall not be liable for monetary relief, or, except as provided in subsection (j), for injunctive or other equitable relief, for infringement of copyright by reason of the provider's transmitting, routing, or providing connections for, material through a system or network controlled or operated by or for the service provider, or by reason of the intermediate and transient storage of that material in the course of such transmitting, routing, or providing connections, if

(1) the transmission of the material was initiated by or at the direction of a person other than the service provider;

(2) the transmission, routing, provision of connections, or storage is carried out through an automatic technical process without selection of the material by the service provider;

(3) the service provider does not select the recipients of the material except as an automatic response to the request of another person;

(4) no copy of the material made by the service provider in the course of such intermediate or transient storage is maintained on the system or network in a manner ordinarily accessible to anyone other than anticipated recipients, and no such copy is maintained on the system or network in a manner ordinarily accessible to such anticipated recipients for a longer period than is reasonably necessary for the transmission, routing, or provision of connections; and

(5) the material is transmitted through the system or network without modification of its content.

(b) System Caching.

(1) Limitation on liability. A service provider shall not be liable for monetary relief, or, except as provided in subsection (j), for injunctive or other equitable relief, for infringement of copyright by reason of the intermediate and temporary storage of material on a system or network controlled or operated by or for the service provider in a case in which

(A) the material is made available online by a person other than the service provider;

(B) the material is transmitted from the person described in subparagraph (A) through the system or network to a person other than the person described in subparagraph (A) at the direction of that other person; and

(C) the storage is carried out through an automatic technical process for the purpose of making the material available to users of the system or network who, after the material is transmitted as described in subparagraph (B), request access to the material from the person described in subparagraph (A), if the conditions set forth in paragraph (2) are met.

(2) Conditions. The conditions referred to in paragraph (1) are that
- (A) the material described in paragraph (1) is transmitted to the subsequent users described in paragraph (1)(C) without modification to its content from the manner in which the material was transmitted from the person described in paragraph (1)(A);
- (B) the service provider described in paragraph (1) complies with rules concerning the refreshing, reloading, or other updating of the material when specified by the person making the material available online in accordance with a generally accepted industry standard data communications protocol for the system or network through which that person makes the material available, except that this subparagraph applies only if those rules are not used by the person described in paragraph (1)(A) to prevent or unreasonably impair the intermediate storage to which this subsection applies;
- (C) the service provider does not interfere with the ability of technology associated with the material to return to the person described in paragraph (1)(A) the information that would have been available to that person if the material had been obtained by the subsequent users described in paragraph (1)(C) directly from that person, except that this subparagraph applies only if that technology
    - (i) does not significantly interfere with the performance of the provider's system or network or with the intermediate storage of the material;
    - (ii) is consistent with generally accepted industry standard communications protocols; and
    - (iii) does not extract information from the provider's system or network other than the information that would have been available to the person described in paragraph (1)(A) if the subsequent users had gained access to the material directly from that person;
- (D) if the person described in paragraph (1)(A) has in effect a condition that a person must meet prior to having access to the material, such as a condition based on payment of a fee or provision of a password or other information, the service provider permits access to the stored material in significant part only to users of its system or network that have met those conditions and only in accordance with those conditions; and
- (E) if the person described in paragraph (1)(A) makes that material available online without the authorization of the copyright owner of the material, the service provider responds expeditiously to remove, or disable access to, the material that is claimed to be infringing upon notification of claimed infringement as described in subsection (c)(3), except that this subparagraph applies only if
    - (i) the material has previously been removed from the originating site or access to it has been disabled, or a court has

ordered that the material be removed from the originating site or that access to the material on the originating site be disabled; and

(ii) the party giving the notification includes in the notification a statement confirming that the material has been removed from the originating site or access to it has been disabled or that a court has ordered that the material be removed from the originating site or that access to the material on the originating site be disabled.

(c) Information Residing on Systems or Networks At Direction of Users.

(1) In general. A service provider shall not be liable for monetary relief, or, except as provided in subsection (j), for injunctive or other equitable relief, for infringement of copyright by reason of the storage at the direction of a user of material that resides on a system or network controlled or operated by or for the service provider, if the service provider

(A)

(i) does not have actual knowledge that the material or an activity using the material on the system or network is infringing;

(ii) in the absence of such actual knowledge, is not aware of facts or circumstances from which infringing activity is apparent; or

(iii) upon obtaining such knowledge or awareness, acts expeditiously to remove, or disable access to, the material;

(B) does not receive a financial benefit directly attributable to the infringing activity, in a case in which the service provider has the right and ability to control such activity; and

(C) upon notification of claimed infringement as described in paragraph (3), responds expeditiously to remove, or disable access to, the material that is claimed to be infringing or to be the subject of infringing activity.

(2) Designated agent. The limitations on liability established in this subsection apply to a service provider only if the service provider has designated an agent to receive notifications of claimed infringement described in paragraph (3), by making available through its service, including on its website in a location accessible to the public, and by providing to the Copyright Office, substantially the following information:

(A) the name, address, phone number, and electronic mail address of the agent.

(B) other contact information which the Register of Copyrights may deem appropriate. The Register of Copyrights shall maintain a current directory of agents available to the public for inspection, including through the Internet, in both electronic and hard copy formats, and may require payment of a fee by service providers to cover the costs of maintaining the directory.

(3) Elements of notification.
    (A) To be effective under this subsection, a notification of claimed infringement must be a written communication provided to the designated agent of a service provider that includes substantially the following:
        (i) A physical or electronic signature of a person authorized to act on behalf of the owner of an exclusive right that is allegedly infringed.
        (ii) Identification of the copyrighted work claimed to have been infringed, or, if multiple copyrighted works at a single online site are covered by a single notification, a representative list of such works at that site.
        (iii) Identification of the material that is claimed to be infringing or to be the subject of infringing activity and that is to be removed or access to which is to be disabled, and information reasonably sufficient to permit the service provider to locate the material.
        (iv) Information reasonably sufficient to permit the service provider to contact the complaining party, such as an address, telephone number, and, if available, an electronic mail address at which the complaining party may be contacted.
        (v) A statement that the complaining party has a good faith belief that use of the material in the manner complained of is not authorized by the copyright owner, its agent, or the law.
        (vi) A statement that the information in the notification is accurate, and under penalty of perjury, that the complaining party is authorized to act on behalf of the owner of an exclusive right that is allegedly infringed.
    (B)
        (i) Subject to clause (ii), a notification from a copyright owner or from a person authorized to act on behalf of the copyright owner that fails to comply substantially with the provisions of subparagraph (A) shall not be considered under paragraph (1)(A) in determining whether a service provider has actual knowledge or is aware of facts or circumstances from which infringing activity is apparent.
        (ii) In a case in which the notification that is provided to the service provider's designated agent fails to comply substantially with all the provisions of subparagraph (A) but substantially complies with clauses (ii), (iii), and (iv) of subparagraph (A), clause (i) of this subparagraph applies only if the service provider promptly attempts to contact the person making the notification or takes other reasonable steps to assist in the receipt of notification that substantially complies with all the provisions of subparagraph (A).

(d) Information Location Tools. A service provider shall not be liable for monetary relief, or, except as provided in subsection (j), for injunctive or other equitable relief, for infringement of copyright by reason of the provider referring or linking users to an online location containing infringing material or infringing activity, by using information location tools, including a directory, index, reference, pointer, or hypertext link, if the service provider

(1)
    (A) does not have actual knowledge that the material or activity is infringing;

    (B) in the absence of such actual knowledge, is not aware of facts or circumstances from which infringing activity is apparent; or

    (C) upon obtaining such knowledge or awareness, acts expeditiously to remove, or disable access to, the material;

(2) does not receive a financial benefit directly attributable to the infringing activity, in a case in which the service provider has the right and ability to control such activity; and

(3) upon notification of claimed infringement as described in subsection (c)(3), responds expeditiously to remove, or disable access to, the material that is claimed to be infringing or to be the subject of infringing activity, except that, for purposes of this paragraph, the information described in subsection (c)(3)(A)(iii) shall be identification of the reference or link, to material or activity claimed to be infringing, that is to be removed or access to which is to be disabled, and information reasonably sufficient to permit the service provider to locate that reference or link.

(e) Limitation on liability of nonprofit educational institutions. (1) When a public or other nonprofit institution of higher education is a service provider, and when a faculty member or graduate student who is an employee of such institution is performing a teaching or research function, for the purposes of subsections (a) and (b) such faculty member or graduate student shall be considered to be a person other than the institution, and for the purposes of subsections (c) and (d) such faculty member's or graduate student's knowledge or awareness of his or her infringing activities shall not be attributed to the institution, if

    (A) such faculty member's or graduate student's infringing activities do not involve the provision of online access to instructional materials that are or were required or recommended, within the preceding 3-year period, for a course taught at the institution by such faculty member or graduate student;

    (B) the institution has not, within the preceding 3-year period, received more than two notifications described in subsection (c)(3) of claimed infringement by such faculty member or graduate student, and such notifications of claimed infringement were not actionable under subsection (f); and

    (C) the institution provides to all users of its system or network informational materials that accurately describe, and promote compliance with, the laws of the United States relating to copyright.

(2) Injunctions. For the purposes of this subsection, the limitations on injunctive relief contained in subsections (j)(2) and (j)(3), but not those in (j)(1), shall apply.

(f) Misrepresentations. Any person who knowingly materially misrepresents under this section

(1) that material or activity is infringing, or

(2) that material or activity was removed or disabled by mistake or misidentification, shall be liable for any damages, including costs and attorneys' fees, incurred by the alleged infringer, by any copyright owner or copyright owner's authorized licensee, or by a service provider, who is injured by such misrepresentation, as the result of the service provider relying upon such misrepresentation in removing or disabling access to the material or activity claimed to be infringing, or in replacing the removed material or ceasing to disable access to it.

(g) Replacement of Removed or Disabled Material and Limitation on Other Liability.

(1) No liability for taking down generally. Subject to paragraph (2), a service provider shall not be liable to any person for any claim based on the service provider's good faith disabling of access to, or removal of, material or activity claimed to be infringing or based on facts or circumstances from which infringing activity is apparent, regardless of whether the material or activity is ultimately determined to be infringing.

(2) Exception. Paragraph (1) shall not apply with respect to material residing at the direction of a subscriber of the service provider on a system or network controlled or operated by or for the service provider that is removed, or to which access is disabled by the service provider, pursuant to a notice provided under subsection (c)(1)(C), unless the service provider

(A) takes reasonable steps promptly to notify the subscriber that it has removed or disabled access to the material;

(B) upon receipt of a counter notification described in paragraph (3), promptly provides the person who provided the notification under subsection (c)(1)(C) with a copy of the counter notification, and informs that person that it will replace the removed material or cease disabling access to it in 10 business days; and

(C) replaces the removed material and ceases disabling access to it not less than 10, nor more than 14, business days following receipt of the counter notice, unless its designated agent first receives notice from the person who submitted the notification under subsection (c)(1)(C) that such person has filed an action seeking a court order to restrain the subscriber from engaging in infringing activity relating to the material on the service provider's system or network.

(3) Contents of counter notification. To be effective under this subsection, a counter notification must be a written communication pro-

vided to the service provider's designated agent that includes substantially the following:

(A) A physical or electronic signature of the subscriber.

(B) Identification of the material that has been removed or to which access has been disabled and the location at which the material appeared before it was removed or access to it was disabled.

(C) A statement under penalty of perjury that the subscriber has a good faith belief that the material was removed or disabled as a result of mistake or misidentification of the material to be removed or disabled.

(D) The subscriber's name, address, and telephone number, and a statement that the subscriber consents to the jurisdiction of Federal District Court for the judicial district in which the address is located, or if the subscriber's address is outside of the United States, for any judicial district in which the service provider may be found, and that the subscriber will accept service of process from the person who provided notification under subsection (c)(1)(C) or an agent of such person.

(4) Limitation on other liability. A service provider's compliance with paragraph (2) shall not subject the service provider to liability for copyright infringement with respect to the material identified in the notice provided under subsection (c)(1)(C).

(h) Subpoena To Identify Infringer.

(1) Request. A copyright owner or a person authorized to act on the owner's behalf may request the clerk of any United States district court to issue a subpoena to a service provider for identification of an alleged infringer in accordance with this subsection.

(2) Contents of request. The request may be made by filing with the clerk

(A) a copy of a notification described in subsection (c)(3)(A);

(B) a proposed subpoena; and

(C) a sworn declaration to the effect that the purpose for which the subpoena is sought is to obtain the identity of an alleged infringer and that such information will only be used for the purpose of protecting rights under this title.

(3) Contents of subpoena. The subpoena shall authorize and order the service provider receiving the notification and the subpoena to expeditiously disclose to the copyright owner or person authorized by the copyright owner information sufficient to identify the alleged infringer of the material described in the notification to the extent such information is available to the service provider.

(4) Basis for granting subpoena. If the notification filed satisfies the provisions of subsection (c)(3)(A), the proposed subpoena is in proper form, and the accompanying declaration is properly executed, the clerk shall expeditiously issue and sign the proposed subpoena and return it to the requester for delivery to the service provider.

(5) Actions of service provider receiving subpoena. Upon receipt of the issued subpoena, either accompanying or subsequent to the receipt

of a notification described in subsection (c)(3)(A), the service provider shall expeditiously disclose to the copyright owner or person authorized by the copyright owner the information required by the subpoena, notwithstanding any other provision of law and regardless of whether the service provider responds to the notification.

(6) Rules applicable to subpoena. Unless otherwise provided by this section or by applicable rules of the court, the procedure for issuance and delivery of the subpoena, and the remedies for noncompliance with the subpoena, shall be governed to the greatest extent practicable by those provisions of the Federal Rules of Civil Procedure governing the issuance, service, and enforcement of a subpoena duces tecum.

(i) Conditions for Eligibility.

(1) Accommodation of technology. The limitations on liability established by this section shall apply to a service provider only if the service provider

(A) has adopted and reasonably implemented, and informs subscribers and account holders of the service provider's system or network of, a policy that provides for the termination in appropriate circumstances of subscribers and account holders of the service provider's system or network who are repeat infringers; and

(B) accommodates and does not interfere with standard technical measures.

(2) Definition. As used in this subsection, the term "standard technical measures" means technical measures that are used by copyright owners to identify or protect copyrighted works and

(A) have been developed pursuant to a broad consensus of copyright owners and service providers in an open, fair, voluntary, multi-industry standards process;

(B) are available to any person on reasonable and nondiscriminatory terms; and

(C) do not impose substantial costs on service providers or substantial burdens on their systems or networks.

(j) Injunctions. The following rules shall apply in the case of any application for an injunction under section 502 against a service provider that is not subject to monetary remedies under this section:

(1) Scope of relief. (A) With respect to conduct other than that which qualifies for the limitation on remedies set forth in subsection (a), the court may grant injunctive relief with respect to a service provider only in one or more of the following forms:

(i) An order restraining the service provider from providing access to infringing material or activity residing at a particular online site on the provider's system or network.

(ii) An order restraining the service provider from providing access to a subscriber or account holder of the service provider's system or network who is engaging in infringing activity and is identified in the order, by terminating the accounts of the subscriber or account holder that are specified in the order.

    (iii) Such other injunctive relief as the court may consider necessary to prevent or restrain infringement of copyrighted material specified in the order of the court at a particular online location, if such relief is the least burdensome to the service provider among the forms of relief comparably effective for that purpose.

(B) If the service provider qualifies for the limitation on remedies described in subsection (a), the court may only grant injunctive relief in one or both of the following forms:

    (i) An order restraining the service provider from providing access to a subscriber or account holder of the service provider's system or network who is using the provider's service to engage in infringing activity and is identified in the order, by terminating the accounts of the subscriber or account holder that are specified in the order.

    (ii) An order restraining the service provider from providing access, by taking reasonable steps specified in the order to block access, to a specific, identified, online location outside the United States.

(2) Considerations. The court, in considering the relevant criteria for injunctive relief under applicable law, shall consider

    (A) whether such an injunction, either alone or in combination with other such injunctions issued against the same service provider under this subsection, would significantly burden either the provider or the operation of the provider's system or network;

    (B) the magnitude of the harm likely to be suffered by the copyright owner in the digital network environment if steps are not taken to prevent or restrain the infringement;

    (C) whether implementation of such an injunction would be technically feasible and effective, and would not interfere with access to noninfringing material at other online locations; and

    (D) whether other less burdensome and comparably effective means of preventing or restraining access to the infringing material are available.

(3) Notice and Ex Parte Orders. Injunctive relief under this subsection shall be available only after notice to the service provider and an opportunity for the service provider to appear are provided, except for orders ensuring the preservation of evidence or other orders having no material adverse effect on the operation of the service provider's communications network.

(k) Definitions.

(1) Service provider. (A) As used in subsection (a), the term "service provider" means an entity offering the transmission, routing, or providing of connections for digital online communications, between or

among points specified by a user, of material of the user's choosing, without modification to the content of the material as sent or received.

(B) As used in this section, other than subsection (a), the term "service provider" means a provider of online services or network access, or the operator of facilities therefor, and includes an entity described in subparagraph (A).

(2) Monetary relief. As used in this section, the term "monetary relief" means damages, costs, attorneys' fees, and any other form of monetary payment.

(l) Other Defenses Not Affected. The failure of a service provider's conduct to qualify for limitation of liability under this section shall not bear adversely upon the consideration of a defense by the service provider that the service provider's conduct is not infringing under this title or any other defense.

(m) Protection of Privacy. Nothing in this section shall be construed to condition the applicability of subsections (a) through (d) on

(1) a service provider monitoring its service or affirmatively seeking facts indicating infringing activity, except to the extent consistent with a standard technical measure complying with the provisions of subsection (i); or

(2) a service provider gaining access to, removing, or disabling access to material in cases in which such conduct is prohibited by law.

(n) Construction. Subsections (a), (b), (c), and (d) describe separate and distinct functions for purposes of applying this section. Whether a service provider qualifies for the limitation on liability in any one of those subsections shall be based solely on the criteria in that subsection, and shall not affect a determination of whether that service provider qualifies for the limitations on liability under any other such subsection.

Source 2
Copyright Term Duration

Note: this is a very simplified summary of copyright terms; see Section 301 *et seq.* of the Copyright Act for the entire text.

WORKS CREATED BUT NOT PUBLISHED BEFORE JANUARY 1, 1978 (§ 303)

(Before the 1976 Copyright Act, copyright began at publication. As a result of the 1976 act, copyright begins at the moment of creation. This section gives protection to works created but not published before the 1976 act was effective.)

- Term as indicated under § 302 (below)
- Copyright deemed to begin January 1, 1978
- In no case shall the term expire before December 31, 2002
- If the work is published on or before December 31, 2002, the term shall not expire before December 31, 2047

WORKS COPYRIGHTED AS OF JANUARY 1, 1978 (§ 304)

(Before the 1976 Copyright Act, the term of copyright was 28 years, renewable at the end of the term for another 28 years if the author was still alive.)

Copyrights in the First Term on January 1, 1978

- The first 28-year term still applies
- If the author owns the copyright, then he or his survivors, or if someone else owns the copyright then that person, is entitled to renewal for a second term of 67 years

181

Copyrights in Their Renewal Term As of January 1, 1999

- Term of 95 years from original copyright date

WORKS CREATED ON OR AFTER JANUARY 1, 1978 (§ 302)

In General

- Copyright begins at creation
- Life plus 70

Joint Authors

- Copyright begins at creation
- Life of last surviving author plus 70

Anonymous and Pseudonymous Works

Earliest of:
- 95 years from first publication
- 120 years from creation

Works Made for Hire

Earliest of:
- 95 years from first publication
- 120 years from creation

Source 3

The Conference on Fair Use: Educational Fair Use Guidelines For Digital Images[1]

TABLE OF CONTENTS:

1. INTRODUCTION:

1.1 Preamble.

Fair use is a legal principle that provides certain limitations on the exclusive rights[2] of copyright holders. The purpose of these guidelines is to provide guidance on the application of fair use principles by educational institutions, educators, scholars, and students who wish to digitize copyrighted visual images under fair use rather than by seeking authorization from the copyright owners for non-commercial educational purposes. These guidelines apply to fair use only in the context of copyright.

There is no simple test to determine what is fair use. Section 107 of the Copyright Act[3] sets forth the four fair use factors which should be assessed in each instance, based on the particular facts of a given case, to determine whether a use is a "fair use": (1) the purpose and character of the use, including whether such use is of a commercial nature or is for nonprofit educational purposes, (2) the nature of the copyrighted work, (3) the amount and substantiality of the portion used in relation to the copyrighted work as a whole, and (4) the effect of the use upon the potential market for or value of the copyrighted work. While only the courts can authoritatively determine whether a particular use is fair use, these guidelines represent the endorsers' consensus of conditions under which fair use should generally apply and examples of when permission is required. Uses that exceed these guidelines may or may not be fair use. The endorsers also agree that the more one exceeds these guidelines, the greater the risk that fair use does not apply.

The limitations and conditions set forth in these guidelines do not apply to works in the public domain—such as U.S. government works or works on which copyright has expired for which there are no copyright restrictions—or to works for which the individual or institution has obtained permission for the particular use. Also, license agreements may govern the uses of some works and users should refer to the applicable license terms for guidance.

The participants who developed these guidelines met for an extended period of time and the result represents their collective understanding in this complex area. Because digital technology is in a dynamic phase, there may come a time when it is necessary to review the guidelines. Nothing in these guidelines should be construed to apply to the fair use privilege in any context outside of educational and scholarly uses of digital images. These guidelines do not cover non-educational or commercial digitization or use at any time, even by non-profit educational institutions. These guidelines are not intended to cover fair use of copyrighted works in other educational contexts such as educational multimedia projects,[4] distance education, or electronic reserves, which may be addressed in other fair use guidelines.

This Preamble is an integral part of these guidelines and should be included whenever the guidelines are reprinted or adopted by organizations and educational institutions. Users are encouraged to reproduce and distribute these guidelines freely without permission; no copyright protection of these guidelines is claimed by any person or entity.

1.2 Background: Rights in Visual Images.

As photographic and electronic technology has advanced, the making of high-quality reproductions of visual images has become easier, cheaper, and more widely accessible. However, the fact that images may be easily available does not automatically mean they can be reproduced and reused without permission. Confusion regarding intellectual property rights in visual images arises from the many ways that images are created and the many sources that may be related to any particular image. Clearing permission, when necessary, requires identifying the holder of the applicable rights. Determining all the holders of the rights connected with an image requires an understanding of the source of the image, the content portrayed, and the creation of the image, both for original visual images and for reproductions of images.

Visual images can be original works or reproductions of other works; in some cases, original works may incorporate reproductions of other works as well. Often, a digital image is several generations removed from the visual image it reproduces. For example, a digital image of a painting may have been scanned from a slide, which was copied from a published book that contained a printed reproduction of the work of art; this reproduction may have been made from a color transparency photographed directly from the original painting. There may be intellectual property rights in the original painting, and each additional stage of reproduction in this chain may involve another layer of rights.

A digital image can be an original visual image, a reproduction, a published reproduction, or a copy of a published reproduction. An original visual image is a work of art or an original work of authorship (or a part of a work), fixed in digital or analog form and expressed in a visual medium. Examples include graphic, sculptural, and architectural works, as well as stills from motion pictures or other audio-visual works. A reproduction is a copy of an original visual image in digital or analog form. The most common forms of reproductions are photographic, including prints, 35mm slides, and color transparencies. The original visual image shown in a reproduction is often referred to as the "underlying work." Digital images can be reproductions of either original visual images or of other reproductions. A published reproduction is a reproduction of an original visual image appearing in a work distributed in copies and made available to the public by sale or other transfer of ownership, or by rental, lease, or lending. Examples include a plate in an exhibition catalog that reproduces a work of art, and a digital image appearing in a CD-ROM or online. A copy of a published reproduction is a subsequent copy made of a published reproduction of an original visual image, for example, a 35mm slide which is a copy of an image in a book.

The rights in images in each of these layers may be held by different rightsholders; obtaining rights to one does not automatically grant rights to use another, and therefore all must be considered when analyzing the rights connected with an image. Rights to use images will vary depending not only on the identities of the layers of rightsholders, but also on other factors such as the terms of any bequest or applicable license.

1.3 Applicability of These Guidelines.

These guidelines apply to the creation of digital images and their use for educational purposes. The guidelines cover (1) pre-existing analog image collections and (2) newly acquired analog visual images. These guidelines do not apply to images acquired in digital form, or to images in the public domain, or to works for which the user has obtained the relevant and necessary rights for the particular use.

Only lawfully acquired copyrighted analog images (including original visual images, reproductions, published reproductions, and copies of published reproductions) may be digitized pursuant to these guidelines. These guidelines apply only to educational institutions, educators, scholars, students, and image collection curators engaging in instructional, research, or scholarly activities at educational institutions for educational purposes.

1.4 Definitions.

Educational institutions are defined as nonprofit organizations whose primary purpose is supporting the nonprofit instructional, research, and scholarly activities of educators, scholars, and students. Examples of educational institutions include K-12 schools, colleges, and universities; libraries, museums, hospitals, and other nonprofit institutions also are considered educational institutions under this definition when they engage in nonprofit instructional, research, or scholarly activities for educational purposes. **Educational purposes** are defined as non-commercial instruction or curriculum-based teaching by educators to students at nonprofit educational institutions, and **research and scholarly activities**, defined as planned non-commercial study or investigation directed toward making a contribution to a field of knowledge and non-commercial presentation of research findings at peer conferences, workshops, or seminars.

Educators are faculty, teachers, instructors, curators, librarians, archivists, or professional staff who engage in instructional, research, or scholarly activities for educational purposes as their assigned responsibilities at educational institutions; independent scholars also are considered educators under this definition when they offer courses at educational institutions. **Students** are participants in instructional, research, or scholarly activities for educational purposes at educational institutions.

A **digital image** is a visual work stored in binary code (bits and bytes). Examples include bitmapped images (encoded as a series of bits and bytes each representing a particular pixel or part of the image) and vector graphics (encoded as equations and/or algorithms representing lines and curves). An **analog image collection** is an assemblage of analog visual images systematically maintained by an educational institution for educational purposes in the form of slides, photographs, or other stand-alone visual media. A **pre-existing analog image collection** is one in existence as of [December 31, 1996]. A **newly acquired analog visual image** is one added to an institution's collection after [December 31, 1996].

A **visual online catalog** is a database consisting of thumbnail images of an institution's lawfully acquired image collection, together with any descriptive text including, for example, provenance and rights information that is searchable by a number of fields, such as source. A **thumbnail image**, as used in a visual online catalog or image browsing display to enable visual identification of records in an educational institution's image collection, is a small scale, typically low resolution, digital reproduction which has no intrinsic commercial or reproductive value.

2. IMAGE DIGITIZATION AND USE BY EDUCATIONAL INSTITUTIONS:

This Section covers digitization by educational institutions of newly acquired analog visual images and Section 6 covers digitization of pre-existing analog image collections. Refer to the applicable section depending on whether you are digitizing newly acquired or pre-existing analog visual works.

2.1 Digitizing by Institutions: Newly Acquired Analog Visual Images.

An educational institution may digitize newly, lawfully, acquired analog visual images to support the permitted educational uses under these guidelines unless such images are readily available in usable digital form for purchase or license at a fair price. Images that are readily available in usable digital form for purchase or license at a fair price should not be digitized for addition to an institutional image collection without permission.

2.2 Creating Thumbnail Images.

An educational institution may create thumbnail images of lawfully acquired images for inclusion in a visual catalog for use at the institution. These thumbnail images may be combined with descriptive text in a visual catalog that is searchable by a number of fields, such as the source.

2.3 Access, Display, and Distribution on an Institution's Secure Electronic Network.

Subject to the time limitations in Section 2.4, an educational institution may display and provide access to images digitized under these guidelines through its own secure electronic network. When displaying digital images on such networks, an educational institution should implement technological controls and institutional policies to protect the rights of copyright owners, and use best efforts to make users aware of those rights. In addition, the educational institution must provide notice stating that digital images on its secure electronic network shall not be downloaded, copied, retained, printed, shared, modified, or otherwise used, except as provided for in the permitted educational uses under these guidelines.

2.3.1 Visual online catalog: An educational institution may display a visual online catalog, which includes the thumbnail images created as part of the institution's digitization process, on the institution's secure electronic network, and may provide access to such catalog by educators, scholars, and students affiliated with the educational institution.

2.3.2 Course compilations of digital images: An educational institution may display an educator's compilation of digital images (see also Section 3.1.2) on the institution's secure electronic network for classroom use, after-class review, or directed study, provided that there are technological limitations (such as a password or PIN) restricting access only to students enrolled in the course. The institution may display such images on its secure electronic network only during the semester or term in which that academic course is given.

2.3.3 Access, display, and distribution beyond the institution's secure electronic network: Electronic access to, or display or distribution of, images digitized under these guidelines, including the thumbnail images in the institution's visual online catalog, is not permitted beyond the institution's own electronic network, even for educational purposes. However, those portions of the visual online catalog which do not contain images digitized under these guidelines, such as public domain images and text, may be accessed, displayed, or distributed beyond the institution's own secure electronic network.

2.4 Time Limitations for Use of Images Digitized by Institutions from Newly Acquired Analog Visual Images.

An educational institution may use and retain in digital image collections images which are digitized from newly acquired analog visual images under these guidelines, as long as the retention and use comply with the following conditions:

2.4.1 Images digitized from a known source and not readily available in usable digital form for purchase or license at a fair price may be used for one academic term and may be retained in digital form while permission is being sought. Permission is required for uses beyond the initial use; if permission is not received, any use is outside the scope of these guidelines and subject to the four-factor fair use analysis (see Section 1.1).

2.4.2 Where the rightsholder of an image is unknown, a digitized image may be used for up to 3 years from first use, provided that a reasonable inquiry (see Section 5.2) is conducted by the institution seeking permission to digitize, retain, and reuse the digitized image. If, after 3 years, the educational institution is unable to identify sufficient information to seek permission, any further use of the image is outside the scope of these guidelines and subject to the four-factor fair use analysis (see Section 1.1).

3. USE BY EDUCATORS, SCHOLARS, AND STUDENTS:

Subject to the time limitations in Section 2.4, images digitized under these guidelines may be used by educators, scholars, and students as follows:

3.1 Educator Use of Images Digitized Under These Guidelines.

3.1.1 An educator may display digital images for educational purposes, including face-to-face teaching of curriculum-based courses, and research and scholarly activities at a non-profit educational institution.

3.1.2 An educator may compile digital images for display on the institution's secure electronic network (see also Section 2.3.2) to students enrolled in a course given by that educator for classroom use, after-class review, or directed study, during the semester or term in which the educator's related course is given.

3.2 Use of Images for Peer Conferences.

Educators, scholars, and students may use or display digital images in connection with lectures or presentations in their fields, including uses at non-commercial professional development seminars, workshops, and conferences where educators meet to discuss issues relevant to their disciplines or present works they created for educational purposes in the course of research, study, or teaching.

3.3 Use of Images for Publications.

These guidelines do not cover reproducing and publishing images in publications, including scholarly publications in print or digital form, for which permission is generally required. Before publishing any images under fair use, even for scholarly and critical purposes, scholars and scholarly publishers should conduct the four-factor fair use analysis (see Section 1.1).

3.4 Student Use of Images Digitized Under These Guidelines.

Students may:

- Use digital images in an academic course assignment such as a term paper or thesis, or in fulfillment of degree requirements.

- Publicly display their academic work incorporating digital images in courses for which they are registered and during formal critiques at a nonprofit educational institution.
- Retain their academic work in their personal portfolios for later uses such as graduate school and employment applications.

Other student uses are outside the scope of these guidelines and are subject to the four-factor fair use analysis (see Section 1.1).

4. IMAGE DIGITIZATION BY EDUCATORS, SCHOLARS, AND STUDENTS FOR SPONTANEOUS USE:

Educators, scholars, and students may digitize lawfully acquired images to support the permitted educational uses under these guidelines if the inspiration and decision to use the work and the moment of its use for maximum teaching effectiveness are so close in time that it would be unreasonable to expect a timely reply to a request for permission. Images digitized for spontaneous use do not automatically become part of the institution's image collection. Permission must be sought for any reuse of such digitized images or their addition to the institution's image collection.

5. IMPORTANT REMINDERS AND FAIR USE LIMITATIONS UNDER THESE GUIDELINES:

5.1 Creation of Digital Image Collections.

When digitizing copyrighted images, as permitted under these guidelines, an educational institution should simultaneously conduct the process of seeking permission to retain and use the images.

Where the rightsholder is unknown, the institution should pursue and is encouraged to keep records of its reasonable inquiry (see Section 5.2). Rightsholders and others who are contacted are encouraged to respond promptly to inquiries.

5.2 Reasonable Inquiry.

A reasonable inquiry by an institution for the purpose of clearing rights to digitize and use digital images includes, but is not limited to, conducting each of the following steps: (1) checking any information within the control of the educational institution, including slide catalogs and logs, regarding the source of the image; (2) asking relevant faculty, departmental staff, and librarians, including visual resource collections administrators, for any information regarding the source of the image; (3) consulting standard reference publications and databases for information regarding the source of the image; and (4) consulting rights reproduction collectives and/or major professional associations representing image creators in the appropriate medium.

5.3 Attribution and Acknowledgment.

Educators, scholars, and students should credit the sources and display the copyright notice(s) with any copyright ownership information shown in the original source, for all images digitized by educators, scholars, and students, including those digitized under fair use. Crediting the source means adequately identifying the source of the work, giving a full bibliographic description where available (including the creator/author, title, publisher, and place and date of publication) or citing the electronic address if the work is from a network source. Educators, scholars, and students should retain any copyright notice or other proprietary rights notice placed by the copyright owner or image archive or collection on the digital image, unless they know that the work has entered the public domain or that the copyright ownership has changed. In those cases when source credits and copyright ownership information cannot be displayed on the screen with the image for educational reasons (e.g., during examinations), this information should still be linked to the image.

5.4 Licenses and Contracts.

Institutions should determine whether specific images are subject to a license or contract; a license or contract may limit the uses of those images.

5.5 Portions from Single Sources Such as Published Compilations or Motion Pictures.

When digitizing and using individual images from a single source such as a published compilation (including but not limited to books, slide sets, and digital image collections), or individual frames from motion pictures or other audiovisual works, institutions and individuals should be aware that fair use limits the number and substantiality of the images that may be used from a single source. In addition, a separate copyright in a compilation may exist. Further, fair use requires consideration of the effect of the use on the potential market for or value of the copyrighted work. The greater the number and substantiality of images taken from a single source, the greater the risk that the use will not be fair use.

5.6 Portions of Individual Images.

Although the use of entire works is usually not permitted under fair use, it is generally appropriate to use images in their entirety in order to respect the integrity of the original visual image, as long as the limitations on use under these guidelines are in place. For purposes of electronic display, however, portions of an image may be used to highlight certain details of the work for educational purposes as long as the full image is displayed or linked to the portion.

5.7 Integrity of Images: Alterations.

In order to maintain the integrity of copyrighted works, educators, scholars, and students are advised to exercise care when making any alterations in a work under fair use for educational purposes such as criticism, comment, teaching, scholarship, and research. Furthermore, educators, scholars, and students should note the nature of any changes they make to original visual images when producing their own digital images.

5.8 Caution in Downloading Images from Other Electronic Sources.

Educators, scholars, and students are advised to exercise caution in using digital images downloaded from other sources, such as the Internet. Such digital environments contain a mix of works protected by copyright and works in the public domain, and some copyrighted works may have been posted to the Internet without authorization of the copyright holder.

6. TRANSITION PERIOD FOR PRE-EXISTING ANALOG IMAGE COLLECTIONS:

6.1 Context.

Pre-existing visual resource collections in educational institutions (referred to in these guidelines as "pre-existing analog image collections") often consist of tens of thousands of images which have been acquired from a wide variety of sources over a period of many years. Many pre-existing collections lack adequate source information for older images and standards for accession practices are still evolving. In addition, publishers and vendors may no longer be in business, and information about specific images may no longer be available. For many images there may also be several layers of rightsholders: the rights in an original visual image are separate from rights in a reproduction of that image and may be held by different rightsholders. All these factors complicate the process of locating rightsholders, and seeking permissions for pre-existing collections will be painstaking and time consuming.

However, there are significant educational benefits to be gained if pre-existing analog image collections can be digitized uniformly and systematically. Digitization will allow educators to employ new technologies using the varied and numerous images necessary in their current curricula. At the same time, rightsholders and educational institutions have concerns that images in some collections may have been acquired without permission or may be subject to restricted uses. In either case, there may be rightsholders whose rights and interests are affected by digitization and other uses.

The approach agreed upon by the representatives who developed these guidelines is to permit educational institutions to digitize lawfully acquired images as a collection and to begin using such images for educational purposes. At the same time, educational institutions should begin to identify the rightsholders and seek permission to retain and use the digitized images for future educational purposes. Continued use depends on the institutions' making a reasonable inquiry (see Section 5.2) to clear the rights in the digitized image. This approach seeks to strike a reasonable balance and workable solution for copyright holders and users who otherwise may not agree on precisely what constitutes fair use in the digital era.

6.2 Digitizing by Institutions: Images in Pre-Existing Analog Image Collections.

6.2.1 Educational institutions may digitize images from pre-existing analog image collections during a reasonable transition period of 7 years (the approximate useful life of a slide) from [December 31, 1996]. In addition, educators, scholars, and students may begin to use those digitized images during the transition period to support the educational uses under these guidelines. When digitizing images during the transition period, institutions should simultaneously begin seeking the permission to digitize, retain, and reuse all such digitized images.

6.2.2 Digitization from pre-existing analog image collections is subject to limitations on portions from single sources such as published compilations or motion pictures (see Section 5.5). Section 6 of these guidelines should not be interpreted to permit the systematic digitization of images from an educational institution's collections of books, films, or periodicals as part of any methodical process of digitizing images from the institution's pre-existing analog image collection during the transition period.

6.2.3 If, after a reasonable inquiry (see Section 5.2), an educational institution is unable to identify sufficient information to seek appropriate permission during the transition period, continued retention and use is outside the scope of these guidelines and subject to the four-factor fair use analysis (see Section 1.1). Similarly, digitization and use of such collections after the expiration of the transition period is outside the scope of these guidelines and subject to the four-factor fair use analysis (see Section 1.1).

NOTES

1. These guidelines shall not be read to supersede other pre-existing educational use guidelines that deal with the 1976 Copyright Act.
2. *See* Section 106 of the Copyright Act.
3. The Copyright Act of 1976, as amended, is codified at 17 U.S.C. Sec. 101 et seq.
4. In general, multimedia projects are stand-alone, interactive programs incorporating both original and pre-existing copyrighted works in various media formats, while visual image archives are databases of individual visual images from which images intended for educational uses may be selected for display.

Source 4_____

The Conference on Fair Use: Fair Use Guidelines for Electronic Reserve Systems*

Revised: March 5, 1996

INTRODUCTION

Many college, university, and school libraries have established reserve operations for readings and other materials that support the instructional requirements of specific courses. Some educational institutions are now providing electronic reserve systems that allow storage of electronic versions of materials that students may retrieve on a computer screen, and from which they may print a copy for their personal study. When materials are included as a matter of fair use, electronic reserve systems should constitute an ad hoc or supplemental source of information for students, beyond a textbook or other materials. If included with permission from the copyright owner, however, the scope and range of materials is potentially unlimited, depending upon the permission granted. Although fair use is determined on a case-by-case basis, the following guidelines identify an understanding of fair use for the reproduction, distribution, display, and performance of materials in the context of creating and using an electronic reserve system.

* Note: These guidelines were written during the Conference on Fair Use process. However, the working group was unable to reach consensus on the guidelines and thus decided that they would not be disseminated as a part of the CONFU Report.

Making materials accessible through electronic reserve systems raises significant copyright issues. Electronic reserve operations include the making of a digital version of text, the distribution and display of that version at workstations, and downloading and printing of copies. The complexities of the electronic environment, and the growing potential for implicating copyright infringements, raise the need for a fresh understanding of fair use. These guidelines are not intended to burden the facilitation of reserves unduly, but instead offer a workable path that educators and librarians may follow in order to exercise a meaningful application of fair use, while also acknowledging and respecting the interests of copyright owners.

These guidelines focus generally on the traditional domain of reserve rooms, particularly copies of journal articles and book chapters, and their accompanying graphics. Nevertheless, they are not meant to apply exclusively to textual materials and may be instructive for the fair use of other media. The guidelines also focus on the use of the complete article or the entire book chapter. Using only brief excerpts from such works would most likely also be fair use, possibly without all of the restrictions or conditions set forth in these guidelines. Operators of reserve systems should also provide safeguards for the integrity of the text and the author's reputation, including verification that the text is correctly scanned.

The guidelines address only those materials protected by copyright and for which the institution has not obtained permission before including them in an electronic reserve system. The Limitations and conditions set forth in these guidelines need not apply to materials in the public domain—such as works of the U.S. government or works on which copyright has expired—or to works for which the institution has obtained permission for inclusion in the electronic reserve system. License agreements may govern the uses of some materials. Persons responsible for electronic reserve systems should refer to applicable license terms for guidance. If an instructor arranges for students to acquire a work by some means that includes permission from the copyright owner, the instructor should not include that same work on an electronic reserve system as a matter of fair use.

These guidelines are the outgrowth of negotiations among diverse parties attending the Conference on Fair Use ("CONFU") meetings sponsored by the Information Infrastructure Task Force's Working Group on Intellectual Property Rights. While endorsements of any guidelines by all conference participants is unlikely, these guidelines have been endorsed by the organizations whose names appear at the end. These guidelines are in furtherance of the Working Group's objective of encouraging negotiated guidelines of fair use.

This introduction is an integral part of these guidelines and should be included with the guidelines wherever they may be reprinted or adopted by a library, academic institution, or other organization or association. No copyright protection of these guidelines is claimed by any person or entity, and anyone is free to reproduce and distribute this document without permission.

A. SCOPE OF MATERIAL

1. In accordance with fair use (Section 107 of the U.S. Copyright Act), electronic reserve systems may include copyrighted materials at the request of a course instructor.
2. Electronic reserve systems may include short items (such as an article from a journal, a chapter from a book or conference proceedings, or a poem from a collected work) or excerpts from longer items. "Longer items" may include articles, chapters, poems, and other works that are of such length as to constitute a substantial portion of a book, journal, or other work of which they may be a part. "Short items" may include articles, chapters, poems, and other works of a customary length and structure as to be a small part of a book, journal, or other work, even if that work may be marketed individually.
3. Electronic reserve systems should not include any material unless the instructor, the library, or another unit of the educational institution possesses a lawfully obtained copy.
4. The total amount of material included in electronic reserve systems for a specific course as a matter of fair use should be a small proportion of the total assigned reading for a particular course.

B. NOTICES AND ATTRIBUTIONS

1. On a preliminary or introductory screen, electronic reserve systems should display a notice, consistent with the notice described in Section 108(f)(1) of the Copyright Act. The notice should include additional language cautioning against further electronic distribution of the digital work.
2. If a notice of copyright appears on the copy of a work that is included in an electronic reserve system, the following statement shall appear at some place where users will likely see it in connection with access to the particular work:
"The work from which this copy is made includes this notice: [restate

the elements of the statutory copyright notice: e.g., Copyright 1996, XXX Corp.]"

3. Materials included in electronic reserve systems should include appropriate citations or attributions to their sources.

C. ACCESS AND USE

1. Electronic reserve systems should be structured to limit access to students registered in the course for which the items have been placed on reserve, and to instructors and staff responsible for the course or the electronic system.
2. The appropriate methods for limiting access will depend on available technology. Solely to suggest and not to prescribe options for implementation, possible methods for limiting access may include one or more of the following or other appropriate methods:
   (a) individual password controls or verification of a student's registration status; or
   (b) password system for each class; or
   (c) retrieval of works by course number or instructor name, but not by author or title of the work; or
   (d) access limited to workstations that are ordinarily used by, or are accessible to, only enrolled students or appropriate staff or faculty.
3. Students should not be charged specifically or directly for access to electronic reserve systems.

D. STORAGE AND REUSE

1. Permission from the copyright holder is required if the item is to be reused in a subsequent academic term for the same course offered by the same instructor, or if the item is a standard assigned or optional reading for an individual course taught in multiple sections by many instructors.
2. Material may be retained in electronic form while permission is being sought or until the next academic term in which the material might be used, but in no event for more than three calendar years, including the year in which the materials are last used.
3. Short-term access to materials included on electronic reserve systems in previous academic terms may be provided to students who have not completed the course.

Source 5

The Conference on Fair Use: Educational Fair Use Guidelines for Distance Learning*

**PERFORMANCE & DISPLAY OF AUDIOVISUAL
AND OTHER COPYRIGHTED WORKS
NOVEMBER 18, 1996**

1.1 Preamble

Fair use is a legal principle that provides certain limitations on the exclusive rights of copyright holders. The purpose of these guidelines is to provide guidance on the application of fair use principles by educational institutions, educators, scholars and students who wish to use copyrighted works for distance education under fair use rather than by seeking authorization from the copyright owners for non-commercial purposes. The guidelines apply to fair use only in the context of copyright.

There is no simple test to determine what is fair use. Section 107 of the Copyright Act sets forth the four fair use factors which should be considered in each instance, based on the particular facts

---

* Note: These Guidelines were written during the Conference on Fair Use process and disseminated as part of the final CONFU Report. However, no general consensus regarding these Guidelines was reached among CONFU participants, due to concerns about the fact that the Guidelines address only real-time transmissions and not asynchronous transmissions as well.

of a given case, to determine whether a use is a fair use: (1) the purpose and character of the use, including whether use is of a commercial nature or is for nonprofit educational purposes, (2) the nature of the copyrighted work, (3) the amount and substantiality of the portion used in relation to the copyrighted work as a whole, and (4) the effect of the use upon the potential market for or value of the copyrighted work.

While only the courts can authoritatively determine whether a particular use is a fair use, these guidelines represent the participants' consensus of conditions under which fair use should generally apply and examples of when permission is required. Uses that exceed these guidelines may or may not be fair use. The participants also agree that the more one exceeds these guidelines, the greater the risk that fair use does not apply. The limitations and conditions set forth in these guidelines do not apply to works in the public domain—such as U.S. government works or works on which the copyright has expired for which there are no copyright restrictions—or to works for which the individual or institution has obtained permission for the particular use. Also, license agreements may govern the uses of some works and users should refer to the applicable license terms for guidance.

The participants who developed these guidelines met for an extended period of time and the result represents their collective understanding in this complex area. Because digital technology is in a dynamic phase, there may come a time when it is necessary to revise these guidelines. Nothing in these guidelines should be construed to apply to the fair use privilege in any context outside of educational and scholarly uses of distance education. The guidelines do not cover non-educational or commercial digitization or use at any time, even by nonprofit educational institutions. The guidelines are not intended to cover fair use of copyrighted works in other educational contexts such as educational multimedia projects, electronic reserves or digital images which may be addressed in other fair use guidelines.

This Preamble is an integral part of these guidelines and should be included whenever the guidelines are reprinted or adopted by organizations and educational institutions. Users are encouraged to reproduce and distribute these guidelines freely without permission; no copyright protection of these guidelines is claimed by any person or entity.

1.2 Background

Section 106 of the Copyright Act defines the right to perform or display a work as an exclusive right of the copyright holder. The Act also provides, however, some exceptions under which it is not necessary to ask the copyright holder's permission to perform or display a work. One is the fair use exception contained in Section 107, which is summarized in the preamble. Another set of exceptions, contained in Sections 110(1)-(2), permit instructors and students to perform or display copyrighted materials without permission from the copyright holder under certain carefully defined conditions.

Section 110(1) permits teachers and students in a nonprofit educational institution to perform or display any copyrighted work in the course of face-to-face teaching activities. In face-to-face instruction, such teachers and students may act out a play, read aloud a poem, display a cartoon or a slide, or play a videotape so long as the copy of the videotape was lawfully obtained. In essence, Section 110(1) permits performance and display of any kind of copyrighted work, and even a complete work, as a part of face-to-face instruction.

Section 110(2) permits performance of a nondramatic literary or musical work or display of any work as a part of a transmission in some distance learning contexts, under the specific conditions set out in that Section. Section 110(2) does not permit performance of dramatic or audiovisual works as a part of a transmission. The statute further requires that the transmission be directly related and of material assistance to the teaching content of the transmission and that the transmission be received in a classroom or other place normally devoted to instruction or by persons whose disabilities or special circumstances prevent attendance at a classroom or other place normally devoted to instruction.

The purpose of these guidelines is to provide guidance for the performance and display of copyrighted works in some of the distance learning environments that have developed since the enactment of Section 110 and that may not meet the specific conditions of Section 110(2). They permit instructors who meet the conditions of these guidelines to perform and display copyrighted works as if they were engaged in face-to-face instruction. They may, for example, perform an audiovisual work, even a complete one, in a one-time transmission to students so long as they meet the other conditions of these guidelines. They may not, however, allow such transmissions to result in copies for students unless they have permission to do so, any more than face-to-face instructors may make copies of audiovisual works for their students without permission.

The developers of these guidelines agree that these guidelines reflect the principles of fair use in combination with the specific provisions of Sections 110(1)-(2). In most respects, they expand the provisions of Section 110(2).

In some cases students and teachers in distance learning situations may want to perform and display only small portions of copyrighted works that may be permissible under the fair use doctrine even in the absence of these guidelines. Given the specific limitations set out in Section 110(2), however, the participants believe that there may be a higher burden of demonstrating that fair use under Section 107 permits performance or display of more than a small portion of a copyrighted work under circumstances not specifically authorized by Section 110(2).

1.3 Distance Learning in General

Broadly viewed, distance learning is an educational process that occurs when instruction is delivered to students physically remote from the location or campus of program origin, the main campus, or the primary resources that support instruction. In this process, the requirements for a course or program may be completed through remote communications with instructional and support staff including either one-way or two-way written, electronic or other media forms.

Distance education involves teaching through the use of telecommunications technologies to transmit and receive various materials through voice, video and data. These avenues of teaching often constitute instruction on a closed system limited to students who are pursuing educational opportunities as part of a systematic teaching activity or curriculum and are officially enrolled in the course. Examples of such analog and digital technologies include telecourses, audio and video teleconferences, closed broadcast and cable television systems, microwave and ITFS, compressed and full-motion video, fiber optic networks, audiographic systems, interactive videodisk, satellite-based and computer networks.

2. APPLICABILITY AND ELIGIBILITY

2.1 Applicability of the Guidelines

These guidelines apply to the performance of lawfully acquired copyrighted works not included under section 110(2) (such as a dramatic work or an audiovisual work) as well as to uses not covered for works that are included in Section 110(2). The covered uses are (1) live interactive distance learning classes (i.e., a teacher in a live class with all or some of the students at remote locations) and (2) faculty instruction recorded without students present for later transmission. They apply to delivery via satellite, closed circuit television or a secure computer network. They do not permit circumventing anti-copying mechanisms embedded in copyrighted works.

These guidelines do not cover asynchronous delivery of distance learning over a computer network, even one that is secure and capable of limiting access to students enrolled in the course through PIN or other identification system. Although the participants believe fair use of copyrighted works applies in some aspects of such instruction, they did not develop fair use guidelines to cover these situations because the area is so unsettled. The technology is rapidly developing, educational institutions are just beginning to experiment with these courses, and publishers and other creators of copyrighted works are in the early stages of developing materials and experimenting with marketing strategies for computer network delivery of distance learning materials. Thus, consideration of whether fair use guidelines are needed for asynchronous computer network delivery of distance learning courses perhaps should be revisited in three to five years.

In some cases, the guidelines do not apply to specific materials because no permission is required, either because the material to be performed or displayed is in the public domain, or because the instructor or the institution controls all relevant copyrights. In other cases, the guidelines do not apply because the copyrighted material is already subject to a specific agreement. For example, if the material was obtained pursuant to a license, the terms of the license apply. If the institution has received permission to use copyrighted material specifically for distance learning, the terms of that permission apply.

2.2 Eligibility

2.2.1 Eligible Educational Institution: These guidelines apply to nonprofit educational institutions at all levels of instruction whose primary focus is supporting research and instructional activities of educators and students but only to their nonprofit activities. They also apply to government agencies that offer instruction to their employees.

2.2.2 Eligible Students: Only students officially enrolled for the course at an eligible institution may view the transmission that contains works covered by these guidelines. This may include students enrolled in the course who are currently matriculated at another eligible institution. These guidelines are also applicable to government agency employees who take the course or program offered by the agency as a part of their official duties.

3. WORKS PERFORMED FOR INSTRUCTION

3.1 Relation to Instruction

Works performed must be integrated into the course, must be part of systematic instruction and must be directly related and of material assistance to the teaching content of the transmission. The performance may not be for entertainment purposes.

4. TRANSMISSION AND RECEPTION

4.1 Transmission (Delivery)

Transmission must be over a secure system with technological limitations on access to the class or program such as a PIN number, password, smartcard or other means of identification of the eligible student.

4.2 Reception

Reception must be in a classroom or other similar place normally devoted to instruction or any other site where the reception can be controlled by the eligible institution. In all such locations, the institution must utilize technological means to prevent copying of the portion of the class session that contains performance of the copyrighted work.

5. LIMITATIONS

5.1 One Time Use

Performance of an entire copyrighted work or a large portion thereof may be transmitted only once for a distance learning course. For subsequent performances, displays or access, permission must be obtained.

5.2 Reproduction and Access to Copies

5.2.1 Receiving Institution: The institution receiving the transmission may record or copy classes that include the performance of an entire copyrighted work, or a large portion thereof, and retain the recording or copy for up to 15 consecutive class days (i.e., days in which the institution is open for regular instruction) for viewing by students enrolled in the course. Access to the recording or copy for such viewing must be in a controlled environment such as a classroom, library or media center, and the institution must prevent copying by students of the portion of the class session that contains the performance of the copyrighted work. If the institution wants to retain the recording or copy of the transmission for a longer period of time, it must obtain permission from the rightsholder or delete the portion which contains the performance of the copyrighted work.

5.2.2 Transmitting Institution: The transmitting institution may, under the same terms, reproduce and provide access to copies of the transmission containing the performance of a copyrighted work; in addition, it can exercise reproduction rights provided in Section 112(b).

6. MULTIMEDIA

6.1 Commercially Produced Multimedia

If the copyrighted multimedia work was obtained pursuant to a license agreement, the terms of the license apply. If, however, there is no license, the performance of the copyrighted elements of the multimedia works may be transmitted in accordance with the provisions of these guidelines.

7. EXAMPLES OF WHEN PERMISSION IS REQUIRED:

7.1 Commercial uses

Any commercial use including the situation where a nonprofit educational institution is conducting courses for a for-profit corporation for a fee such as supervisory training courses or safety training for the corporation's employees.

7.2 Dissemination of recorded courses

An institution offering instruction via distance learning under these guidelines wants to further disseminate the recordings of the course or portions that contain performance of a copyrighted work.

7.3 Uncontrolled access to classes

An institution (agency) wants to offer a course or program that contains the performance of copyrighted works to non-employees.

7.4 Use beyond the 15–day limitation

An institution wishes to retain the recorded or copied class session that contains the performance of a copyrighted work not covered in Section 110(2). (It also could delete the portion of the recorded class session that contains the performance.)

ENDORSING ORGANIZATIONS

Organizations Participating in Developing but not Necessarily
Endorsing or Supporting These Guidelines:

American Association of Community Colleges
American Association of Law Libraries
American Council of Learned Societies
Association of American Publishers
Association of American Universities
Association of College and Research Libraries
Association of Research Libraries
Broadcast Music, Inc.
City University of New York
Coalition of College and University Media Centers
Creative Incentive Coalition
Houghton Mifflin
Indiana Partnership
John Wiley & Sons, Inc.
Kent State University
National Association of State Universities and Land Grant
     Colleges
National Geographic
National School Board Association
Special Libraries Association
State University of New York
U.S. Copyright Office
University of Texas System
Viacom

Source 6

The Conference on Fair Use: Fair Use Guidelines for Educational Multimedia*

TABLE OF CONTENTS

*Note: These Guidelines were written during the Conference on Fair Use process and disseminated as part of the final CONFU Report. However, no general consensus regarding these Guidelines was reached among CONFU participants, especially representatives of some academic and educational institutions and representatives of library concerns.[1]

1. INTRODUCTION

1.1 Preamble

Fair use is a legal principle that defines the limitations on the exclusive rights[2] of copyright holders. The purpose of these guidelines is to provide guidance on the application of fair use principles by educators, scholars and students who develop multimedia projects using portions of copyrighted works under fair use rather than by seeking authorization for non-commercial educational uses. These guidelines apply only to fair use in the context of copyright and to no other rights.

There is no simple test to determine what is fair use. Section 107 of the Copyright Act[3] sets forth the four fair use factors which should be considered in each instance, based on particular facts of a given case, to determine whether a use is a "fair use": (1) the purpose and character of use, including whether such use is of a commercial nature or is for nonprofit educational purposes, (2) the nature of the copyrighted work, (3) the amount and substantiality of the portion used in relation to the copyrighted work as a whole, and (4) the effect of the use upon the potential market for or value of the copyrighted work.

While only the courts can authoritatively determine whether a particular use is fair use, these guidelines represent the participants[4] consensus of conditions under which fair use should generally apply and examples of when permission is required. Uses that exceed these guidelines may nor may not be fair use. The participants also agree that the more one exceeds these guidelines, the greater the risk that fair use does not apply.

The limitations and conditions set forth in these guidelines do not apply to works in the public domain—such as U.S. Government works or works on which copyright has expired for which there are no copyright restrictions—or to works for which the individual or institution has obtained permission for the particular use. Also, license agreements may govern the uses of some works and users should refer to the applicable license terms for guidance.

The participants who developed these guidelines met for an extended period of time and the result represents their collective understanding in this complex area. Because digital technology is in a dynamic phase, there may come a time when it is necessary to review the guidelines. Nothing in these guidelines shall be construed to apply to the fair use privilege in any context outside of educational and scholarly uses of educational multimedia projects.

This Preamble is an integral part of these guidelines and should be included whenever the guidelines are reprinted or adopted by organizations and educational institutions. Users are encouraged to reproduce and distribute these guidelines freely without permission; no copyright protection of these guidelines is claimed by any person or entity.

1.2 Background

These guidelines clarify the application of fair use of copyrighted works as teaching methods are adapted to new learning environments. Educators have traditionally brought copyrighted books, videos, slides, sound recordings and other media into the classroom, along with accompanying projection and playback equipment. Multimedia creators integrated these individual instructional resources with their own original works in a meaningful way, providing compact educational tools that allow great flexibility in teaching and learning. Material is stored so that it may be retrieved in a nonlinear fashion, depending on the needs or interests of learners. Educators can use multimedia projects to respond spontaneously to students' questions by referring quickly to relevant portions. In addition, students can use multimedia projects to pursue independent study according to their needs or at a pace appropriate to their capabilities. Educators and students want guidance about the application of fair use principles when creating their own multimedia projects to meet specific instructional objectives.

1.3 Applicability of These Guidelines

(Certain basic terms used throughout these guidelines are identified in bold and defined in this section.)
These guidelines apply to the use, without permission, of portions of lawfully acquired copyrighted works in educational multimedia projects which are created by educators or students as part of a systematic learning activity by nonprint educational institutions.

Educational multimedia projects created under these guidelines incorporate students' or educators' original material, such as course notes or commentary, together with various copyrighted media formats including but not limited to, motion media, music, text material, graphics, illustrations, photographs and digital software which are combined into an integrated presentation. Educational institutions are defined as nonprofit organizations whose primary focus is supporting research and instructional activities of educators and students for noncommercial purposes.

For the purposes of the guidelines, educators include faculty, teachers, instructors, and others who engage in scholarly, research and instructional activities for educational institutions. The copyrighted works used under these guidelines are lawfully acquired if obtained by the institution or individual through lawful means such as purchase, gift or license agreement but not pirated copies. Educational multimedia projects which incorporate portions of copyrighted works under these guidelines may be used only for educational purposes in systematic learning activities including use in connection with non-commercial curriculum-based learning and teaching activities by educators to students enrolled in courses at nonprofit educational institutions or otherwise permitted under Section 3. While these guidelines refer to the creation and use of educational multimedia projects, readers are advised that in some instances other fair use guidelines such as those for off-air taping may be relevant.

2. PREPARATION OF EDUCATIONAL MULTIMEDIA PROJECTS USING PORTIONS OF COPYRIGHTED WORKS

These uses are subject to the Portion Limitations listed in Section 4. They should include proper attribution and citation as defined in Sections 6.2.

2.1 By students:

Students may incorporate portions of lawfully acquired copyrighted works when producing their own educational multimedia projects for a specific course.

2.2 By Educators for Curriculum-Based Instruction:

Educators may incorporate portions of lawfully acquired copyrighted works when producing their own educational multimedia programs for their own teaching tools in support of curriculum-based instructional activities at educational institutions.

3. PERMITTED USES OF EDUCATIONAL MULTIMEDIA PROGRAMS CREATED UNDER THESE GUIDELINES

Uses of educational multimedia projects created under these guidelines are subject to the Time, Portion, Copying and Distribution Limitations listed in Section 4.

3.1 Student Use:

Students may perform and display their own educational multimedia projects created under Section 2 of these guidelines for educational uses in the course for which they were created and may use them in their own portfolios as examples of their academic work for later personal uses such as job and graduate school interviews

3.2 Educator Use for Curriculum-Based Instruction:

Educators may perform and display their own educational multimedia projects created under Section 2 for curriculum-based instruction to students in the following situations:

3.2.1 for face-to-face instruction,

3.2.2 assigned to students for directed self-study,

3.2.3 for remote instruction to students enrolled in curriculum-based courses and located at remote sites, provided over the educational institution's secure electronic network in real-time, or for after class review or directed self-study, provided there are technological limitations on access to the network and educational multimedia project (such as a password or PIN) and provided further that the technology prevents the making of copies of copyrighted material.

If the educational institution's network or technology used to access the educational multimedia project created under Section 2 of these guidelines cannot prevent duplication of copyrighted material, students or educators may use the multimedia educational projects over an otherwise secure network for a period of only 15 days after its initial real-time remote use in the course of instruction or 15 days after its assignment for directed self-study. After that period, one of the two use copies of the educational multimedia project may be placed on reserve in a learning resource center, library or similar facility for on-site use by students enrolled in the course. Students shall be advised that they are not permitted to make their own copies of the multimedia project.

3.3 Educator Use for Peer Conferences:

Educators may perform or display their own multimedia projects created under Section 2 of these guidelines in presentations to their peers, for example, at workshops and conferences.

3.4 Educator Use for Professional Portfolio

Educators may retain educational multimedia projects created under Section 2 of these guidelines in their personal portfolios for later personal uses such as tenure review or job interviews.

4. LIMITATIONS—TIME, PORTION, COPYING AND DISTRIBUTION

The preparation of educational multimedia projects incorporating copyrighted works under Section 2, and the use of such projects under Section 3, are subject to the limitations noted below.

4.1 Time Limitations

Educators may use their educational multimedia projects created for educational purposes under Section 2 of these guidelines for teaching courses, for a period of up to two years after the first instructional use with a class. Use beyond that time period, even for educational purposes, requires permission for each copyrighted portion incorporated in the production. Students may use their educational multimedia projects as noted in Section 3.1.

4.2 Portion Limitations

Portion limitations mean the amount of a copyrighted work that can reasonably be used in educational multimedia projects under these guidelines regardless of the original medium from which the copyrighted works are taken. In the aggregate means the total amount of copyrighted material from a single copyrighted work that is permitted to be used in an educational multimedia project without permission under these guidelines. These limits apply cumulatively to each educator's or student's multimedia project(s) for the same academic semester, cycle or term. All students should be instructed about the reasons for copyright protection and the need to follow these guidelines. It is understood, however, that students in kindergarten through grade six may not be able to adhere rigidly to the portion limitations in this section in their independent development of educational multimedia projects. In any event, each such project retained under Sections 3.1 and 4.3 should comply with the portion limitaitons in this section.

4.2.1 Motion Media

Up to 10% or 3 minutes, whichever is less, in the aggregate of a copyrighted motion media work may be reproduced or otherwise incorporated as part of a multimedia project created under Section 2 of these guidelines.

4.2.2 Text Material

Up to 10% or 1000 words, whichever is less, in the aggregate of a copyrighted work consisting of text material may be reproduced or otherwise incorporated as part of a multimedia project created under Section 2 of these guidelines. An entire poem of less than 250 words may be used, but no more than three poems by one poet, or five poems by different poets from any anthology may be used. For poems of greater length, 250 words may be used but no more than three excerpts by a poet, or five excerpts by different poets from a single anthology may be used.

4.2.3 Music, Lyrics, and Music Video

Up to 10%, but in no event more than 30 seconds, of the music and lyrics from an individual musical work (or in the aggregate of extracts from an individual work), whether the musical work is embodied in copies, or audio or audiovisual works, may be reproduced or otherwise incorporated as a part of a multimedia project created under Section 2. Any alterations to a musical work shall not change the basic melody or the fundamental character of the work.

4.2.4 Illustrations and Photographs

The reproduction or incorporation of photographs and illustrations is more difficult to define with regard to fair use because fair use usually precludes the use of an entire work. Under these guidelines a photograph or illustration may be used in its entirety but no more than 5 images by an artist or photographer may be reproduced or otherwise incorporated as part of an educational multimedia project created under Section 2. When using photographs and illustrations from a published collective work, not more than

10% or 15 images, whichever is less, may be reproduced or otherwise incorporated as part of an educational multimedia project created under Section 2.

4.2.5 Numerical Data Sets

Up to 10% or 2500 fields or cell entries, whichever is less, from a copyrighted database or data table may be reproduced or otherwise incorporated as part of a educational multimedia project created under Section 2 of these guidelines. A field entry is defined as a specific item of information, such as a name or Social Security number, in a record of a database file. A cell entry is defined as the intersection where a row and a column meet on a spreadsheet.

4.3 Copying and Distribution Limitations

Only a limited number of copies, including the original, may be made of an educator's educational multimedia project. For all of the uses permitted by Section 3, there may be no more than two use copies only one of which may be placed on reserve as described in Section 3.2.3.

An additional copy may be made for preservation purposes but may only be used or copied to replace a use copy that has been lost, stolen, or damaged. In the case of a jointly created educational multimedia project, each principal creator may retain one copy but only for the purposes described in Sections 3.3 and 3.4 for educators and Section 3.1 for students.

5. EXAMPLES OF WHEN PERMISSION IS REQUIRED

5.1 Using Multimedia Projects for Non-Educational or Commercial Purposes

Educators and students must seek individual permissions (licenses) before using copyrighted works in educational multimedia projects for commercial reproduction and distribution.

5.2 Duplication of Multimedia Projects Beyond Limitations Listed in These Guidelines

Even for educational uses, educators and students must seek individual permissions for all copyrighted works incorporated in their

personally created educational multimedia projects before repli-
cating or distributing beyond the limitations listed in Section 4.3.

5.3 Distribution of Multimedia Projects Beyond Limitations Listed in These Guidelines

Educators and students may not use their personally created educational multimedia projects over electronic networks, except for
uses as described in Section 3.2.3, without obtaining permissions
for all copyrighted works incorporated in the program.

6. IMPORTANT REMINDERS

6.1 Caution in Downloading Material from the Internet

Educators and students are advised to exercise caution in using
digital material downloaded from the Internet in producing their
own educational multimedia projects, because there is a mix of
works protected by copyright and works in the public domain on
the network. Access to works on the Internet does not automatically mean that these can be reproduced and reused without permission or royalty payment and, furthermore, some copyrighted
works may have been posted to the Internet without authorization
of the copyright holder.

6.2 Attribution and Acknowledgment

Educators and students are reminded to credit the sources and display the copyright notice © and copyright ownership information
if this is shown in the original source, for all works incorporated as
part of the educational multimedia projects prepared by educators
and students, including those prepared under fair use. Crediting
the source must adequately identify the source of the work, giving
a full bibliographic description where available (including author,
title, publisher, and place and date of publication). The copyright
ownership information includes the copyright notice (©, year of first
publication and name of the copyright holder).

The credit and copyright notice information may be combined
and shown in a separate section of the educational multimedia
project (e.g. credit section) except for images incorporated into the
project for the uses described in Section 3.2.3. In such cases, the

copyright notice and the name of the creator of the image must be incorporated into the image when, and to the extent, such information is reasonably available; credit and copyright notice information is considered "incorporated" if it is attached to the image file and appears on the screen when the image is viewed. In those cases when displaying source credits and copyright ownership information on the screen with the image would be mutually exclusive with an instructional objective (e.g. during examinations in which the source credits and/or copyright information would be relevant to the examination questions), those images may be displayed without such information being simultaneously displayed on the screen. In such cases, this information should be linked to the image in a manner compatible with such instructional objectives.

6.3 Notice of Use Restrictions

Educators and students are advised that they must include on the opening screen of their multimedia program and any accompanying print material a notice that certain materials are included under the fair use exemption of the U.S. Copyright Law and have been prepared according to the multimedia fair use guidelines and are restricted from further use.

6.4 Future Uses Beyond Fair Use

Educators and students are advised to note that if there is a possibility that their own educational multimedia project incorporating copyrighted works under fair use could later result in broader dissemination, whether or not as commercial product, it is strongly recommended that they take steps to obtain permissions during the development process for all copyrighted portions rather than waiting until after completion of the project.

6.5 Integrity of Copyrighted Works: Alterations

Educators and students may make alterations in the portions of the copyrighted works they incorporate as part of an educational multimedia project only if the alterations support specific instructional objectives. Educators and students are advised to note that alterations have been made.

6.6 Reproduction or Decompilation of Copyrighted Computer Programs

Educators and students should be aware that reproduction or decompilation of copyrighted computer programs and portions thereof, for example the transfer of underlying code or control mechanisms, even for educational uses, are outside the scope of these guidelines.

6.7 Licenses and Contracts

Educators and students should determine whether specific copyrighted works, or other data or information are subject to a license or contract. Fair use and these guidelines shall not preempt or supersede licenses and contractual obligations.

NOTES

1. These Guidelines shall not be read to supersede other preexisting education fair use guidelines that deal with the Copyright Act of 1976.
2. See Section 106 of the Copyright Act.
3. The Copyright Act of 1976, as amended, is codified at 17 U.S.C. Sec.101 et seq.
4. The names of the various organizations participating in this dialog appear at the end of these guidelines and clearly indicate the variety of interest groups involved, both from the standpoint of the users of copyrighted material and also from the standpoint of the copyright owners.

*Source 7*_____

Final Report of the National Commission on New Technological Uses of Copyrighted Works, July 31, 1978, Library of Congress, Washington, DC, 1979, pages 54–55.

CONTU GUIDELINES ON PHOTOCOPYING UNDER INTERLIBRARY LOAN ARRANGEMENTS

The CONTU guidelines were developed to assist librarians and copyright proprietors in understanding the amount of photocopying for use in interlibrary loan arrangements permitted under the copyright law. In the spring of 1976 there was realistic expectation that a new copyright law, under consideration for nearly twenty years, would be enacted during that session of Congress. It had become apparent that the House subcommittee was giving serious consideration to modifying the language concerning "systematic reproduction" by libraries in Section 108(g)(2) of the Senate-passed bill to permit photocopying under interlibrary arrangements, unless such arrangements resulted in the borrowing libraries obtaining "such aggregate quantities as to substitute for a subscription to or purchase of" copyrighted works.

The Commission discussed this proposed amendment to the Senate bill at its meeting on April 2, 1976. Pursuant to a request made at that meeting by the Register of Copyrights, serving in her ex officio role, the Commission agreed that it might aid the House and Senate subcommittees by offering its good offices in bringing the principal parties together to see whether agreement could be reached on a definition of "such aggregate quantities." This offer was accepted by the House and Senate subcommittees and the interested parties, and much of the summer of 1976 was spent by the Commission in working with the parties to secure agreement on "guidelines" interpreting what was to become the proviso in Section 108(g)(2) relating to "systematic reproduction" by libraries. The pertinent parts of that section, with the proviso added by the House emphasized, follow:

> (g) The rights of reproduction and distribution under this section extend to the isolated and unrelated reproduction or distribution of a single copy or phonorecord of the same material on separate occasions, but do not extend to cases where the library or archives, or its employee...
>
> (2) engages in the systematic reproduction or distribution of single or multiple copies or phonorecords of material described in subsection (d):
>
> Provided, That nothing in this clause prevents a library or archives from participating in interlibrary arrangements that do not have, as their purpose of effect, that the library or archives receiving such copies or phonorecords for distribution does so in such aggregate quantities as to substitute for a subscription to or purchase of such work.

Before enactment of the new copyright law, the principal library, publisher, and author organizations agreed to the following detailed guidelines defining what "aggregate quantities" would constitute the "systematic reproduction" that would exceed the statutory limitations on a library's photocopying activities.

PHOTOCOPYING-INTERLIBRARY ARRANGEMENTS

Introduction

Subsection 108(g)(2) of the bill deals, among other things, with limits on interlibrary arrangements for photocopying. It prohibits systematic photocopying of copyrighted materials but permits interlibrary arrangements "that do not have, as their purpose or effect, that the library or archives receiving such copies or phonorecords for distribution does so in such aggregate quantities as to substitute for a subscription to or purchase of such work."

The National Commission on New Technological Uses of Copyrighted Works offered its good offices to the House and Senate subcommittees in bringing the interested parties together to see if agreement could be reached on what a realistic definition would be of "such aggregate quantities." The Commission consulted with the parties and suggested the interpretation which follows, on which there has been substantial agreement by the principal library, publisher, and author organizations. The Commission considers the guidelines which follow to be a workable and fair interpretation of the intent of the proviso portion of subsection 108(g)(2).

These guidelines are intended to provide guidance in the application of section 108 to the most frequently encountered interlibrary case: a library's obtaining from another library, in lieu of interlibrary loan, copies of articles from relatively recent issues of periodicals—those published within five years prior to the date of the request. The guidelines do not specify what aggregate quantity of copies of an article or articles published in a periodical, the issue date of which is more than five years prior to the date when the request for the copy thereof is made, constitutes a substitute for a subscription to such periodical. The meaning of the proviso to subsection 108(g)(2) in such case is left to future interpretation.

The point has been made that the present practice on interlibrary loans and use of photocopies in lieu of loans may be supplemented or even largely replaced by a system in which one or more agencies or institutions, public or private, exist for the specific purpose of providing a central source for photocopies. Of course, these guidelines would not apply to such a situation.

GUIDELINES FOR THE PROVISO OF SUBSECTION 108(G)(2)

1. As used in the proviso of subsection 108(g)(2), the words "...such aggregate quantities as to substitute for a subscription to or purchase of such work" shall mean:
   (a) with respect to any given periodical (as opposed to any given issue of a periodical), filled requests of a library or archives (a "requesting entity") within any calendar year for a total of six or more copies of an article or articles published in such periodical within five years prior to the date of the request. These

guidelines specifically shall not apply, directly or indirectly, to any request of a requesting entity for a copy or copies of an article or articles published in any issue of a periodical, the publication date of which is more than five years prior to the date when the request is made. These guidelines do not define the meaning, with respect to such a request, of "...such aggregate quantities as to substitute for a subscription to [such periodical]."

(b) With respect to any other material described in subsection 108(d), including fiction and poetry), filled requests of a requesting entity within any calendar year for a total of six or more copies or phonorecords of or from any given work (including a collective work) during the entire period when such material shall be protected by copyright.

2. In the event that a requesting entity:

(a) shall have in force or shall have entered an order for a subscription to a periodical, or

(b) has within its collection, or shall have entered an order for, a copy of phonorecord of any other copyrighted work, materials from either category of which it desires to obtain by copy from another library or archives (the "supplying entity"), because the material to be copied is not reasonably available for use by the requesting entity itself, then the fulfillment of such request shall be treated as though the requesting entity made such copy from its own collection. A library or archives may request a copy or phonorecord from a supplying entity only under those circumstances where the requesting entity would have been able, under the other provisos of section 108, to supply such copy from materials in its own collection.

3. No request for a copy or phonorecord of any materials to which these guidelines apply may be fulfilled by the supplying entity unless such request is accompanied by a representation by the requesting entity that the request was made in conformity with these guidelines.

4. The requesting entity shall maintain records of all requests made by it for copies or phonorecords of any materials to which these guidelines apply and shall maintain records of the fulfillment of such requests, which records shall be retained until the end of the third complete calendar year after the end of the calendar year in which the respective request shall have been made.

5. As part of the review provided for in subsection 108(i), these guidelines shall be reviewed not later than five years from the effective date of this bill.

These guidelines were accepted by the Conference Committee and were incorporated into its report on the new act. During the ensuing twenty months, both library and publisher organizations have reported considerable progress toward adapting their practices to conform with the CONTU guidelines.

The guidelines specifically leave the status of periodical articles more than five years old to future determination. Moreover, institutions set up for the specific purpose of supplying photocopies of copyrighted material are excluded from coverage of the guidelines.

Source 8

American Library Association Model Policy Concerning College and University Photocopying for Classroom, Research and Library Reserve Use

(Permission granted by the American Library Association, 2001)

This model policy, another in a series of copyright advisory documents developed by the American Library Association (ALA), is intended for the guidance and use of academic librarians, faculty, administrators, and legal counsel in response to implementation of the rights and responsibilities provisions of Public Law 94–553, General Revision of the Copyright Law, which took effect on January 1, 1978.

Prepared by ALA Legal Counsel Mary Hutchings of the law firm Sidley & Austin, with advise and assistance from the Copyright Subcommittee (ad hoc) of ALA's Legislation Committee, Association of College and Research Libraries (ACRL) Copyright Committee, Association of Research Libraries (ARL) and other academic librarians and copyright attorneys, the model policy outlines "fair use" rights in the academic environment for classroom teaching, research activities and library services. Please note that it does not address other library photocopying which may be permitted under other sections of the Copyright Law, e.g., § 108 (Reproduction by Libraries and Archives).

Too often, members of the academic community have been reluctant or hesitant to exercise their rights of fair use under the law for fear of courting an infringement suit. It is important to understand that in U.S. law, copyright is a limited statutory monopoly and the public's right to use materials must be protected. Safeguards have been written into the legislative history accompanying the new copyright law protecting librarians, teachers, researchers and scholars and guaranteeing their rights of access to information as they carry out their responsibilities for educating or conducting research. It is, therefore, important to heed the advise of a former U.S. Register of Copyrights: "If you don't use fair use, you will lose it!"

I. THE COPYRIGHT ACT AND PHOTOCOPYING

From time to time, the faculty and staff of this University [College] may use photocopied materials to supplement research and teaching. In many cases, photocopying can facilitate the University's [College's] mission; that is, the development and transmission of information. However, the photocopying of copyrighted materials is a right granted under the copyright law's doctrine of "fair use" which must not be abused. This report will explain the University's [College's] policy concerning the photocopying of copyrighted materials by faculty and library staff. Please note that this policy does not address other library photocopying which may be permitted under sections of the copyright law, e.g., 17 U.S.C. § 108.

Copyright is a constitutionally conceived property right which is designed to promote the progress of science and the useful arts by securing for an author the benefits of his or her original work of authorship for a limited time. U.S. Constitution, Art. I, Sec. 8. The Copyright statute, 17 U.S.C.§ 101 et seq., implements this policy by balancing the author's interest against the public interest in the dissemination of information affecting areas of universal concern, such as art, science, history and business. The grand design of this delicate balance is to foster the creation and dissemination of intellectual works for the general public.

The Copyright Act defines the rights of a copyright holder and how they may be enforced against an infringer. Included within the Copyright Act is the "fair use" doctrine which allows, under certain conditions, the copying of copyrighted material. While the

Act lists general factors under the heading of "fair use" it provides little in the way of specific directions for what constitutes fair use. The law states:

17 U.S.C. § 107. Limitations on exclusive rights: Fair use

Notwithstanding the provisions of section 106, the fair use of a copyrighted work, including such use by reproduction in copies or phonorecords or by any other means specified by that section, for purposes such as criticism, comment, news reporting, teaching (including multiple copies for classroom use), scholarship, or research, is not an infringement of copyright. In determining whether the use made of a work in any particular case is a fair use the factors to be considered shall include

    (1) the purpose and character of the use, including whether such use is of a commercial nature or is for nonprofit educational purposes;

    (2) the nature of copyrighted work;

    (3) the amount and substantiality of the portion used in relation to the copyrighted work as a whole; and

    (4) the effect of the use upon the potential market for or value of the copyrighted work.

The purpose of this report is to provide you, the faculty and staff of this University [College], with an explanation of when the photocopying of copyrighted material in our opinion is permitted under the fair use doctrine. Where possible, common examples of research, classroom, and library reserve photocopying have been included to illustrate what we believe to be the reach and limits of fair use.

Please note that the copyright law applies to all forms of photocopying, whether it is undertaken at a commercial copying center, at the University's [College's] central or departmental copying facilities or at a self-service machine. While you are free to use the services of a commercial establishment, you should be prepared to provide documentation of permission from the publisher (if such permission is necessary under this policy), since many commercial copiers will require such proof.

We hope this report will give you an appreciation of the factors which weight in favor of fair use and those factors which weigh against fair use, but faculty members must determine for themselves which works will be photocopied. This University [College] does not condone a policy of photocopying instead of purchasing copyrighted works where such photocopying would constitute an infringement under the Copyright law, but it does encourage faculty members to exercise good judgment in serving the best interests of students in an efficient manner.

Instructions for securing permission to photocopy copyrighted works when such copying is beyond the limits of fair use appear at the end of this report. It is the policy of this University that the user (faculty, staff or librarian) secure such permission whenever it is legally necessary.

II. UNRESTRICTED PHOTOCOPYING

A. Uncopyrighted Published Works

Writing published before January 1, 1978 which have never been copyrighted may be photocopied without restriction. Copies of works protected by copyright must bear a copyright notice, which consists of the letter "c" in a circle, or the word "Copyright", or the abbreviation "Copr.", plus the year of first publication, plus the name of the copyright owner. 17 U.S.C. § 401. As to works published before January 1, 1978, in the case of a book, the notice must be placed on the title page or the reverse side of the title page. In the case of a periodical the notice must be placed either on the title page, the first page of text, or in the masthead. A pre-1978 failure to comply with the notice requirements results in the work being injected into the public domain, i.e., unprotected. Copyright notice requirements have been relaxed since 1978, so that the absence of notice on copies of a work published after January 1, 1978 does not necessarily mean the work in the public domain. 17 U.S.C. § 405 (a) and (c). However, you will not be liable for damages for copyright infringement of works published after that date, if, after normal inspection, you photocopy a work on which you cannot find a copyright symbol and you have not received actual notice of the fact the work is copyrighted. 17 U.S.C. § 405(b).

However, a copyright owner who found out about your photocopying would have the right to prevent further distribution of the copies if in fact the work were copyrighted and the copies are infringing. 17 U.S.C. § 405(b).

B. Published Works with Expired Copyrights

Writings with expired copyrights may be photocopied without restriction. All copyrights prior to 1906 have expired. 17 U.S.C. § 304(b). Copyrights granted after 1906 may have been renewed; however the writing will probably not contain notice of the renewal. Therefore, it should be assumed all writings dated 1906 or later are covered by a valid copyright, unless information to the contrary is obtained from the owner or the U.S. Copyright Office (see Copyright Office Circular 15t).

Copyright Office Circular R22 explains how to investigate the copyright status of a work. One way is to use the Catalog of Copyright Entries published by the Copyright Office and available in [the University Library] many libraries. Alternatively you may request the Copyright Office to conduct a search of its registration and/or assignment records. The Office charges an hourly fee for this service. You will need to submit as much information as you have concerning the work in which you are interested, such as the title, author, approximate date of publication, the type of work or any available copyright data. The Copyright Office does caution that its searches are not conclusive; for instance, if a work obtained copyright less than 28 years ago, it may be fully protected although there has been no registration or deposit.

C. Unpublished Works

Unpublished works, such as theses and dissertations, may be protected by copyright. If such a work was created before January 1, 1978 and has not been copyrighted or published without copyright notice, the work is protected under the new Act for the life of the author plus fifty years, 17 U.S.C. § 303, but in no case earlier than December 31, 2002. If such a work is published on or before that date, the copyright will not expire before December 31, 2027. Works created after January 1, 1978 and not published enjoy copyright protection for the life of the author plus fifty years. 17 U.S.C. § 302.

D. U.S. Government Publications

All U.S. Government publications with the possible exception of some National Technical Information Service Publications less than five years old may be photocopied without restrictions, except to the extent they contain copyrighted materials from other sources. 17 U.S.C. § 105. U.S. Government publications are documents prepared by an official or employee of the government in an official capacity. 17 U.S.C. § 101.

Government publications include the opinions of courts in legal cases, Congressional Reports on proposed bills, testimony offered at Congressional hearings and the works of government employees in their official capacities. Works prepared by outside authors on contract to the government may or may not be protected by copyright, depending on the specifics of the contract. In the absence of copyright notice on such works, it would be reasonable to assume they are government works in the public domain. It should be noted that state government works may be protected by copyright. See, 17 U.S.C. § 105. However, the opinions of state courts are not protected.

III. PERMISSIBLE PHOTOCOPYING OF COPYRIGHTED WORKS

The Copyright Act allows anyone to photocopy copyrighted works without securing permission from the copyright owner when the photocopying amounts to a "fair use" of the material. 17 U.S.C. § 107. The guidelines in this report discuss the boundaries for fair use of photocopied material used in research or the classroom or in a library reserve operation. Fair use cannot always be expressed in numbers—either the number of pages copied or the number of copies distributed. Therefore, you should wight the various factors listed in the Act and judge whether the intended use of photocopied, copyrighted material is within the spirit of the fair use doctrine. Any serious questions concerning whether a particular photocopying constitutes fair use should be directed to University [College] counsel.

A. Research Uses

At the very least, instructors may make a single copy of any of the following for scholarly research or use in teaching or preparing to teach a class:
1. a chapter from a book;
2. an article from a periodical or newspaper;
3. a short story, short essay, or short poem, whether or not from a collective work;
4. a chart, diagram, graph, drawing, cartoon or picture from a book, periodical, or newspaper.

These examples reflect the most conservative guidelines for fair use. They do not represent inviolate ceilings for the amount of copyrighted material which can be photocopied within the boundaries of fair use. When exceeding these minimum levels, however, you again should consider the four factors listed in Section 107 of the Copyright Act to make sure that any additional photocopying is justified. The following demonstrate situations where increased levels of photocopying would continue to remain within the ambit of fair use:

1. the inability to obtain another copy of the work because it is not available from another library or source cannot be obtained within your time constraints;
2. the intention to photocopy the material only once and not to distribute the material to others;
3. the ability to keep the amount of material photocopied within a reasonable proportion to the entire work (the larger the work, the greater amount of material which may be photocopied).

Most single-copy photocopying for your personal use in research—even when it involves a substantial portion of a work—may well constitute fair use.

B. Classroom Uses

Primary and secondary school educators have, with publishers, developed the following guidelines, which allow a teacher to distribute photocopied material to students in a class without the publisher's prior permission, under the following conditions:

1. the distribution of the same photocopied material does not occur every semester;
2. only one copy is distributed for each student which copy must become the student's property;
3. the material includes a copyright notice on the first page of the portion of material photocopied;
4. the students are not assessed any fee beyond the actual cost of the photocopying.

In addition, the educators agreed that the amount of material distributed should not exceed certain brevity standards. Under those guidelines, a prose work may be reproduced in its entirety if it is less than 2500 words in length. If the work exceeds such length, the excerpt reproduced may not exceed 1000 words, or 10% of the work, whichever is less. In the case of poetry, 250 words is the maximum permitted.

These minimum standards normally would not be realistic in the University setting. Faculty members needing to exceed these limits for college education should not feel hampered by these guidelines, although they should attempt a "selective and sparing" use of photocopied, copyrighted material.

The photocopying practices of an instructor should not have a significant detrimental impact on the market for the copyrighted work. 17 U.S.C. § 107(4). To guard against this effect, you usually should restrict use of an item of photocopied material to one course and you should not repeatedly photocopy excepts from one periodical or author without the permission of the copyright owner.

C. Library Reserve Uses

At the request of a faculty member, a library may photocopy and place on reserve excerpts from copyrighted works in its collection in accordance with guidelines similar to those governing formal classroom distribution for face-to-face teaching discussed above. This University [College] believes that these guidelines apply to the library reserve shelf to the extent it functions as an extension of classroom readings or reflects an individual student's right to photocopy for his personal scholastic use under the doctrine of fair use. In general, librarians may photocopy materials for reserve room use for the convenience of students both in preparing class assignments and in pursuing informal educational activities which higher education requires, such as advanced independent study and research.

If the request calls for only one copy to be placed on reserve, the library may photocopy an entire article, or an entire chapter from a book, or an entire poem. Requests for multiple copies on reserve should meet the following guidelines:

1. the amount of material should be reasonable in relation to the total amount of material assigned for one term of a course taking into account the nature of the course, its subject matter and level, 17 U.S.C. § 107(1) and (3);

2. the number of copies should be reasonable in light of the number of students enrolled, the difficulty and timing of assignments, and the number of other courses which may assign the same material, 17 U.S.C. § 107(1) and (3);

3. the material should contain a notice of copyright, see 17 U.S.C. § 401;

4. the effect of photocopying the material should not be detrimental to the market for the work. (In general, the library should own at least one copy of the work.) 17 U.S.C. § 107(4).

For example, a professor may place on reserve as a supplement to the course textbook a reasonable number of copies of article from academic journals or chapters from trade books. A reasonable number of copies will in most instances be less than six, but factors such as the length or difficulty of the assignment, the number of enrolled students and the length of time allowed for completion of the assignment may permit more in unusual circumstances.

In addition, a faculty member may also request that multiple copies of photocopied, copyrighted material be placed on the reserve shelf if there is insufficient time to obtain permission from the copyright owner. For example, a professor may place on reserve several photocopies of an entire article from a recent issue of *Time* magazine or the *New York Times* in lieu of distributing a copy to each member of the class. If you are in doubt as to whether a particular instance of photocopying is fair use in the reserve reading room, you should waive any fee for such a use.

D. Uses of Photocopied Material Requiring Permission

1. repetitive copying: The classroom or reserve use of photocopied materials in multiple courses or successive years will normally require advance permission from the owner of the copyright, 17 U.S.C. § 107(3).
2. copying for profit: Faculty should not charge students more than the actual cost of photocopying the material, 17 U.S.C. § 107(1).
3. consumable works: The duplication of works that are consumed in the classroom, such as standardized tests, exercises, and workbooks, normally requires permission from the copyright owner, 17 U.S.C. § 107(4).
4. creation of anthologies as basic text material for a course: Creation of a collective work or anthology by photocopying a number of copyrighted articles and excerpts to be purchased and used together as the basic text for a course will in most instances require the permission of the copyrighted owners. Such photocopying of a book and thus less likely to be deemed fair use, 17 U.S.C. § 107(4).

E. How to Obtain Permission

When a use of photocopied material requires that you request permission, you should communicate complete and accurate information to the copyright owner. The American Association of Publishers suggests that the following information be included in a permission request letter in order to expedite the process:

1. Title, author and/or editor, and edition of materials to be duplicated.
2. Exact material to be used, giving amount, page numbers, chapters and, if possible, a photocopy of the material.
3. Number of copies to be made.
4. Use to be made of duplicated materials.
5. Form of distribution (classroom, newsletter, etc.).
6. Whether or not the material is to be sold.
7. Type of reprint (ditto, photography, offset, typeset).

The request should be sent, together with a self-addressed return envelope, to the permissions department of the publisher in question. If the address of the publisher does not appear at the front of the material, it may be readily obtained in a publication entitled *The Literary Marketplace*, published by the R. R. Bowker Company and available in all libraries.

The process of granting permission requires time for the publisher to check the status of the copyright and to evaluate the nature of the request. It is advisable, therefore, to allow enough lead time to obtain permission before the materials are needed. In some instances, the publisher may assess a fee for the permission. It is not inappropriate to pass this fee on to the student who receive copies of the photocopied material.

The Copyright Clearance Center also has the right to grant permission and collect fees for photocopying rights for certain publications. Libraries may copy from any journal which is registered with the CCC and report the copying beyond fair use to CCC and pay the set fee. A list of publications for which the CCC handles fees and permissions is available from CCC, 310 Madison Avenue, New York, N.Y. 10017.

Agreement on Guidelines for Classroom Copying in Not-For-Profit Educational Institutions (from the House Committee on the Judiciary, Report on the Copyright Act of 1976.)

WITH RESPECT TO BOOKS AND PERIODICALS

The purpose of the following guidelines is to state the minimum standards of educational fair use under Section 107 of H.R. 2223. The parties agree that the conditions determining the extent of permissible copying for educational purposes may change in the future; that certain types of copying permitted under these guidelines may not be permissible in the future; and conversely that in the future other types of copying not permitted under these guidelines may be permissible under revised guidelines.

Moreover, the following statement of guidelines is not intended to limit the types of copying permitted under the standards of fair use under judicial decision and which are stated in Section 107 of the Copyright Revision Bill. There may be instances in which copying which does not fall within the guidelines stated below may nonetheless be permitted under the criteria of fair use.

GUIDELINES

I. *Single Copying for Teachers*

A single copy may be made of any of the following by or for a teacher at his or her individual request for his or her scholarly research or use in teaching or preparation to teach a class:

A. A chapter from a book;
B. An article from a periodical or newspaper;
C. A short story, short essay or short poem, whether or not from a collective work;
D. A chart, graph, diagram, drawing, cartoon or picture from a book, periodical, or newspaper.

II. *Multiple Copies for Classroom Use*

Multiple copies (not to exceed in any event more than one copy per pupil in a course) may be made by or for the teacher giving the course for classroom use or discussion; provided that:

A. The copying meets the tests of brevity and spontaneity as defined below; and,
B. Meets the cumulative effect test as defined below; and,
C. Each copy includes a notice of copyright.

DEFINITIONS

Brevity

(*i*) Poetry: (a) A complete poem if less than 250 words and if printed on not more than two pages or, (b) from a longer poem, an excerpt of not more than 250 words.

(*ii*) Prose: (a) Either a complete article, story or essay of less than 2,500 words, or (b) an excerpt from any prose work of not more than 1,000 words or 10% of the work, whichever is less, but in any event a minimum of 500 words.

[Each of the numerical limits stated in "i" and "ii" above may be expanded to permit the completion of an unfinished line of a poem or of an unfinished prose paragraph.]

(*iii*) Illustration: one chart, graph, diagram, drawing, cartoon or picture per book or per periodical issue.

(*iv*) "Special" works: Certain works in poetry, prose or in "poetic prose" which often combine language with illustrations and which are intended sometimes for children and at other times for a more general audience fall short of 2,500 words in their entirety. Paragraph "ii" above notwithstanding such "special works" may not be reproduced in their entirety; however, an excerpt comprising not more than two of the published pages of such special work and containing not more than 10% of the words found in the text thereof, may be reproduced.

Spontaneity

(*i*) The copying is at the instance and inspiration of the individual teacher, and

(*ii*) The inspiration and decision to use the work and the moment of its use for maximum teaching effectiveness are so close in time that it would be unreasonable to expect a timely reply to a request for permission.

Cumulative Effect

(*i*) The copying of the material is for only one course in the school in which the copies are made.

(*ii*) Not more than one short poem, article, story, essay or two excerpts may be copied from the same author, nor more than three from the same collective work or periodical volume during one class term.

(*iii*) There shall not be more than nine instances of such multiple copying for one course during one class term.

[The limitations stated in "ii" and "iii" above shall not apply to current news periodicals and newspapers and current news sections of other periodicals.]

III. *Prohibitions as to I and II Above*

Notwithstanding any of the above, the following shall be prohibited:

(A) Copying shall not be used to create or to replace or substitute for anthologies, compilations or collective works. Such replacement or substitution may occur whether copies of various works or excerpts therefrom are accumulated or reproduced and used separately.

(B) There shall be no copying of or from works intended to be "consumable" in the course of study or of teaching. These include workbooks, exercises, standardized tests and test booklets and answer sheets and like consumable material.

(C) Copying shall not:

   (a) substitute for the purchase of books, publishers' reprints or periodicals;

   (b) be directed by higher authority;

   (c) be repeated with respect to the same item by the same teacher from term to term.

(D) No charge shall be made to the student beyond the actual cost of the photocopying.

Source 10_____
How to Get Permission to
Use Copyrighted Material

During the process of writing the 1976 Copyright Act, Congress at some point realized that there was no centralized, easily accessible method of gaining permission to use a copyrighted work. In an effort to make it easier for libraries and others to enjoy legal uses of works that did not fall under any of the exceptions, such as that for library photocopying, the Senate recommended that "workable clearance and licensing procedures be developed." At the time, one of the main concerns was library photocopying. Now, of course, the Internet introduces an entirely new area of need. The Copyright Clearance Center (CCC), established in response to the 1976 act, provides licensing services for the reproduction and distribution of copyrighted materials in both print and electronic formats internationally. The CCC, however, cannot cover everything ever published, and the Internet makes this more true than ever.

Of course, the Internet presents some challenges not seen in the photocopying arena, namely self-publishing. With so much material available on the Internet, and so much of it not related to any formal publishing organization, not to mention the speed with which pages change, it is more difficult for collective licensing organizations to establish relations with owners of copyright in Web pages than in published books. Nonetheless, many collective licensing organizations have expanded their services to included licensing of Web pages.

If you want to seek permission to use material on a Web page then, you have a few avenues to pursue. First, many commercial copyright owners will allow *limited* use of their works for nonprofit educational purposes, though remember that this is the owner's option, unless your use is a fair use. If you believe your use falls into this category, you should contact the "publisher" of the page directly. The copyright owner will probably want a description of exactly what material you wish to use and how. If your use does not fall into this category, the path you choose first might depend on whether the page is authored by an individual, corporation, institution, or other large entity. Note that if your own pages do not fall into the nonprofit, educational category, you should be prepared to pay for your use. If the author is an individual, it might be easiest to send a letter to the copyright owner asking for permission and describing how you intend to use the information. Letters with original signatures from the copyright owner are preferable to emails, which may or may not be recognized by the courts. Be sure to keep records of your communications and to abide by any agreement you reach with the copyright owner.

If you wish to use information from a site where the copyright is owned by an institution—say you want to include a picture of the new electric car from Ford Motor Company's Web pages on your pages about alternative energy—you still have a few options. First, look over the pages to see if they provide contact information for seeking copyright permission. If not, you might contact the organization directly, but it might be quicker and easier to use a licensing organization, namely the CCC. Keep in mind that you may not find a licensing organization that will work with the entity in which you are interested. The Copyright Clearance Center may be reached at:

www.copyright.com
(978) 750–8400
info@copyright.com

Source 11

How to Protect Your Work

REGISTERING FOR COPYRIGHT[1]

Keep in mind that a work is protected by copyright the minute it is "fixed in a tangible medium." You do *not* need to register your work with the Copyright Office in order to ensure copyright protection. However, several benefits inure to registered works:

- Registration establishes a public record of the copyright claim.
- In order to file a claim of infringement, the work in question must be registered.
- Registration made within five years of publication establishes prima facie evidence of the validity of the copyright. This means that if your work is registered, the other guy in the battle has the burden of proving your copyright to be invalid, rather than you having to prove its validity.
- If a work is registered within three months of publication, or prior to an infringement of the work, you as the injured copyright owner may recover statutory damages and attorney's fees. If the work is not registered until after the infringement occurs, you may receive only actual damages and profits as awards in a suit against an infringer.
- Registration provides the U.S. Customs Service with the information they need to protect against the importation of infringing copies of your work.

A major benefit also inures to the Library of Congress (LC) from copyright registrations. The registration process requires the author to submit two copies of his work. These copies are sent to the Library of Congress. Registration is, in part, meant to ensure and build the LC's collection. As you might imagine, this is a controversial practice for various reasons.

Registering a work is quite simple and inexpensive. As the author, you must file with the Copyright Office a completed registration form, submit a fee of $30 (as of summer 2000), and deposit two copies of the work with the office. Different forms are filed for different types of work, but they are all quite simple to complete. Remember, the Copyright Office is trying to encourage registration, so they want to make it as painless as possible. In some cases, different requirements for the deposit of copies exist as well, depending on the type of work.

The Copyright Office publishes a wide range of pamphlets, called "circulars," which are very good at explaining the why's and how's of copyright law and registration. The circulars, as well as registration forms, are all available on the Copyright Office's Web site, in text, PDF, or HTML format: *www.loc.gov/copyright/*

MAKING IT EASY FOR OTHERS TO RESPECT YOUR RIGHTS

Keep in mind that, especially in the cyberworld, many infringers have no idea that they are doing anything wrong. Some may assume that copyright does not apply in cyberspace at all. Others may assume that if a work does not have a copyright statement on it, it is up for grabs. Either way, you may prevent ignorant infringements by making it easy for users to see that your page is copyrighted and to contact you for permissions. Place a copyright notice on every page. Your notice should consist of the © symbol, the word "copyrighted," or the abbreviation "copr."; *and* the year of publication of the work; *and* the name of the copyright owner. Thus, appropriate statements would look like:

© Gretchen McCord Hoffmann, 2000
copyright Gretchen McCord Hoffmann, 2000
copr. Gretchen McCord Hoffmann, 2000

An additional benefit of placing notices on your pages is that a defendant cannot then claim innocent infringement, which a court may consider in awarding damages.

You might also include statements giving your position on others' use of your page. If you are happy to allow others to use your page if they simply note that they have received permission, say so. If you are willing to allow certain uses, such as for educational or nonprofit uses, say so. Otherwise, a statement such as, "Copyright owner may be contacted to seek permission for use of this page at . . . ," in addition to being a courtesy, may reinforce the fact that no one can legally use your page without your permission.

USING TECHNOLOGY TO PROTECT YOUR DIGITAL WORKS

Technology may be used to protect your online works to some extent. Such measures include marking a page as your own, so that if someone tries to download print, or copy the page, your mark comes through as a "watermark." You may have seen similar watermarks on some paper when you attempt to photocopy it. For example, some college transcripts will produce photocopies with a huge watermark proclaiming the fact that "this is a photocopy, not an original." Other means might enable you to limit access to your online works, allowing users to read a Web page but not download or print it. These technologies are in their infancy, but expect to see a rapid growth in availability over the next few years, due in part to the strong protection given by the Digital Millennium Copyright Act.

MONITORING INFRINGEMENT OF YOUR WORK ON THE WEB

Registration doesn't prevent someone from infringing your work; instead, it puts you in a stronger position and gives you more options should an infringer come along. Even technological tricks are no guarantee that your work won't be infringed. If a surefire means of preventing infringement existed, we wouldn't be having this conversation. Perhaps the better question is: How do you know when someone infringes your work?

If you are seriously concerned about infringement, you should use a combination of methods to combat it, including registering your work, placing notices on every page, and implementing some technological protections. You may also consider investing the time to monitor potential infringements on the Web. This involves setting aside time on a regular basis to search the Web for your pages, or parts thereof, on someone else's server.

"But that's ridiculous," you're saying. "How can I search for each phrase on each of my pages every month?" Practically speaking, it would be impossible to literally search for any infringement of any portion of your pages. But you can use tricks that may make your searching a little easier.

Keep in mind that many people who infringe on the Internet are simply ignorant of copyright laws and don't realize that they are doing something illegal. Thus, they probably won't take the time to "doctor" up a page to make it less identifiable as the original. One of my friends, an instruction librarian, identified an infringer who fell in this category by using metatags. (Metatags are discussed in Chapter 9) Metatags are extremely easy to insert in your HTML code and are not seen by those viewing your page. You might include in metatags copyright statements or inventive words that are unlikely to be used by other Web pages, so that you can use search engines to search for "copyright University of America Library, 2000" or "Supercalifragilisticexpialidocious," or simply your name, none of which are likely to turn up on too many pages other than your own. Should someone stealing your page realize that she is stealing, she can easily remove the metatags, however, so this is certainly not foolproof.

The bottom line is that there is no certain way to prevent infringement or to detect every infringement. This was true long before the Internet existed, as well. For this reason, the more techniques you use in combination, the more likely you will be able to both prevent and detect infringements.

RESPONDING TO AN INFRINGEMENT

The first thing you should do if you discover someone infringing a work you have created as part of your job is to contact your institution's legal counsel with the information of what is being infringed, how or how much, and the URLs of the infringing pages. Discuss with your legal counsel whether she or you should contact the infringer to request that he stop his infringing actions. Keep monitoring the infringing page, and if the material is not removed, keep in touch with your counsel about pursuing the matter.

If you believe that your personal pages, in which you own the copyright, have been infringed, you might contact the infringer yourself to explain what you believe he is doing wrong and why. If you are willing for him to use your material as long as he includes a permission statement or to enter into some other compromise, let him know that. If not, ask him to take down the material and let him know that you will be talking to an attorney if he does not. You might ask your institution's legal counsel for a suggestion of attorneys to contact for help.

As a practical matter, the same path is usually taken in most infringement cases that are not major commercial infringements. First, a cease-and-desist letter is sent to the infringer. Usually, that's the end of it. If not, he will be notified that further legal action will be pursued should he not respond immediately to your request. Then, your legal counsel would file a complaint in court. Often, that will persuade the infringer to cease and desist. Seldom will such a case actually go to trial.

The main things for you to keep in mind are that you should always be in touch with legal counsel and you should keep records of all your communications with that person and the infringer, should you have any direct contact, as well as records of the infringing acts and the dates on which you discovered them.

NOTE

1. Should you wish to register works that you have created as part of your job, such as your library's Web pages, chences are those works will be considered "works for hire," which means that your employer owns the copyright, not you. If you are uncertain, clear this up before registering a work.

How to Fulfill Your Responsibility as an Information Professional to Represent the Needs of Your Library and Your Users

If you've even skimmed the main contents of this book, you realize how unsettled, to say the least, copyright law is concerning the Internet. As a librarian, you realize how important the Internet is to your job. Of course, there are many issues concerning the Internet other than copyright and many legal issues affecting libraries other than those concerning the Internet. Has a thought like any of the following crossed your mind while reading this book?

- "What a mess! Why doesn't somebody with some experience and know-how get in there and clean it up?"
- "Even *I* could have done a better job deciding that case or writing that law!"
- "What's going to happen to our library services if that law doesn't change or gets decided in the wrong way?"
- Or, even more simply: "What a bunch of ignoramuses!"

I've certainly had all of those thoughts and more as I learn more and more about the issues set forth in this book, and others as well, like funding for libraries. But do you see what the answer to each of these questions is?

- *You* are the one with the experience and know-how to clean up the mess.
- Yes, *you* probably could have done a better job! Why? Because you know what the case or law means to libraries, library users, and Internet users.
- *You* need to see that this doesn't happen.
- Of course "they" are "ignoramuses." By definition, they don't know any better—but *you* do.

You are the key here. *You* know what libraries need, what your users need, how your users use the library and the Internet, and even how the Internet works. Most members of Congress, judges, lawyers, and state legislators know little of these things. Our system of government is a *representative* democracy. Congress relies on its constituents to tell it what they need. It is our job as information professionals to make sure that Congress knows what our users and our institutions need.

"Does this really make a difference?" you ask. Let me give my favorite personal anecdote and a well-known aspect of the development of the current law. During my first year as a professional librarian, I participated in the Texas Library Association's Legislative Day, in which librarians spend a day visiting their representatives in the state legislature to inform them about and discuss with them issues of concern. This was in the early 1990s, when resource sharing was just beginning to develop. A mandate had been issued by the lieutenant governor (the most powerful position in Texas government) that no new funds were to be given out during that session.

I was lucky enough to be a part of the group who visited Lt. Gov. Bob Bullock during Legislative Day. The library association had invested a lot of time over the previous years getting to know Bullock and familiarizing him with our issues. Our big issue that year was requesting three million dollars as seed money for a statewide resource-sharing project. We gave him the pitch. He asked why we needed the project. We explained, with personal stories and statistics to support our argument. He, who had just mandated that no new money be given out, turned to his aide and said, "We can find three million for these people, can't we?" Now would that have happened if we had all been hard at work behind the reference desk, cataloging books, and teaching classes, instead of lobbying our representatives?

On a national level, it is clear that the participation of librarians and library organizations has helped tremendously in sustaining the balance in copyright law, and specifically in including exemptions for libraries in the statute. Think for a moment about how this works: How likely is it that a member of the committee working on an amendment to the copyright law would have the sudden thought, "Hey, what can we do for libraries with this bill?" We have to be there. We have to let our representatives know what we need. It is their job to try to meet our needs, but it is our job to inform them of those needs.

"But I really and truly hate public speaking/begging/politics/ fill-in-the-blank." There are many ways you can get involved in the political process to help your profession. The key is to get involved.

First, you need to keep up to date on what is going on:

- The American Library Association distributes via email the ALA Washington Office Newsline, a free, irregularly issued publication that updates you on what is going on in Washington that affects libraries and tells you when response from the library community is needed. To subscribe, send an email message to *listproc@ala1.ala.org*. Leave the subject line blank. As the first and only line of text in the message, type "subscribe ala-wo YourFirstName YourLastName" (for example, subscribe ala-wo Melville Dewey).
- You can also review past issues of ALAWON at *www.ala.org/washoff/ alawon/index.html*.
- The ALA Washington Office Web pages also provide information about current issues, explaining the background and why librarians should be concerned, at *www.ala.org/washoff/*.
- The ALA Washington Office has recently begun a Copyright Education Program to inform librarians and library supporters about issues specifically related to copyright: *http://copyright.ala.org*.
- Other library associations, including some state associations, also provide information about legislative and policy issues. Check with your organization about its legislative and policy work.
- Other Web sites with similar interests, listed in Sources 14 and 15 include Digital Future Coalition and Electronic Frontier Foundation.

Then, you need to get to know your representatives and keep in contact with them. ALA also provides material to help you out with this, at *www.ala.org/washoff/advocacy.html*. This site includes online brochures such as *Library Advocacy Pocket Checklist, Effective Ways to Communicate With Legislators*, and *How to Write a Letter to Your Legislator*.

Both ALA and many state library associations sponsor legislative days, when librarians and library supporters meet with state legislators or members of Congress. In most cases, the association will organize the event and train you on the issues and how to speak to your representative. You don't have to know anything going into it except what your patrons need. The association will explain the issues and tell you how to present them in two minutes flat (legislators like short meetings!). You probably will not have to meet with a representative alone, so you will have moral support with you.

I encourage librarians to get involved in legislative days, but it is at least as important to keep in touch with your legislators via letters, email, faxes, and phone calls throughout the sessions. We don't want our issues and concerns to be totally new when our group walks into a legislator's office. We need to let our legislators know that we are paying attention and that we care.

You should also keep up with what is going on in your state and your community. Talk to your state library association, your local city council, and library boards. Watch their agendas. Is an upcoming item "mandating filters on all computers in public libraries"? Talk to your colleagues, organize a group to attend the meeting, designate someone to speak out for you.

Your libraries and your library users depend on you to represent their needs. No one else but you can do it. And there is strength in numbers. This is part of your professional duty, and there are many organizations and people out there to help you. You truly can make a difference in the future of libraries, information users, and the information society.

Source 13
Resources: Organizations

United States Copyright Office
U.S. Copyright Office
Library of Congress
101 Independence Avenue, S.E.
Washington, DC 20559–6000
(202) 707–3000
www.loc.gov/copyright

American Library Association Washington Office
1301 Pennsylvania Avenue, N.W.
Suite 403
Washington, DC 20004
(202) 628–8419
www.ala.org/washoff

American Library Association Office for Information Technology Policy
1301 Pennsylvania Avenue, N.W.
Suite 403
Washington, DC 20004
(202) 628–8424
www.ala.org/oitp

Copyright Clearance Center
222 Rosewood Drive
Danvers, MA 01923
(978) 750–8400
info@copyright.com

Electronic Frontier Foundation
1550 Bryant Street, Suite 725
San Francisco CA 94103
(415) 436–9333
www.eff.org

Source 14
Resources: Publications

Bielefield, Arlene, and Lawrence Cheeseman. 1993. *Libraries and Copyright Law*. New York: Neal-Schuman Publishers, Inc.

Bruwelheide, Janis H. 1995. *The Copyright Primer for Librarians and Educators*. 2nd ed. Chicago: American Library Association.

Fishman, Stephen. 1994. *The Copyright Handbook: How to Protect and Use Written Works*. 2nd ed. Berkeley: Nolo Press.

Gasaway, Laura N., ed. 1997. *Growing Pains: Adapting Copyright for Libraries, Education, and Society*. Littleton, Co. Fred B. Rothman & Co.

Gasaway, Laura N., and Sarah K. Wiant. 1994. *Libraries and Copyright: A Guide to Copyright Law in the 1990s*. Washington, D.C.: Special Libraries Association.

Hayes, David L. "Advanced Copyright Issues on the Internet," *Texas Intellectual Property Law Journal* 7, no. 1, (Fall 1998): 2.

Leaffer, Marshall. 1995. *Understanding Copyright Law*. 2nd ed. New York: Matthew Bender & Co., Inc.

Lehman, Bruce A. 1998. *The Conference on Fair Use: Final Report to the Commissioner on the Conclusion of the Conference on Fair Use*. Washington, D.C.: U.S. Patent and Trademark Office.

———. 1995. *Intellectual Property and the National Information Infrastructure: The Report of the Working Group on Intellectual Property Rights*. Washington, D.C.: U.S. Patent and Trademark Office.

Patterson, L. Ray, and Stanley W. Lindberg. 1991. *The Nature of Copyright: A Law of Users' Rights*. Athens: University of Georgia Press.

Source 15
Resources: Web Pages

American Library Association
www.ala.org

American Library Association Washington Office
www.ala.org/washoff

American Library Association Washington Office Copyright Education Program
http://copyright.ala.org

Association of Research Libraries
http://arl.cni.org/info/frn/copy/copytoc.html

Brinson, J. Dianne, and Mark F. Radcliffe. 1998. *An Intellectual Property Law Primer for Multimedia and Web Developers.* Cyberspace and New Media Law Center. *www2.viaweb.com/lib/laderapress/primer.html*

CONFU: The Conference on Fair Use
www.utsystem.edu/ogc/intellectualproperty/confu.htm

Copyright Clearance Center, Inc.
www.copyright.com

Copyright on the Internet, Franklin Pierce Law Center
www.fplc.edu/tfield/copynet.htm

Cyberlaw Encyclopedia
www.gahtan.com/cyberlaw/Copyright_Law/

Daily IP News
www.ipmag.com

Digital Future Coalition
www.dfc.org

Electronic Frontier Foundation
www.eff.org

FindLaw: Copyright
www.findlaw.com/01topics/23intellectprop/01copyright/index.html

Harper, Georgia. *Copyright Crash Course.*
www.utsystem.edu/ogc/intellectualproperty/cprtindx.htm

Intellectual Property Reference Library
www.servtech.com/~mbobb/

Internet Law News
http://bna.com/ilaw
(you can subscribe for free to receive this via daily email.)

Legal Information Institute
www.law.cornell.edu/topics/copyright.html

Lutzker, Arnold P. *Primer on the Digital Millennium: What the Digital Millennium Copyright Act and the Copyright Term Extension Act Mean for the Library Community.*
www.ala.org/washoff/primer.html

Stanford University Libraries. *Copyright and Fair Use.*
http://fairuse.stanford.edu/

United States Copyright Office
http://lcweb.loc.gov/copyright/

United States Copyright Act
www.law.cornell.edu/uscode/17/

Index

About the Author

Gretchen McCord Hoffmann will earn her J.D. from the University of Texas School of Law in May 2001. She will then join the Austin, Texas, office of the law firm of Fulbright & Jaworski as an associate in their Intellectual Property and Technology Section. At the UT School of Law, Gretchen serves as Chief Articles Editor of the *Texas Intellectual Property Law Journal* and as Co-Editor-in-Chief of the *Texas Journal of Women and the Law*. During law school, Gretchen interned for the Texas Supreme Court and the Senate Jurisprudence Committee of the Texas Legislature and worked for the Texas Library Association as a legislative assistant on the Uniform Computer Information Transaction Act.

Gretchen earned a B.A. from Rice University in sociology and psychology in 1991 and an M.S.I.S. from the University of North Texas in 1992. She worked for two years as a reference librarian at the University of Texas at San Antonio, then for four years as the Coordinator of Library Instruction at the University of Houston. During her career as a librarian, Gretchen was very active in the Texas Library Association. Her activities include serving on the TLA Legislative Committee since 1993, participating in legislative days at both state and national levels, and participating in other legislative activities. She also served on various committees and round tables, including as Chair of the TLA Library Instruction Round Table. Gretchen also has participated in American Library Association legislative activities. Gretchen continues to serve on the TLA Legislative Committee and the Legal Resources Working Group of the TLA UCITA Task Force.